THE JUNIOR HIGH

School in Search of a Mission

Kenneth A. Tye

UNIVERSITY
PRESS OF
AMERICA

LANHAM • NEW YORK • LONDON

Copyright © 1985 by

University Press of America,™ Inc.

4720 Boston Way
Lanham, MD 20706

3 Henrietta Street
London WC2E 8LU England

Printed in the United States of America

ISBN (Perfect): 0-8191-4465-7
ISBN   (Cloth): 0-8191-4464-9

Grateful acknowledgment is made to Bobbs-Merrill Educational Publishing, a subsidiary of ITT, for permission to reprint excerpts from William Van Til, Gordon S. Vars, and John Lounsbury, *Modern Education for the Junior High Years,* 1967.

All University Press of America books are produced on acid-free paper which exceeds the minimum standards set by the National Historical Publications and Records Commission.

THIS BOOK IS DEDICATED TO MY WIFE, BARBARA, AND TO MY CHILDREN, STEVE, DEBBIE, AND MIKE.

iii

ACKNOWLEDGMENTS

There were three sets of people who made the writing of this book possible. To begin with there were the teachers, administrators, parents, students, and other support personnel in the twelve junior highs who answered questions, were observed, and/or who gave materials so that staff members of A Study of Schooling could understand what went on in their schools. To them I am very grateful.

Throughout the volume, I draw from one technical report or another prepared by staff members of A Study of Schooling. There were far more people involved in the Study than are represented by the few names which have eventually appeared as claiming authorship to the few books and several technical reports which ultimately resulted from the Study. There were over 50 people who were staff members at one time or another during the eight years it took to conceptualize the Study and collect, organize, analyze, and report the data from A Study of Schooling. The contribution of each person was critical whether as data collector, programmer, fund raiser, typist, manager, or conceptualizer. I thank each person who was part of the Study.

We also owe a debt of gratitude to the various agencies which provided grant support so that A Study of Schooling could be carried out. Those agencies were:

The Danforth Foundation
The Ford Foundation
International Paper Company Foundation
The JDR 3rd Fund
Martha Holden Jennings Foundation
Charles F. Kettering Foundation
Lilly Endowment, Inc.
Charles Stewart Mott Foundation
National Institute of Education
The Needmor Fund
Pedamorphosis, Inc.
The Rockefeller Foundation
The Spencer Foundation
U.S. Office of Education

There were individuals to whom I owe a special debt of thanks, also. My wife, Barbara, who has her own parallel book from the Study, <u>Multiple Realities: A Study of 13 American High Schools</u>, and I spent countless hours discussing, analyzing, reviewing, and commiserating about our works. Bette Overman and Paula de Fusco provided us with data reports, suggestions, and much moral support. Masako Oshita was my loyal and hardworking secretary throughout the eight years of the Study and more. Martha Twelvetree was the unsung office manager heroine who kept the accounts and did the countless other things which kept the project operating. The one person who was not around at the end of the Study to reap its rewards but who early in its history helped with funding, arranging for schools, and with the design of the parent study was Charles Wall. Chuck was critical to the Study and he was a friend. Finally, the inspiration and the focal point of the entire project was its Director, John Goodlad. Without John there would have been no Study and this book would not have been written. I shall always be grateful to him for the intellectual stimulation and interesting work he made possible for me during the 14 years of our association at the Research Division, Institute for the Development of Educational Activities, Inc., under whose auspices A Study of Schooling was conducted.

TABLE OF CONTENTS

This book grew out of A Study of Schooling, a comprehensive inquiry into elementary and secondary education that spanned in its duration the concluding years of the 1970's and the early years of the 1980's. Schools in seven regions of the United States were studied in triples: elementary schools passing their students into middle schools from which they progressed to senior high schools. The 38 schools comprising the sample were selected so as to be as representative as possible of the nation's schools--in diversity of location, size, socio-economic status of students' families, and so on. They were studied in depth and breadth from the perspective of students enrolled, their teachers, their parents, the principals, and others. The data encompassed nearly 18,000 students, approximately 1,350 teachers, and some 8,600 parents. In addition, carefully trained observers recorded human interactions, pedagogical procedures, curricular content, and instructional materials in 1,016 class-rooms.

Overall findings, as well as personal observations on the data and dozens of recommendations for improvement are reported in my book, A Place Called School (McGraw-Hill, 1984). But the data bank is so enormous and the ways of coming to grips with the information so varied that one book simply does not do justice to what many reviewers have described as the most comprehensive study of schooling ever conducted. Consequently, three additional books, including this one, are going to press almost simultaneously and another is in preparation. All four of these manuscripts represent the work of senior members of the research staff of A Study of Schooling whose long and deep involvement in conceptualization, data gathering, and data analysis lend authority to their conclusions and interpretations.

These authors benefitted also from having the opportunity to note the emphases and omissions in my book, as well as from having available nearly all of the technical reports on segments of A Study of Schooling. They both expand on topics and themes addressed by me and introduce new ones. The result is a more exhaustive treatment of what they chose to focus upon and, overall, a more comprehensive understanding of schooling at each level. Without this understanding, recommendations for reform tend to fall short of what is required.

The present volume focuses on the junior high school, an institution marvelously conceived that largely lost its way. Unless we have some understanding of what this middle school in the precollegiate hierarchy was intended to be, we lose the poignancy inherent in the gap between what it generally is and what we once had in mind for it. Once this gap becomes apparent and understood, it is difficult to be other than impatient with those who believe a longer school day, some more courses in mathematics and science, and tighter teacher control constitute the basic reforms needed by this institution in stress.

The author, Dr. Kenneth A. Tye, lays bare in unique fashion the distance between idealistic aspirations for the junior high school and how it currently appears to function day by day. This school, he observes, was intended to provide young people with opportunities to discover and explore, to make intelligent decisions, to become appropriately socialized to society, and to progress reflectively and successfully through a special stage of development. These expectations are presented in such a way as to provide a value screen through which the data can be observed. One might construct a different value screen but, if one accepts and uses the one Dr. Tye develops--and it is difficult to ignore his rationale and the base on which it rests--then the data put before the reader are sobering, indeed.

Directions for change arise out of a reasonably clear map of where we are and a vision of where we want to be. But, for change to take place, there also must be knowledge of the terrain lying ahead, or the effort to reach another part of the forest, a clearing, or higher ground may be so fraught with frustration that cynicism or despair or both may set in. The efforts to effect fundamental change in schools are testimony to the difficulties involved. The most cynical of these have been undertaken on the assumption that educators are mindless, or uncaring, or incompetent, or all of these things together and so they must be told what to do. But the mandates and requirements imposed on

x

teachers to assure their accountability in schools and classrooms have done little to change the circumstances under which teachers teach and students learn.

Ken Tye knows this. Before we studied the circumstances of teaching and learning in A Study of Schooling, we studied the circumstances giving rise to change in these processes. He and I and others followed over a period of six years the efforts of principals and teachers to improve the quality of life and of teaching and learning in 18 schools. We learned a lot about what is required for fundamental change to occur. Dr. Tye co-authored one of the half-dozen books in which we described and reflected on our experiences in studying educational change and in seeking to improve schools as the key units of change.

He uses this earlier work as a backdrop against which to analyze some of the data we gathered in A Study of Schooling. It becomes clear that prevailing paradigms of school improvement and the practices stemming from them are not likely to effect the needed reconstruction. Teachers are isolated from each other in their daily work. Staff development in school districts may help them refine some of their present teaching practices, but does not come close to tackling the conditions in schools that prevent teachers from doing as well as they know how to do. Teachers rarely work on school-wide problems together; when they do so, the efforts tend to be short, peripheral, and often discouraging. Teachers have no time for sustained attention to conditions in their own schools. Neither does anyone else. And so, the most troublesome problems of schools remain chronic and endemic.

In spite of this, Dr. Tye ends on a somewhat cautious but nonetheless upbeat note. Better visions of what might be and better understanding of what is together provide basic preparation for the challenges of reconstruction. The idealized junior high school he describes should be a source of guidance for principals and teachers, in particular, at a time when the improvement of schooling is again on national, state, and local agendas.

Ken Tye is a friend and colleague of long standing. He and I, with other friends and colleagues, have developed over the years a set of beliefs about human beings, education, schools, and teaching and learning that come together at various places in our writing and professional activities. Our efforts to understand how institutions and people change and what this understanding means for schools and the people most closely associated with them have spanned some 16 years. I am pleased now to introduce a book that represents one of the tangible outcomes of the journey we enjoyed together.

Our work in the study of schools and how to go about making them better has been supported by the Charles F. Kettering Foundation through what was formerly its education arm, the Institute for Development of Educational Activities, Inc. For A Study of Schooling, the Kettering Foundation was joined by 11 other philanthropic foundations and two agencies of the federal government in what probably was the largest consortium of funding bodies ever put together in support of a single project. On behalf of my colleagues and myself, I thank those persons associated with these institutions for both the funds that made our inquiries possible and the moral support that came with them.

John I. Goodlad
October, 1984

CHAPTER I

THE PURPOSE AND ORGANIZATION OF THE BOOK

Some Personal Reflections

I spent nine years working in junior highs, working at various jobs. For five years I taught English, social studies, physical education, drama and/or journalism in various combinations. One year, the worst of the nine for me, I was a vice-principal in charge of everything from the bookroom to the cafeteria to the buses to disciplining the students who "misbehaved." One year I was a curriculum coordinator. During that year, it was my job to organize committees of teachers who "wrote curriculum" in various subject areas. For two years, the best of the nine for me, I taught all subjects to approximately 25 students in grades five through eight in one room of an elementary school where I was also the principal.

During four of the five years that I taught specific subjects, when I was a vice-principal, and when I was a curriculum coordinator, I worked in large junior high schools where students were "grouped by ability." That is, in all cases, some criterion or criteria was or were applied to each student to determine in which class he or she was to be placed. Interesting things happened as a result of this process. In one school where I worked, students were grouped on the basis of reading achievement. One class I taught was a "Z" group. In X-Y-Z parlance that meant that the students in my class couldn't read too well. It also meant that there were more Mexican-Americans than in other classes, a higher absence rate, more "behavior" problems, and more students who just didn't like school. That "Z" students didn't like school was not surprising since success in school is so closely related to verbal ability and since most adults at schools don't really care to work with "Z" students anyway.

In the schools where I worked, adults, including teachers, assumed that some students were going on to college and that others were not. The college bound were really the favored ones (The "Xs"). But even

1

deeper than that: a fundamental premise of American education has always been that schooling is competitive. Not everyone can succeed; someone has to lose. Unfortunately, Americans accept this as a fact of life and they can see no reason why it shouldn't be true in schools, too.

In general, my recollections of students in all the schools where I worked was that they were very sensitive, very changeable, and terribly curious about a whole lot of things. I remember how badly most of my students wanted to be accepted and liked by other students and how important it was for them to wear just the right clothes, say the right things, and be seen at the right places. I always marvelled at how, on the one hand, each one so much wanted to be accepted; but, on the other hand, how many could be terribly cruel to other students who did not quite measure up to group norms because of their clothes, or size or for some other reason. At the same time, they had a wonderful sense of fairness which adults just don't have. It is now hard to imagine that these young people had all of these feelings while at the same time they also knew that "someone had to fail."

Even though they were self-centered, sensitive, and changeable, I found junior high students a lot of fun to work with. I think this was due to the fact that most of them were so curious. A lot of this curiosity was personalized; that is, much of it had to do with things that affected their daily lives. Also, a lot was generalized. They were curious about what they read in books or newspapers and what they saw on T.V. or in the movies. Having taught many of these naturally curious young people, I cannot understand reports which say that junior high school students find science and social studies "uninteresting." These are just the subjects which should appeal to the "curious."

The teachers, counselors and administrators I worked with during my nine years in junior high schools, by and large, were dedicated and hard-working. As I reflect upon those years, I realize that single sets of descriptors do not do justice to them. They were as different individually as any group of people in our society.

The one sure thing I can say about all of the people at the junior high schools where I worked,

2

including myself, was that we weren't really certain about what we were supposed to be doing. That's not to say that we were bad, stupid, lazy or unprofessional. We could describe, in one form or another, the Cardinal Principles of Education or some other such lofty set of goals for formal schooling. However, at another level, there were some real differences of opinion among staff members about purposes and about what we actually should be doing.

There were a number of teachers and administrators who thought we were supposed to be teaching our subjects: math, science, English, home economics, whatever. Many of these people were on their way to jobs at a nearby high school, for in most of the places where I worked you were paid more and it was more prestigious at the high school. It was also usually the case where I worked that pupil-teacher ratios, facilities and teacher materials were better or more available at the high school than at the junior high school.

There were other staff members who viewed each day as a war between themselves, as representatives of "correct" patterns of human behavior, and students, who were seen as having to learn these patterns. As the years have passed, it has become obvious to many of these people that the "war" has intensified and that students have become more hopeless.

Some staff members held the view that junior high school students were also people trying to grow up and that the school was a place to help make that possible. They tended to use words like core class, block time, subject integration, homeroom, counseling and exploration. Not all, but a lot, of these people had been elementary school teachers at one time. They had made the change to junior high school for a variety of reasons: prestige, more pay, a free period for planning, their own children had become early adolescents and the challenge of working with this age group had become obvious. Interestingly, in my whole nine years of work in junior highs, I met only one person who had attended a teacher training college in a course specifically designed to prepare people to work with early adolescents.

There are some other things I remember about the people I worked with at junior high schools. For

3

example, I remember that almost every married teacher had a spouse who worked, too. Also, most of the teachers I knew, of necessity, were good at other things: carpentry, auto repair, planning and preparing food, sewing. Additionally, many teachers had other jobs in the evenings and/or on the weekends. Salaries weren't so high, but people compensated through being in two-income families, through do-it-yourself projects at home and/or through having second jobs.

The schools where I worked were quite different places, one from the other. Some of these differences were because of the communities in which the schools were located. For example, at one school there was a kind of unspoken assumption that we were preparing students for college. At that school there were frequent contacts with parents who were quite concerned about their children's progress lest those children ultimately not graduate from college. At another school the staff generally bemoaned the lack of parent interest in the program. Not many children there were expected to go to college. Parent energies were mostly put into earning enough money to subsist.

The most interesting school was probably the one sociologists would label as being in transition. That is, in this case, most students in earlier years at the school had gone on to high school and then college. However, by the time I taught there, over half of the students and their parents were not much interested in college. That was particularly hard on those staff members I described earlier who believed in their subject and/or who felt they were fighting a "war."

In addition to differences in the schools because of community factors and to the outlooks of the staffs, there were also differences because of leadership. As a teacher, I worked with principals who were very helpful and supportive. I also worked in schools where I hardly ever saw the principal because he or she was always busy "managing." I remember an old and simple adage about schools--"turned-on teachers will produce turned-on kids." I somehow feel that I worked harder and was even a better teacher in those schools where there was an interested and supportive principal.

4

Underlying Assumptions

This book is about junior high schools. It, along with several companion volumes about other levels of schooling and about other schooling topics, reports data from A Study of Schooling carried out by the Research Division, I/D/E/A directed by John Goodlad.

A Study of Schooling was not designed to test a set of preconceived hypotheses. Rather it sought to describe the schools studied in such a way that hypotheses could be generated by the staff and by other researchers who may also examine the accumulated descriptive data.

The need for a study which described practice was identified by Goodlad and his associates as a result of previous work. First, during the mid 60s, a group of experienced teachers from the University Elementary School at UCLA utilized a framework that they agreed upon to examine the effects of elementary school programs reported to be "innovative." What was found, and what was confirmed in a replication by the I/D/E/A staff, was that such innovations--described and extolled in the literature and/or by school district and school staff personnel--were not really in operation in the classroom. They had been "blunted on the classroom door."[1]

In the late 60s, the Research Division of I/D/E/A conducted the Study of Change and School Improvement. That Study led to the development of the DDAE model of school-based problem-solving: Dialog, Decision-Making, Action, and Evaluation. This model, along with a "network" which linked together 18 school staffs in a search for better ways to individualize instruction, combined to become a successful strategy for educational change through the development of self-renewing schools.[2]

As a result of these studies, Goodlad and his associates concluded that if we really wish to improve American schooling, we need to invest in the single school. It is that unit, the school with its teachers, administrators, students and parents, and supported by the district and state, which has the necessary combined arrangements and resources to make possible the change process.

5

This assumption about the importance of the single school was critical to the development of A Study of Schooling. The Study was designed to gather a comprehensive set of data about a relatively small set of schools. It was thought that the process of generating hypotheses relevant to change in schools was better served by a comprehensive data set than by data on a limited set of variables from a large, more generalizable sample.

A second assumption which guided the design of the data collection was that schools are organic; they are systems with interrelated parts. Even though we had this ecological view, we had to eventually limit the amount of data we could collect. It was just not possible to ask teachers, for example, to fill out questionnaires for more than five or six hours. For this reason, it became critical for us to "guess at" what we thought were the issues to examine and the questions to ask. Those "guesses," sometimes carefully thought through and at other times hurriedly made, directed us to the questions we asked and the data we collected.

A third closely related assumption was critical to the development of the Study. We assumed that because so much data was to be collected we would find that a quite unique picture would emerge for each school. At the same time, we felt that the schools would share a great many common characteristics. It was these differences and similarities which we felt would become the focus of the greatest number of the hypotheses we would be generating.

Many of my own beliefs and biases about junior high schools were shaped by the nine years briefly described at the beginning of this chapter. Some arose from other professional experiences, not the least of which were those gained with the earlier I/D/E/A study, the Study of Change and School Improvement. Other beliefs and biases developed as I came in contact with the research and/or theories of scholars. Many were formed as a result of my observations of the experiences of my own three children as they passed through their early adolescence.

At this point, then, it becomes necessary for me to set forth those assumptions about junior high school education which guided the writing of this book. They are few and, I believe, fairly straightforward:

-- The school with its staff, students, parents, and resources is the logical unit upon which to focus change efforts. The superordinate levels of schooling (district, state) should encourage and support, rather than direct, school-based efforts.

-- The principal is the key person in the process of change. The degree to which he/she motivates, supports, and provides leadership to the staff determines to a great extent the willingness of the school staff to work to improve the schooling program.

-- Ability grouping of students, which is intended to facilitate teaching and learning, actually discriminates against students on the basis of economic status, ethnicity, academic achievement and aspiration. Heterogeneous grouping should be encouraged.

-- At present, the traditions of the various subject areas (e.g., mathematics, English/language arts, science, etc.) are more important in the determination of school programs than are the characteristics of the students or the needs of the society. The characteristics of early adolescents should be considered far more carefully in program planning than they now are.

-- The so-called "middle school" is a recent organizational design intended to better bridge the educational gap between the elementary school and the high school. While there are a number of structural differences between middle schools and junior highs, the actual educational differences are usually few, at least in current practice.

-- Early adolescents are sensitive, changeable, extremely curious and in need of educational opportunities quite different from those needed by adolescents of high school age. Unfortunately, most contemporary junior high schools tend to be closely patterned after the high school.

7

-- Most junior high schools are just that, "junior." Pupil teacher ratios are higher at the junior high, teacher salaries are lower, materials and supplies are fewer, and buildings are older. Communities and educators tend to value high schools more than junior highs. The schools of different levels need to be valued equally for the different tasks they perform for students and for society.

-- A fundamental premise of American education is that it is and should be competitive and that some students will succeed and some will fail. Such an attitude, particularly addressed to very sensitive early adolescents, is destructive of personalities. This is not an acceptable state of affairs. Competition should be minimized and opportunities for success and cooperation need to be designed for all junior high school students.

-- What happens in school is related to the greater society except that the school usually lags quite far behind the society. For example, in a time of rapid changes in work and leisure time activities, the school is still viewed as and still operates as an institution which prepares people for the world of work. The learning and practice of skills, the exploration of interests and abilities, and the development of aptitudes have intrinsic value for the early adolescent. They should not be confused with preparation for work or education for careers.

A Study of Schooling

We studied the schools in sets of three. First, a high school was chosen. Then a feeder junior high was added which had a student population as nearly like that at the high school as possible. Finally, using the same criteria, a feeder elementary school was chosen.[3] We hoped to get a picture of the total school experience, grades 1-12. Aspects of the community in which each "triple" was located were also studied.

Of the twelve junior high schools studied, three were large, six were medium-sized, and three were

8

small. Four were urban, three were rural, and five were suburban. As to socioeconomic status (SES), six were middle, two were low, three were mid/low and one was hi/mid.[4] Ethnically, six were virtually all white, one was 99% black, one was nearly all Hispanic, and four were ethnically heterogeneous with an almost-equal number of white and nonwhite students. At several schools, languages other than English were spoken. The Study instruments were produced in Spanish, Korean, and Armenian as well as in English.

Each of the twelve junior high schools and its community reflected a combination of the four demographic factors listed above: size, location, socioeconomic status, and ethnicity.

Intermediate agencies or district offices in the communities worked with I/D/E/A to select the schools for the Study. One county school office and two regional service centers actually coordinated data collection in six triples, after working with the school districts to select the schools. In all other cases, school districts were approached to select schools, but data collections were coordinated by persons directly employed by I/D/E/A. In one case, agreement regarding the data collection was sought and received from the local American Federation of Teacher (AFT) executive group. The cooperation of all of these agencies and groups was outstanding.

Teacher reactions to participation in the Study were also favorable. Each school participant received $25.00, but that was hardly adequate compensation for five to ten hours of work, which included responding to questionnaires, providing curriculum materials, being interviewed and being observed while teaching. Four factors seemed to account for the generally favorable response from teachers. First, they were promised, and received, both school-general and classroom-specific feedback from the data collected. Second, they were well-oriented to the purposes and procedures of the Study. Third, the Study staff, including intermediate agency and county office personnel, and particularly site coordinators, were quite sensitive to the particular needs of each school. Finally, most staff members themselves were basically open, cooperative, and curious people who saw participation as a professional responsibility.

9

Each triple was studied for one month during 1977 by a team of approximately 24 locally-recruited data collectors. Overall, 9,106 questionnaires were received from 6,042 junior high school students.[5] These 6,042 students represented 60% of the total student population (10,109) in the twelve schools, and the range was from 98% in a small school to 46% in the largest school. Some 400 questionnaires were received from 431 junior high school teachers. These 431 teachers represented 88% of the total teacher population (479) and the range was from 52% to 100%. Of these, 337 were interviewed and 362 had their classes observed.[6] The Study received packages of curriculum materials from 366 classes. The packages included lists of topics and skills taught, of books and other materials used, and samples of tests, quizzes, and worksheets used.

Sample classes were identified as to track level after the data were collected: low, average, or high ability track, or heterogeneous grouping.[7]

Questionnaires and interviews were completed by all twelve principals. Most of the vice-principals, counselors, librarians, and other non-teaching staff also completed questionnaires, and many were interviewed as well.

In each school district, information was gathered from the business division, adult and pupil personnel service offices, curriculum specialists, and superintendents. Members of the Board of Education were interviewed and completed questionnaires. Some 2,688 parent questionnaires were received. Master schedules, student and teacher handbooks, records of school publicity, school newspapers, and anecdotal data (including unsolicited notes or letters) from students and teachers were collected, as were state and district curriculum guides. Finally, data collectors kept daily logs of their experiences and the coordinators of the data collections at all sites shared their impressions in taped interviews after the data collection phase was over.

The Schools

Below is a brief description of each of the twelve junior highs in which data were collected by A Study of

10

Schooling. Individual schools are often discussed in subsequent chapters. The reader may find it helpful to occasionally refer back to these descriptions.

Atwater. Atwater Junior High was the only junior high in a district which served a predominantly white, middle class suburban community adjacent to a large city in the Northwest. Atwater had no central business district of its own. Residents shopped in the city at large suburban shopping centers. At the time of the Study, busing for integration was being discussed for the neighboring urban school district and metropolitan busing, which surely would have involved Atwater, was one option under consideration.

The school was an old, two-storied building. The original structure was built in the 30s and had been the high school. It was in relatively good repair and had extra space for other than regular classroom programs. There was an in-school suspension program, for example. The school was situated on a large, eight-acre site.

The school had 24 teachers and 496 students in grades 7-9. The sample consisted of 23 teachers (96%), 342 pupils (69%) and 157 parents (38%). There was a vice-principal, two counselors, a librarian and an attendance officer. A nurse, speech therapist, psychologist, psychometrist, and curriculum specialist were all available to the school.

The school generally had high marks on adult climate measures. The Staff Job Satisfaction score was the highest of all junior highs in the Study. The school appeared to be a good place to work. In part, this was attributable to the new, young principal who was highly regarded.

Aside from a strong arts program, the general impression of the school was that it had a very average curriculum. There was not a lot of in-service activity. However, there had been human relations training involving teachers with students and initiated by the principal.

Teachers had a good impression of the teaching at the school. While there was considerable student turnover (23%), there was little teacher turnover. The teachers, basically, were an older group who pretty well "knew the ropes," or so they thought. They gave the school a grade of "B." Parents generally agreed, giving a grade of "B-." Students, however, gave it a "C+." They were not so satisfied.

Bradford. Bradford Junior High was located in a predominantly white, lower middle class community not far from a large Midwestern city. Most jobs were associated with major industries in the greater metropolitan area and layoffs had been common during periods of recession. There was a considerable amount of fear in the community about the possible spread of the blacks in the nearby city to Bradford. Additionally, there was some fear of the possibility of court-ordered metropolitan busing.

Forty percent of the sampled Bradford parents said they had not finished high school and no one reported being a college graduate. They tended to be long-term residents, they were the youngest 'respondent group of parents of all the junior highs in the Study, and their level of participation in school related activities was the lowest of all junior highs.

The school was five years old at the time of the Study. Some of the buildings had been constructed as open space so that there could be team teaching. However, during my visit to the school, the principal pointed out with some pride how all the folding walls were closed and how each teacher had his/her own class.

Bradford had 35 teachers and 858 students in grades 7-9. The sample consisted of 28 teachers (80%), 657 students (77%), and 211 parents (31%). There was a vice-principal, three counselors, a learning consultant, and a half-time librarian and nurse. There were other support persons available from the district and county office of education.

On the Work Environment Inventory, Bradford teachers scored at about the mean or slightly below in comparison to the other junior highs in the Study. In short, this was a workplace where teachers felt that some things were O.K. and a few weren't. They were moderately positive about the principal. He was not seen as very open nor was he seen as providing leadership in curriculum and instruction. The teachers were particularly pleased with the fact that there had been a real "tightening up" of discipline at the school.

The school had a strange set of curriculum offerings derived from tradition, the desires of the staff, a particular "hobby horse" of someone or ones at the district level (i.e., swimming), and piecemeal responses to societal pressure (i.e., "careers"). The school was an example of how one program could dominate a school and upset any kind of curriculum balance. For example, band was the only music offered at the school and, yet, every student had swimming for two semesters at a minimum. Teachers at Bradford participated in very few in-service training activities. What little there was appeared to be highly individual and taken outside of the school and district.

Teachers had a fairly positive impression of the quality of teaching at the school. This relatively young staff had taught for 10 years, on the average. They graded the school "B-," as did both the parents and students.

Crestview. Crestview Middle School was the only junior high in a district which was in a rural/suburban area just outside a medium-sized Midwestern city. The area was a low-to-middle class community with extremes of income that ranged from below poverty level--old people living solely on Social Security; young single-parent families on welfare--to a large number of middle-class employees of both light and heavy industry in and around the nearby city. There was not a strong sense of "community" in Crestview. There was much transciency. The area was virtually all white and many residents had moved there from Appalachian states and had brought their cultural values with them (e.g., woman's role was seen as wife and mother and many female teens married and left school or married immediately after high school graduation).

The school was in a well-kept, old, two-storied building. The oldest building was built in 1925 and the school had originally been the high school. The staff was not particularly happy with the facility.

Crestview Middle School had 32 teachers and 725 students in grades 6-8. The sample consisted of 32 teachers, 430 students (59%), and 257 parents (41%).

13

There was no vice-principal, one counselor, a school psychologist, a nurse and speech therapist part-time, and an attendance officer one day per week. Curriculum services were available from the county. All in all, the school had a very low ratio of support and administrative personnel.

On the Work Environment Inventory, teachers at Crestview scored the principal quite low in comparison to the other junior highs in the Study. In terms of Staff Cohesiveness, scores were at about the mean, but other scores were below the mean. In other words, the staff members related well enough to their fellow workers but they were less positive about the principal and the "situation."

The class schedule was about the most straightforward of all the junior highs. At all grade levels, students were enrolled in a two hour language arts block and one period each of math, science and social studies. Physical education and a course entitled Unified Arts alternated with each other every other day for the three years (See chapter 4). Students could substitute band or chorus for Unified Arts. Several teachers had a period of "noon duty" in lieu of one teaching period--and they were not happy about it! Teachers had no planning period and they each taught six periods, with some splitting their time between the middle school and the high school.

Crestview teachers, a relatively young group, participated in a number of in-service training activities, many at the school. Teachers believed that there was good teaching at the school. However, they gave the school a grade of "C+," expressing their dissatisfaction with their work conditions, including what they perceived to be a lack of supplies and equipment. Parents and students also gave the school a grade of "C+."

Euclid. Euclid Junior High served a large, sparsely populated farming and ranching area covering 724 square miles in the Great Plain, west of the Mississippi River and east of the Rocky Mountains. The population, almost totally white, was made up mostly of long-term residents.

The school served as a community center. Over 60% of the parent sample said that they had participated at the school by helping at special events. Nearly 40% had attended community meetings of one kind or another at the school. The impression I got from our data was of a very supportive parent group.

The junior and senior high shared one building. It was an old building--the oldest part dated from 1937. A new agriculture building had been completed just a few months before our data collection. The school was on an 11.4 acre site, with nine acres given over to playground and field areas.

The school had 13 teachers and 133 students in grades 7-8. Classes were very small. The sample consisted of 12 teachers (92%), 128 students (96%), and only 41 parents (32%). The principal was the only administrator for the school. There was one full-time counselor and one librarian for both the junior and senior high and there was one full-time psychologist for the elementary and secondary school in the district.

On the Work Environment Inventory, Euclid ranked above the mean on all scales when compared to the other junior highs in the Study. Over half of the teachers indicated that the administration at the school was a minor problem. This did not seem directed at the new principal. The staff, in fact, was positive about her leadership. (She was the only woman principal in our junior high sample and had taught 23 years before becoming an administrator). The problem seemed to arise from the fact that the high school and junior high shared the campus, the counselor, and even most teachers. There was some evidence, from teacher interview responses, of cliques at the school.

The Euclid teachers were the youngest junior high group in the Study. On the average, they had taught just less than seven years. Several departments were one-person departments and teachers were given their assignments and then pretty much left to do the best they could. Evidence suggested that there were a few quite creative teachers but that most did a pretty routine job. There was relatively little in-service activity at the school. One human relations program and one behavioral objective training program were school-based.

Teachers were quite positive about the teaching at the school. Further, they were only one of two junior high groups which, on the average, disagreed with the statement, "Many of the students at this school don't care about learning." They gave the school a grade of "B+" as did parents. Students graded the school "B."

Fairfield. This community, located near a large city in the Southwest, encompassed an area of 148 square miles. It was made of two quite distinct regions. The largest portion, about 125 square miles, was made up of farms and ranches. The remaining 23 square miles was a fairly densely populated suburban area with a large proportion of its adult population employed by two large, nearby military bases. The population was quite transient. Ethnically, about 48% of the population was Hispanic, 46% was white, and the others were black, Asian and American Indian. The community was low to middle income, on the average, and over 30% of the parent sample had not graduated from high school.

Fairfield High, Junior High and Elementary School were all grouped together on a common 30 acre site. The junior high was built in about 1950 and was originally the high school. It was a single-storied "finger" building with outside hallways, typical of the American Southwest. The building was somewhat in disrepair at the time of the Study. I noted unpainted areas, chuckholes in the paved play areas and holes in walls when I visited the school. The teachers' workroom was partly unpainted and contained worn-out furniture. One teacher said when interviewed, "...The maintenance is horrible around here. They haven't cleaned my room in a month." There was a large set of vocational educational buildings for the two secondary schools standing by themselves some distance from the regular sites.

Fairfield Junior High had 42 teachers and 764 students in grades 7-8. The sample consisted of 35 teachers (83%), 462 students (60%), and 218 parents (33%). We had no information on the number of administrative and professional staff at or available to the school. The school did have a full-time librarian and there was a quite good regional educational service center nearby which fulfilled requests for services. How much it was called upon we do not know.

16

On the Work Environment Inventory, this school ranked lowest of all junior highs on every scale and sub-scale. In addition, the gap between Fairfield scores and scores for the next-lowest school was usually quite large. The work environment here was truly poor. Salaries were low and teacher turnover was an amazing 57% during the year prior to the Study. The administration of the school was seen as a problem by nearly 80% of the teachers. This is the only junior high in our sample where <u>fewer</u> than half of the students responded "yes" to the questions, "The principal is friendly" and "The principal is helpful." The picture is one of a weak principal. However, such a statement does not go far enough. Data from the total triple suggests that the district administration, and in particular the superintendent, was where the problem resided. Teacher interview comments indicated constant turnover of principals, and, yet, district administration and school board membership never changed.

The general impression of the curriculum at this school was that it was very unremarkable. Language arts and math functioned at a very low level suggesting a kind of operational self-fulfilling prophesy: "These kids can't perform well so we won't push them; sure enough they don't perform well." There was a very large vocational program focused on specific trades (e.g., general mechanical repair, building maintenance, office assistance) which was administered separately from both the junior and senior highs and did not appear to be well-coordinated. The one art course was started in mid-year with no pre-planning, equipment or materials. There was little in-service participation by teachers.

About 48% of the students were Hispanic as were only about 6% of the teachers. Teachers were only lukewarm concerning the quality of education at the school. They gave the school a grade of "C-," the lowest given by any junior high staff in the Study. Parents graded the school "C+," and students "C."

<u>Laurel</u>. The rural town of Laurel was located about an hour's drive from a major city in the South. Small farms from 50 to 300 acres comprised most of the 400 square miles of the school district and many students came to school by bus. The total population of the district at the time of the Study was approximately

17

3,000, just about evenly divided between whites and blacks. The schools had been desegregated five years before our data collection and at the time of the Study many whites were still uneasy about the unified system. Over one-half of the population earned less than $5,000 per year and almost one-half of our parent sample said they had not finished high school. Over half also said they had resided in the area for nine or more years.

The school was located near the center of town, on an attractive, tree-shaded 15 acre lot which it shared with the immediately adjacent high school. The two schools were connected by a covered walkway and gave the impression of being a single school. Although the middle school was old (it had originally been the high school), teachers were quite satisfied with it.

Laurel Middle School had 24 teachers and 276 students in grades 6-8. The sample consisted of 21 teachers (88%), 270 students (98%), and 81 parents (33%). Over 90% of the teachers were under 40. On the average, they had taught only 4.4 years and nearly 30% of them were in their first year. With half the student body black, two-thirds of the teachers were white. The principal was black. The median salary on the salary schedule was lowest of the junior highs in the Study and teacher turnover was a high 38% during the year prior to the Study.

In addition to the principal, professional support staff included a curriculum specialist, a librarian and a counselor. The Laurel School District was one of a very few in the state which had not consolidated with a large city or county. Because of this, there were no services to it from such a source. However, the district had a sizeable amount of federal funding. Here, then, was a district which fiercely maintained its local autonomy but which opted for federal monies.

On the Work Environment Inventory, the school ranked next to last among the junior highs in the Study on the Composite Leadership Scale and was below the mean on all sub-scales. Some 65% of the teachers said that the administration was a problem at the school.

There was a strong Title I-ESEA program in basic language arts and math. Also, there was what appeared to be an extensive, activity-based science program. Teachers were involved in little in-service training,

18

however. What there was was pursued by individuals on their own time.

Teachers were only mildly enthusiastic about the teaching at the school. They graded the school a "C+." Parents were more positive, giving it a "B-." Students were most positive, they said "B."

Manchester. The Manchester community was located within a large city in the Midwest. Its population of 65,236 at the time of the Study was about two-thirds black and one-third white. The school population was almost totally black. The community was once all white and the whites who remained were older home owners. Manchester was basically a residential community. Most people who lived there commuted to work in others parts of the city or were retired. While there was a wide range of incomes, we classified the community as middle-class. About 20% of our parent sample were college graduates and another 60% had some higher education. The average length of residence in the community of parents in our sample was about six years.

Manchester Middle School was a relatively new, very well-kept building with typically Midwestern enclosed hallways. It was located on a spacious 20.82 acre site. When I visited the school, parents were in evidence as "hall monitors." I got the impression that everyone from the principal through the students was very proud of the school. Vandalism was negligible.

The school had 62 teachers and 1,547 students in grades 6-8. The sample consisted of 32 teachers (52%), 790 students (51%), and 301 parents (24%). The faculty was an older group, salaries were high, and there was little teacher turnover. Over half of the teachers were black, as was the principal. There were two full-time assistant principals, six full-time counselors and a full-time librarian. In addition, a social worker and a speech therapist were at the school two days per week and a psychologist, an attendance officer and curriculum specialists were available from the regional or district offices.

On the Work Environment Inventory, Manchester Middle School ranked high on the Composite Principal Leadership Scale. The principal had been at the school for nine years. There was teacher dissatisfaction but

19

it was not directed at him. The district had recently lost a millage and there was much "belt tightening."

From the schedule, I got the impression that Manchester Middle School was a pretty standard, large city junior high except that it served grades 6-8 rather than 7-9. It seemed to have more in common with Newport Junior High, for example, than it did with Crestview Middle School. Teachers reported participation in a good deal of in-service. Much of it was school-based and some was initiated by the district. Also, a wide variety of topics was covered.

Teachers felt that they were doing a good job and that students received a lot of individual attention. They graded the school "B-" as did parents. Students, however, while proud of the building, were less enthusiastic about the program. They gave a grade of "C+."

Newport. The Newport community was part of a large city in the West. Its most distinctive feature was its remarkable ethnic heterogeneity. The Study identified 58 nationalities and 36 different languages in the community. The population was very mobile in comparison to the other communities in the Study. Apartments were far more numerous than single family dwellings. The community had its full share of urban problems including crowded living conditions, traffic congestion, poor public recreation facilities, drug abuse, transiency and crime. About one-third of the parent sample had completed four or more years of college and only 16% had not completed high school.

The school occupied a city block, was old and shabby looking inside and out. Many "portable" classrooms--more permanent than temporary--were in evidence. The playground was quite limited, all asphalt and surrounded by high chain link fencing. There was a lot of graffiti in evidence and teachers were quite dissatisfied with the facilities.

Newport Junior High had 75 teachers and 1,649 students in grades 7-9. The sample consisted of 58 teachers (77%), 757 students (46%), and 260 parents (17%). The school had a full-time vice principal, four full-time counselors and a full-time nurse and librarian. In addition, there was a psychometrist and a speech therapist at the school one day per week, a

20

school psychologist available upon request, three part-time attendance officers and a school physician one day per month. Home visiting teachers and curriculum specialists were also available upon request. All of the above people were available from the district. In theory, the school could have requested assistance from the county office, too. However, as is the case with most big city schools, this was never done.

On the Work Environment Inventory, the school ranked just below the mean of all the junior highs in the Study on the Composite Leadership Scale and quite low on all other scales. From teacher interviews, I got the impression of a number of teachers frustrated by an old building, a changing student population and changing standards. Some were also frustrated with a new but experienced principal who was perceived as quite laissez-faire.

The school appeared to have the most balanced set of arts, P.E. and vocational education offerings of all the junior highs in the Study. There was also an extensive array of electives. There was little evidence of departmental cooperation except for reading teachers who had developed a structured management system which made extensive use of progress checklists and learning centers. There seemed to be a good deal of attention paid to high-interest, low-level reading materials for slow readers in English classes. Teachers participated in a fair amount of in-service training, some of which was school-based. Topics were quite varied.

Despite the comparative strength of the school curriculum, teachers were only mildly positive about teaching at the school. This was an older, experienced staff and they graded the school "B-" as did parents. The students were even more negative. They gave the school a "C+."

Palisades. This community was located in an affluent section of a major city in the South. The population in the community was predominantly white. However, approximately half of the students in the schools in the area were bused in from an affluent black neighborhood across the city. The population of that area was relatively young and quite well educated, on the average. Because both white and black students came from upper middle class families, racial tensions often aggravated by economic class differences appeared to be minimal. People in the community, as well as in the entire city, seemed proud of the fact that desegregation had been brought about with a minimum of problems even though the process was one of one-way busing.

The school was a multi-storied brick building built in the mid-50s. Until five years before the Study, it had been the high school. It was well kept and was located in a beautiful wooded area on a large, well maintained grassy campus.

Palisades Middle School had 49 teachers and 825 students in grades 6-8. The sample consisted of 41 teachers (84%), 492 students (60%), and 305 parents (39%). The teaching staff was one of the oldest in the Study and 42% were black. The white and black teachers tended to remain separated from each other, eating and otherwise relaxing in their own groups. There was one assistant principal, two counselors, a librarian, and a nurse, all full-time. In addition there was a psychologist, a psychometrist, a social worker and a speech therapist, all part-time. Home visiting teachers and curriculum specialists were available as necessary. Counselors had no secretarial support, however.

There was an interesting pattern to the scores on the Work Environment Inventory. Scores on principal scales and task oriented scales (e.g., Problem Solving/ Decision Making) were all at about the mean for all the junior highs in the Study. However, the scores for Staff Openness and Staff-to-Staff Affection scales were among the lowest in the sample, reflecting the racial split among the teachers.

Although the school was called a Middle School and the students were in grades 6-8, the curriculum looked remarkably like an urban junior high with students having six separate subjects each day at every grade level. Except for a Title I reading course, all students had a standard mixture of required and elective courses. There was a good deal of in-service training and much of it was school-based.

Teachers felt strongly that there was good teaching at the school. They gave the school a grade of "B+." Parents graded the school "B" and students gave it a "B-."

22

Rosemont. This community was in a large city in the Southwest. The population was almost totally Mexican-American. The average family income was under $5,000 annually, the lowest in our sample. About 45% of the homes were rental units, many in low-income housing projects. The area was experiencing a population decline and there did not appear to be an influx of new immigrants from Mexico. Parent respondents at the school had the lowest average education level of any sample in the Study. Almost 62% had less than an eighth grade education and another 17% had only some high school. Also, our parent sample ranked second among the junior highs in terms of length of residence. Over 60% had lived in the area for nine or more years.

The school was a single-storied, relatively new building in good repair. It had outside, open hallways. Teachers were very positive about the facilities.

Rosemont Middle School had 44 teachers and 993 students in grades 6-8. The sample consisted of 42 teachers (95%), 591 students (60%), and 156 parents (20%). Only about 20% of the teachers were Hispanic, but the principal was. The school had a vice-principal and two counselors full-time. There was a full-time nurse and a full-time librarian. Also, there was a part-time home visiting teacher and a school psychologist available on-call. Curriculum specialists and other service personnel were available from the nearby regional education service center.

Scores on the Work Environment Inventory were all at or above the mean for the junior highs in our Study. Our evidence seemed to suggest that the principal did a good job and that he was respected.

About half the students were in an English As A Second Language (ESL) Program and many students were scheduled into remedial reading or math classes instead of having an elective. Otherwise, this "middle school" had a curriculum which looked like most city junior highs. Teachers reported only moderate participation in in-service training activities, most of which were sponsored by the district or the regional service center.

Teachers were positive about the teaching at the school. They gave the school a grade of "B-." Parents were more positive, clearly valued education for their children, and clearly thought the school was doing a good job. They gave the school a "B+." Students gave it a "B."

Vista. The Vista School District covered 44 square miles and included a small suburban community as well as rural areas. It was near a medium-sized Midwestern city. It was virtually all white and "white flight" was characteristic of many of the newer residents who had moved out of the nearby city. Many commuted to work there. Nearly one-quarter of our parent sample were college graduates.

The school was a relatively new, single-storied building with inside hallways. It was set off from nearby houses; was in good repair; and was surrounded by large, well kept fields and playgrounds. Teachers were the most satisfied of all junior high teachers concerning facilities.

Vista Junior High had 49 teachers and 1,188 students in grades 7-8. The sample consisted of 48 teachers (98%), 662 students (56%), and 416 parents (37%). The school had a vice-principal, a librarian, and four full-time counselors. The school nurse was half-time and a school psychologist, pupil attendance officer and speech therapist were available as needed. Curriculum specialists and other service personnel were also available from the nearby county education office.

On the Work Environment Inventory, Vista ranked first of all junior highs in the sample on all scales except one which measured principal behavior. Teachers were very positive about the principal and all other dimensions of the work environment.

All students had one semester of typing, there were study halls and English and math courses were semester courses. Otherwise, this was a junior high where students had virtually no choice of courses and all teachers at a given grade level in a subject taught the same things, with only slight variations for different ability levels of the classes. The teachers reported only moderate participation in in-service training and most of that was on an individual basis at one or other of the local teacher training institutions.

24

Teachers had a very positive view of teaching at the school. They gave the school a "B+" as did the parent sample. Students graded it a "B." There was generally a good feeling about this homogeneous, traditional school.

Woodlake. The Woodlake School District was a rural/suburban area about 90 miles from a large city in the Northwest. It was 55 square miles in size and was greatly affected by the existence of a large military base. Fully one-third of the people in the area were either military personnel on active duty, reservists, retired military personnel and/or civilian employees on the base. A large number of Woodlake teachers were wives of naval personnel. The community was definitely upper middle-class. I saw mostly single family dwellings with good-sized, neat yards. Our parent sample was well-educated with about two-thirds of them having some education beyond high school. They were also quite mobile. Their level of participation in school activities was quite low.

The school building was "vintage 50s," single-storied, with inside hallways. The only junior high in the district, it came off poorly when compared to the new high school which had won statewide prizes for its construction. The school was located on a large, 17 acre site.

Woodlake Junior High had 30 teachers and 655 students in grades 7-9. The sample consisted of 27 teachers (90%), 461 students (70%), and 285 parents (52%). There were a full-time vice principal and librarian. There were 1½ counselors, a school psychologist and a speech therapist available from the district. Curriculum specialists, a social worker, and other service personnel were available from the nearby regional educational service center.

Scores on the Work Environment Inventory were well above the mean of the sampled junior highs on ten of the eleven dimensions. On the eleventh dimension, Principal Leadership, the score was positive but just below the mean. The Staff Job Satisfaction score for teachers was one of the highest in the sample. The school appeared to be a good place to work and the principal, in his second year, seemed to be doing a relatively good job.

There were some special interest science courses
(i.e., applied science, engines, marine biology, space
science) and a fairly extensive foreign language
program. Otherwise, the school had a rather conventional junior high curriculum. The language arts
program did stand out as organized and comprehensive--
basics and beyond. Teachers reported almost no school-
based in-service training. There was some sponsored by
the district or the nearby regional educational center
and individuals took courses at nearby teacher training
institutions.

Teachers were quite satisfied with the teaching at
the school. They gave the school a "B+." However,
both students and parents gave only a "B-."

Organization of the Book

The book consists of ten chapters, organized into
three sections. Section One sets forth the rationale
for the book and presents the background necessary to
an analysis of data about junior high schools collected
by A Study of Schooling.

I began Chapter 1 by describing some of my own
personal experiences in junior high schools. It was
these experiences which served to create my own views
of what junior highs are like and of how they might be.
I also set forth in this chapter a handful of assumptions which serve to guide the writing of the remainder
of the book. Finally, in Chapter 1, I describe A Study
of Schooling itself, the schools in the sample, and the
organization of the book.

Chapter 2 provides grounding for the remainder of
the book by weaving together a literature review with
selected data from the Study. First, the nature of
junior high age students is explored through a review
of literature about the so-called "developmental tasks"
of adolescence. This is contrasted with data from the
Study having to do with student self-concept and future
educational plans. Against this background, the
chapter traces the history of the junior high from its
beginning early in the twentieth century (when it was
designed so that college bound students could begin
their academic studies sooner), to the emergence of the
so-called middle school, which is purported to better
meet the unique social, psychological, and intellectual

needs of early adolescents. Then, the chapter describes the six classic aims of the junior high school: integration, exploration, guidance, differentiation, socialization, and articulation. The chapter ends with Study data about the perceptions of students, parents, and teachers of the functions of junior high schools.

Section Two of the book contains an in-depth description of the programs of the twelve schools in the sample. All chapters are data-based and each is organized around one of the aims of junior high schools discussed in Chapter 2.

Chapter 3 describes, from a variety of perspectives, the degree to which the junior high school is structured to encourage integrative behavior on the part of students. Data from teachers, students and class observations are presented which tell what teaching/ learning activities are actually carried out in classrooms and how students and teachers feel about them. Class schedules are examined for evidence of core and/or block scheduling.

The chapter on exploration, Chapter 4, describes the degree to which the junior high is organized to encourage students to discover and explore their aptitudes, interests and abilities. It looks at the schedules of the sample schools to determine what latitude students have in selecting class options and it describes student attitudes toward the various school subjects. Within classes, it describes student and teacher data about the materials and equipment which are used to facilitate teaching/learning. Student participation in extracurricular activities and data about the degree to which students are involved in decision-making are detailed and the arts are examined as a special case of exploration.

The data on guidance are examined in Chapter 5. The question is, "How does the school assist pupils to make intelligent decisions regarding their present educational activities and how does it prepare them for future decision-making?" The chapter examines the perceptions of students, parents and teachers about the counseling services of the school, and data about home-school relations are also discussed.

At the classroom level, data on teaching practices relating to both instructional and interpersonal

27

guidance are examined in light of teachers' age, sex, educational beliefs and satisfaction with aspects of their careers.

Differentiation is the subject of Chapter 6. Assumptions which undergird the practice of tracking as well as data about its pervasiveness are examined. The nature and effects of tracking are described. Data on in-class and in-school grouping are reviewed and the implications of such groupings are looked at.

Chapter 7 is about the socialization of students. It looks at student, teacher and observer data to see just how time is spent in classrooms and it examines data about how students interact in and out of class. As an example of contemporary attitudes toward the school's role in the socialization process, student, teacher and parent responses to selected items about the teaching of global understanding and other social issues are presented.

The final chapter in this section, Chapter 8, is about articulation. Thus, critical data which have been previously presented are re-examined and statements made about the degree to which the junior high school bridges the gap between the students' elementary school and high school experiences.

There are two chapters in the third and final section of the book. In Chapter 9, I discuss the difficulties which will be involved in attempting to bring about change in present junior highs and middle schools. Data are presented about (1) external influences upon teachers, (2) the work environment of the schools, and (3) the personal and professional characteristics of teachers. Essentially, these data suggest a systemic predisposition against change.

The final chapter, Chapter 10, summarizes the data and makes numerous recommendations for the improvement of junior high school education. Summaries and recommendations are organized around four headings: school organization, curriculum, teaching/learning, and guidance. Following the summaries and recommendations, I propose concrete ways in which change can be brought about. In so doing, I take into account the conditions, described in Chapter 9, which mitigate against change. I conclude Chapter 10 with the proposal of an updated set of aims for junior high school education.

Limitations

Several caveats need to be stated at this point. Most importantly, the findings which follow are based on the study of only twelve junior high schools and are reported as such. These findings are not generalizable beyond this sample. In the final section, the data are used as a basis for speculation about a number of issues critical to the schooling of early adolescents. Questions are raised and hypotheses proposed in keeping with the original purposes of the Study of Schooling.

A special caution is given about parent data. While student and teacher responses were collected by questionnaires administered at the schools themselves, parent responses were collected by mail. A low return rate resulted in small parent samples at some schools even though there were some follow-up phone calls and/or home visits.

Readers should also be aware that the parent sample was not always representative. Often the people who returned the completed questionnaires were people (1) whose value patterns included compliance with requests such as this; (2) whose attitudes towards this study were positive; and/or (3) who, for whatever reasons, welcomed a chance to critique the schools in their community. We do know, from subsequent analysis of the parent data, that the parents who did respond tended to be slightly more affluent than the average for their community. We also know that minority parents were underrepresented in our sample relative to their numbers in the population at-large. For these reasons, caution in the interpretation of parent data is recommended.

Since A Study of Schooling was designed as an attempt to understand the internal dynamics of schools rather than their outcomes, no student achievement data were collected. Instead, the Study focused on processes, relationships, and attitudes towards the daily experiences of schooling.

And finally, readers are asked to bear in mind that the interpretations of Study data presented in this book are those of the author. Alternative explanations and hypotheses will occur to every reader who is closely involved with the day-to-day business of schooling as well as to researchers who may be interested in the education of early adolescents. Educators interested in doing secondary analysis of the data should write to the ERIC Document Reproduction Service, P.O. Box 190, Arlington, VA 22210.

1. John I. Goodlad, M. Frances Klein and Associates, <u>Behind the Classroom Door</u>. Worthington, Ohio: Charles A Jones, rev. ed., 1974.

2. A number of books, articles and dissertations resulted from this Study. The most important among these are: (a) John I. Goodlad, <u>The Dynamics of Educational Change: Toward Responsive Schools</u>, New York: McGraw-Hill Book Co., 1975; (b) Mary Bentzen, <u>Changing Schools: The Magic Feather Principle</u>, New York: McGraw-Hill Book Co., 1974; (c) Kenneth A. Tye, and Jerrold M. Novotney, <u>Schools in Transition: The Practitioner as Change Agent</u>, New York: McGraw-Hill Book Co., 1975.

3. This book is one of a series covering all three levels of schooling. The other two books are: Barbara Tye, <u>Multiple Realities: A Study of 13 American High Schools</u>. Lanham, MD: University Press of America, 1984 and M. Frances Klein, <u>Inside Elementary Classrooms</u> (in process). The summary volume for the entire Study is: Goodlad, John I. <u>A Place Called School: Prospects for the Future</u>. New York: McGraw-Hill Book Co., 1984.

4. There were 13 "triples" studied. However, one rural secondary school (grades 7-12) is not included in this write-up but is in the Barbara Tye high school book. Large schools = student population over 1,000; medium = 500-1000; small = under 500. SES of the community was defined by school district personnel.

5. Due to sample design, which involved questionnairing and observing in a cross-section of classes in every subject area, some students were questionnaired more than once about class-specific data.

6. Each class was observed three times. The subject area distribution of observed classes was as follows: English--73, math--70, social studies--54, science--42, arts--45, foreign language--11, vocational and career education--49, physical education--25. There were 369 classes observed.

7. See: Jeannie Oakes, <u>Tracking Policies and Practices: School by School Summaries</u>, I/D/E/A Study of Schooling Technical Report 25, ERIC Document Reproduction Service, 1981.

31

CHAPTER II

THE ORIGIN, HISTORY AND FUNCTIONS

OF THE JUNIOR HIGH

The junior high school in the United States today is much like the early adolescent it purports to serve. It is in search of its own identity. This is not surprising since it tends to operate ahistorically. That is, as is the case with many institutions in the United States, the people there do what they do because they do it and there is often no more significance to it than that. As Eichorn says, "...Unlike the elementary and secondary education phases of schooling, the transitional school [junior high] has not developed a set role in the total scheme of school organization..."[1]

But the junior high school movement in the United States does have a history, and in that history is its reason for existence. This chapter examines that history and, in so doing, hopes to shed light upon the question of what the junior high school in the United States is supposed to be and what it is supposed to do for the students it services.

The Early History of the Junior High

The date of the establishment of the first junior high school in the United States is debated in the literature. Van Til, et al., tell of Columbus, Ohio in 1909 and Berkeley, California in 1910.[2] Heironomous says Richmond, Indiana in 1895.[3] No matter; the idea caught on and spread rapidly.

The standard organizational pattern for public schooling in the United States after the Civil War was the 8-4 plan although some southern states provided only eleven years of schooling (7-4) and there were some 8-5 plans in New England.

According to Van Til, et al., the first prompting for the junior high school came in a report of a

33

subcommittee of the now famous Committee of Ten on Secondary School Studies.[4] As can be seen from the statement quoted below, it was a desire to have students begin academic studies sooner which motivated the initial, although indirect, call for the junior high school:

> In the opinion of the committee, several subjects now reserved for high schools--such as algebra, geometry, natural science, and foreign languages--should be begun earlier than now, and therefore within the schools classified as elementary; or as an alternative, the secondary school period should be made to begin two years earlier than at present, leaving six years instead of eight for the elementary school period.[5]

This pressure for beginning academic studies earlier came not from the high schools of the day; but, rather, from leaders of higher education. In fact, the composition of the Committee of Ten was: five college presidents, one college professor, two private school headmasters, one high school principal, and the U.S. Commissioner of Education.

In the late nineteenth century in the United States, there was hardly universal secondary education. Most secondary schools were college preparatory schools and many were private rather than supported by public funds. As Van Til, et al. pointed out:

> That college presidents took the lead in a matter of secondary education in the late nineteenth century is not surprising. College presidents had more prestige than high school administrators. Secondary education was regarded by the public largely as preparation of a few for college and college presidents naturally were concerned with the improvement of preparatory work.[6]

Clearly, the issues were economy of time and the early introduction of college-level work into the secondary school curriculum. These issues were hotly debated for some time with the advocates of college preparatory work on one side, and generally, superintendents of large city school systems on the other. This latter group, through the Committee of Fifteen, appointed by

34

the Department of Superintendence of the NEA in 1895 opposed the reduction of elementary schooling.

The debate for a long while did not suggest the formation of a separate school known as a junior high school. To be sure, junior high schools began to appear circa 1900. However, there was neither national support for the movement nor expansion of the issues beyond the issue of economy of time until 1918 and the now famous Cardinal Principles of Secondary Education developed by the Commission on the Reorganization of Secondary Education.

The most critical sections of the Commission report were:

> We . . . recommend a reorganization of the school system whereby the first six years shall be devoted to elementary education designed to meet the needs of pupils approximately 6 to 12 years of age, and the second six years to secondary education designed to meet the needs of pupils approximately 12 to 18 years of age.
>
> The six years to be devoted to secondary education may well be divided into two periods which may be designated as the junior and senior periods. In the junior period emphasis should be placed upon the attempt to help the pupil explore his own aptitudes and to make at least provisional choice of the kinds of work to which he shall devote himself. In the senior period emphasis should be given to training in the fields thus chosen. This distinction lies at the basis of the organization of the junior and senior high schools.
>
> In the junior high school there should be a gradual introduction of departmental instruction, some choice of subjects under guidance, promotion by subjects, prevoca- tional courses, and a social organization that calls for the initiative and develops the sense of personal responsibility for the welfare of the group.

As junior high schools actually began to appear in many education systems, primarily in the cities, it was still not clear what their role was to be. The initial notion of the junior high school as a way of starting certain academic subjects earlier and lowering the college entrance age was gradually giving way to the notion that the formation of a separate junior high school was a way to provide for the peculiar educational needs of early adolescents.

Studies of Early Adolescence

Early Studies. Early studies of pupils of junior high age added weight to the argument for a separate school to provide for the unique educational needs of early adolescents. For example, between 1907 and 1911 several educators as well as psychologists studied the problem of retention and drop-outs.

Three of these studies became very famous and their results were widely circulated. E.L. Thorndike, the noted psychologist, studied drop-outs in twenty-three cities with populations of 25,000 or more and reported his findings in The Elimination of Pupils from School.[8] Leonard P. Ayers gathered data in fifty-nine cities and wrote an influential book with a dramatic title, Laggards in Our Schools.[9] George D. Strayer conducted a study in 319 cities and entitled his report of conclusions, Age and Grade Census of Schools and Colleges.[10]

These studies showed a high drop-out rate beyond fifth grade. Only slightly more than one in three students who entered public school even reached ninth grade and only approximately one in ten completed high school. About one-third of the school children of the time were retained at one time or another while they were in school and about one in six children at any grade was a repeater in that grade.

There were many reasons for drop-outs and retentions--illness, late entrance, low intelligence, irregular attendance, lack of family support for schooling. However, there can be no doubt that the poor quality of the school program, itself, was a major contributor. Van Til and his colleagues describe that program as follows:

In the early twentieth century, schools were predominantly formal and traditional. Many pupils understandably felt that schoolwork had little or no relationship to their lives. They saw no connection between school learning and out-of-school experiences and interests. The same academic diet day after day resulted in a loss of appetite for education. The average and below average child in particular found the heavily academic character of the work tedious and difficult. Poor readers were severely and continuously handicapped, because the school program was almost exclusively based on the printed word. At the ninth grade, the opening of the high school years, the content became still more academic and the method still more formal. Suddenly, the student was confronted with many teachers instructing him in the formal subjects that almost exclusively made up the high school program. The result was often failure. The outcome of failure was often withdrawal. The very ones who dropped out were the ones least prepared to succeed in an increasingly complex and competitive society.[11]

Along with the drop-out and retention studies, there were also other works about adolescence and individuality which gave impetus to the fledgling junior high school movement of the early twentieth century.

G. Stanley Hall was a very influential early psychologist. In today's world he would probably be viewed as a reactionary. Certainly his theories would be considered strange. He developed the culture-epoch theory which stated that the growth of the individual paralleled the development of mankind. What was memorable, however, was his focus upon the importance of adolescence. He characterized this period of life as one of upheaval, of new interests, deepening feelings, and of a widened outlook upon life. It was a period of radical change--physical, social, emotional and intellectual.[12] The physiological advent of puberty, in Hall's view, was responsible for these radical changes. Educators took Hall's views seriously. For example, R. A. Mackie said:

The young adolescent is a new kind of being which demands a new environment, new methods

and new matter...We must take into account the
nature of the great upheaval at the dawn of the
teens, which marks the pubescent ferment, and
which requires distinct change in matter and
method of education.[13]

These were new ideas for educators and, indeed, for
society. Heretofore, children had rather abruptly
moved to adulthood, going from school and/or the
protected home environment into the adult world of
work. Given that there was a transitional stage in
life called adolescence, it seemed only logical that
there should be a transitional school which dealt
specifically with early adolescents. Thus, the rationale for the junior high school was strengthened.

Additionally, the study of individual differences
by psychologists such as James M. Cattell and E. L.
Thorndike added to the idea that early adolescents
needed a separate school, one which was more flexible
and which catered at once to a range of prepubescent,
pubescent and postpubescent characteristics and behaviors.

Today's Early Adolescents. "I feel that I am learning
kind of and kind of not but I don't feel like I am
going to fail, which I hope I don't."

This statement was uttered by a junior high school
student in response to the question, "What is the most
important thing that you have learned or done so far in
this class?" It is typical of the uncertainty and/or
ambivalence of early adolescence and suggests the
difficulty of designing a school program to meet the
educational and emotional needs of the young people of
this age group.

The physical, psychological and social characteristics of early adolescence have long been a concern of
those who have advocated junior high schools separated
from the upper secondary phase of schooling. I would
suggest that this is a proper concern. However, I also
believe that we have done an injustice to the concept
of developmental characteristics in at least three
ways: 1) such characteristics, while identified, have
not been utilized in program development; 2) such
characteristics have been used after the fact, to
justify decisions made about school organization which

38

were made for other than developmental reasons; and 3) as society has changed so have the characteristics of youth, including early adolescents and our schools have not kept up with such changes.

Many state departments of education, school districts, and even schools have produced lists of the developmental characteristics of children or youth in the age group(s) they have been commissioned to serve. However, in most instances there has been little relationship between such lists and actual practice. We need to do a better job of linking student needs to the actual program of the school.

The so-called sexual revolution, television, changes in family patterns (i.e., working mothers, divorce) are commonly recognized as influencing the lives of children and youth. And yet, these new social forces are not often taken into account when "developmental characteristics" are considered in the planning of school programs. As Lipsitz says:

> We grow up in historical contexts and in particular communities. Becoming an adolescent during the Depression had a different meaning from growing up during the expanding economy of the 1950s, which was different from entering adolescence during the 1970s, with shrinking job markets and growing inflation....[14]

The program of today's junior high school more likely than not is designed for early adolescents of several decades ago. We need to be conscious of the current characteristics of our students. To this end, data from A Study of Schooling should be helpful.

The classic work on developmental characteristics is Developmental Tasks and Education first published in 1948 and now in its third edition. A developmental task is defined as

> ...a task which arises at or about a certain period in the life of an individual, successful achievement of which leads to his happiness and to success with later tasks, while failure leads to unhappiness to the individual, disapproval by society, and difficulty with later tasks.[15]

The developmental tasks of adolescence fall into eight categories:

1. Achieving new and more mature relations with age-mates of both sexes.

2. Achieving a masculine or feminine social role.

3. Accepting one's physique and using the body effectively.

4. Achieving emotional independence of parents and other adults.

5. Preparing for marriage and family life.

6. Preparing for an economic career.

7. Acquiring a set of values and an ethical system as a guide to behavior.

8. Desiring and achieving socially responsible behavior.[16]

Psychologists have tended to agree that the predominant characteristic of early adolescents is that "...at no other age are children so different from each other...."[17]

Differences in physical maturity are perhaps the most obvious. Growth rates differ between the sexes. Girls tend to grow rapidly to approximately their 13th birthday after which their growth rate slows. They are generally taller and heavier than boys until they are 13. The growth rate of boys is greater between 12 and 16. Rapid muscular development occurs for both sexes during early adolescence. None of them seem to be satisfied with themselves: they are too tall, too short, too fat, too thin, too under-developed and/or too clumsy.[18]

Early adolescents are also quite different from each other with regard to their intellectual interests and accomplishments. The obvious differences have to do with achievement: reading level, math achievement, ability to use the English language. They also have different intellectual interests as well as avocational

40

and recreational interests. Special talents in sports and the arts begin to appear and develop.

This age period is a time of change in the social relationship among individuals. Before junior high school, most boys prefer to associate only with their own sex. Many boys and girls make the transition from group to paired boy-girl relationships during the junior high years.

During early adolescence there is a great drive to establish an independent personality. Noar describes this drive as follows:

> The establishment of an independent personality involves emancipation from parental control and securing equality of status in the adult world. It is this need that lies at the root of so much misunderstanding and conflict in the home and the school. If rebellion against grown-ups could be regarded as evidence of maturity, adults would look upon it with favor...Teachers who do not fully understand the need for independence are prone to bemoan the seeming loss of respect for their authority...Instead of encouraging growth in these directions the school too often makes rules and regulations that deprive the pupils of independence of thought and action...[19]

While early adolescents desire freedom, they also tend to want security. Ties which bind them to their age-mates become stronger. This creates certain pressures for conformity and is the reason why early adolescents often are so precise about kinds of clothes they must have, their hair styles, and the like. As Grooms suggests, "Peer acceptance is exceedingly important to future behavior patterns. Peer rejection often leads to development of solitary behavior models."[20]

A significant number of developmental tasks for early adolescents have to do with their adjustment to the social order: preparing for marriage and family life, acquiring a set of values, and acquiring socially acceptable behavior. However, junior highs have done a poor job of dealing with this set of student needs. Partly, this is due to the fact that there is no traditional subject area which deals specifically with areas of social adjustment and teachers are reluctant to give up precious time from "regular" content. Secondly, teachers are not taught in teacher training institutions how to teach to such needs and therefore are reluctant to do so. Finally, topics to be dealt with are most often controversial (e.g., sex roles, labor-management relations, environmental issues, race relations) and are avoided or only "taught about." When students are denied the means of achieving socially responsible behavior, the result often is socially undesirable and/or irresponsible behavior. It is important that we give more attention to the designing of curricula and the training of teachers for junior high schools so that early adolescents are enabled to meet the bio-socio-psychological tasks that are the basis for success throughout life.

It is also argued that intellectual growth goes through various "stages of development." For example, according to Erikson, adolescence is a period that "simultaneously recapitulates all the earlier stages of development and anticipates all those to come...."[21] Likewise, on the basis of his research into the cognitive processes of children over several decades, Piaget theorizes that intellectual capability is linked to maturation. He identifies four developmental stages:

1. The sensory-motor stage (first two years) - the child learns to control perception and motor responses in dealing with physical objects and language.

2. The preoperational or representational stage (to about age six or seven) - the child learns to extract concepts from experience and later to make perceptual and intuitive judgments.

3. The stage of concrete operations (between ages seven and eleven) - the child learns to solve physical problems by anticipating consequences perceptually.

4. The stage of formal operations (late childhood or early adolescence) - the child learns to think hypothetically, to theorize and to experiment.[22]

While stages overlap somewhat, according to Piaget, they cannot be telescoped or accelerated. Each stage is a necessary prerequisite to later intellectual development.[23] Thus, at the junior high school level according to this view of intellectual development, curricula should be designed which cause students to inquire, hypothesize, experiment, test assumptions and theorize.

Recent research into intellectual development suggests that because of a plateau period of brain growth from approximately age 12 to 14, caution should be taken to assess student readiness for formal operations learning and care should be taken not to put children under too much pressure in this regard.[24]

Study of Schooling Data. Two sets of data from A Study of Schooling are examined here because they relate directly to the developmental needs of students. These were data on self-concept and the future educational plans of students.

There were a relatively small number of questions in the survey which asked students about their general self-esteem (SC-GEN), peer relationships (SC-PEERS), and academic success (SC-ACAD). The following report of those data draws heavily from the unpublished report, Student Life, Chapter Two, "Student and Self: The Personal Domain" by Barbara Benham Tye.[25]

The item breakdown resulted from a factor analysis and formed the three scales shown below:

GENERAL (SC-GEN) (8)
-4. At times I think I'm no good at all.
-7. There are a lot of things about myself I'd change if I could.
-8. Most people are better liked than I am.
-9. I often feel like giving up when I can't do my schoolwork.
10. I'm pretty sure of myself.
-11. Kids often pick on me.
-13. I often wish I were someone else.
-18. I get upset easily when I'm scolded.

PEERS (SC-PEER) (4)
1. I'm easy to like.
3. I'm popular with kids my own age.
6. Kids usually follow my ideas.
16. I'm a lot of fun to be with.

ACADEMIC (SC-ACAD)   (6)

-2. I'm not doing as well as I'd like to in school.
 5. I am a good reader.
12. I'm proud of my schoolwork.
15. I'm good at math.
17. I'm doing the best work that I can.
19. I am able to do schoolwork at least as well as most other students.

The scales were identical for both upper elementary and secondary students; the response modes, however, differed: upper elementary students were asked to indicate whether the statement was "usually true" or "usually false," while the secondary students were asked to select one of four possible responses (strongly agree; mildly agree; mildly disagree; strongly disagree).

The junior high school self-concept data take on extraordinary meaning when they are juxtaposed against the elementary and senior high school data. Table 2.1 shows the level mean for all three types of self-concept for upper elementary, junior high, and senior high students.

The SC-Peers means were the highest scores of the three types of self-concept for both junior high and high school, followed by SC-Acad and then SC-Gen.

Overall, the General Self-Concept (SC-Gen) and the Self-Concept in Relation to Peers (SC-Peers) scores were higher at the high school level than at the junior high level. However, the Academic Self-Concept (SC-Acad) scores were higher at the junior high level.

Conclusions drawn about schooling vis-a-vis these self-concept scores can be speculative at best. There are so many limitations. There needs to be more work on the validity of the items/scales. So many factors other than school factors come into play to influence self-concept. Deriving scores from paper-and-pencil measures of complex attitudinal and emotional constructs is a problem. However, some patterns appeared to be so marked that they, at least, were worth noting and suggestive of areas for possible further study. B. Tye, in her Student Life report, examined grade-by-grade trends in self-concept scores. She noted a

44

steady rise in SC-Gen through the grades and a steady decline in the SC-Acad from grade 4 through grade 9. There was no marked change in SC-Peer scores until high school when they rose slightly from grades 9 through 12.

Table 2.1

Comparison of Self-Concept Scores at Three Levels of Schooling

	Mean	Standard Deviation	N
Upper Elementary			
SC-Gen	1.52	0.25	1641
SC-Peers	1.65	0.29	1637
SC-Acad	1.73	0.23	1640
Junior High			
SC-Gen	2.52	0.56	5642
SC-Peers	2.95	0.52	5635
SC-Acad	2.92	0.52	5642
Senior High			
SC-Gen	2.71	0.53	7237
SC-Peers	3.03	0.47	7238
SC-Acad	2.79	0.51	7238

A number of interesting questions were raised about the steady drop in SC-Acad. For example, it appeared that teachers in the lower grades made more of an effort to help each child feel good about his or her school work. Perhaps elementary school teachers, responsible basically for one set of about 30 students each day rather than the 150-200 students seen daily by high school teachers, are better able to exhibit such supportive behavior. Or perhaps there is just more pressure for academic accomplishment at the higher grade levels. Tye noted that observation data from the Study of Schooling showed that elementary teachers exhibited more supportive behavior. By senior high, in fact, the frequency of teacher praise, encouragement, correction with guidance, and positive interactions with students dropped by almost 50% from the number of observed occurrences at the early elementary level.

Such data raise questions about staffing practices and organizational patterns for junior high schools. It is common in American junior high schools to hire teachers with high school teaching experience and/or training. If the needs of early adolescents are generally different from those of adolescents, perhaps this staffing practice, at least in terms of its potential impact on SC-Acad, should be re-examined. Similarly, the movement of students from teacher to teacher, subject to subject, at the junior high school level may need to be re-examined. This data supports the notion of core classes, block time, and/or home-rooms.

B. Tye also examined differences between boys' and girls' self-concept scores. Table 2.2 reports these scores for junior high students.

Where significant differences existed between boys' and girls' scores, the boys' scores were higher than the girls' on SC-Gen and lower on SC-Acad. There were no significant differences between the scores of girls and boys on the SC-Peers subscale.

With regard to SC-Gen, the gap between boys and girls seemed to widen through the grades at the junior high school level. That is, mean scores increased for boys from grades six through nine while girls' mean scores stayed pretty constant. Tye found that these scores increased at about the same rate for girls and boys at the high school level. On the one hand, this seemed to indicate that girls' general self-concept could be considered more stable at the junior high school. On the other hand, it also indicated that attention needs to be paid to the poorer general self-concept of girls. Clearly, these differences need further examination.

Black junior high school students in our sample scored relatively high on all self-concept measures, regardless of whether they were in all black schools or in schools with mixed racial populations. The self-concept scores of Hispanic populations were generally lower. This data may suggest that it is far easier to get Black students to believe that "Black is beautiful" than it is to get Hispanic students to believe that

46

Table 2.2

Self-Concept by Grade and Sex
at the Junior High Level

Grade/Sex		$\bar{X}$	Sd	N	sig.
			SC-Gen		
6	B	2.49	.57	353	NS
	G	2.50	.62	331	
7	B	2.54	.56	1064	.01
	G	2.47	.58	1092	
8	B	2.60	.54	1009	.001
	G	2.49	.55	1098	
9	B	2.64	.55	356	.001
	G	2.49	.54	340	
			SC-Acad		
6	B	3.02	.51	353	.05
	G	3.10	.52	331	
7	B	2.91	.53	1064	.05
	G	2.96	.52	1092	
8	B	2.87	.52	1009	NS
	G	2.88	.53	1097	
9	B	2.82	.51	355	NS
	G	2.8	.52	341	
			SC-Peer		
6	B	2.96	.57	352	NS
	G	2.94	.59	331	
7	B	2.93	.54	1065	NS
	G	2.95	.53	1092	
8	B	2.97	.50	1008	NS
	G	2.95	.51	1094	
9	B	2.96	.48	353	NS
	G	2.94	.46	340	

"Brown is beautiful." The degree to which cultural and/or language factors might be involved was in no way examined.

The student survey also contained three questions about students' future plans:
A-12 "If I could do anything I want, I would like to--"
A-13 "I think my parents would like me to--"
A-14 "Actually, I will probably--"

The seven possible responses to these questions were:
--Quit school as soon as possible
--Finish high school
--Go to trade or technical school
--Go to junior college
--Go to a four-year college or university
--Go to graduate school after college
--Don't know

Table 2.3 shows the responses of junior high students to the three questions. These responses, overall, were very similar to those by senior high students indicating that students' expectations and perceptions of their parents' expectations were pretty well set by junior high.

The largest percentages were those for "Go To A Four-Year College," followed closely by "Finish High School." This nearly equal split may be an important indicator of other aspects of students' experiences in school, since the distinction between "college-prep" and "non-college prep" is one that usually shapes these experiences in major ways. We will return to this issue in later chapters when "differentiation" and "tracking" are examined in concept and in practice.

Another interesting pattern was that which involved a comparison of each response across all three questions. For example, slightly less than 30% of the students said "I would like to go to a four-year college or university." However, slightly more than 40% thought that "My parents would like me to go to a four-year college or university." When it finally came to "Actually, I will probably go to a four-year college or university," approximately 35% responded. Thus, a number of students felt that their parents had higher expectations for them than they did for themselves. A number also thought they would actually go to college even though they didn't want to. This was an indication that at least some students go on to college because their parents want them to rather than because they want to themselves.

Table 2.3

Junior High Student Responses to Three
Questions About Their Future Plans

	A-12 "I would like to--"	A-13 "My parents would like me to--"	A-14 "Actually, I will probably--"
Quit	5.7%	1.2%	3.2%
Finish High School	25.9	29.5	28.4
Trade/Tech	6.1	4.4	6.4
Jr. College	4.4	5.5	7.8
4-Year College	28.9	41.4	34.6
Graduate School	7.0	11.9	8.0
Don't Know	21.9	6.0	11.6
N	N=5254	N=5225	N=5222

At the school level, two data sets seemed worth reporting. These were: (1) the data on students who felt they would "like to quit" and (2) the data on students who said they would "like to go to a four-year college."

Data on junior high students who said they would "like to quit" are reported in Table 2.4.

In all schools, fewer than 5% of the students responded "Actually, I will probably quit" while the responses to "I would like to quit" ranged from 2.8% at Woodlake to 13.3% at Laurel.

In every case except one, higher percentages of students said they would like to quit than believed they actually would quit. In that one case, the percentages were exactly the same.

Table 2.4

Junior High Student Desire To
Quit School - Percentages

School	"I would like to quit"	"Actually, I will probably quit"	Drop-out rate First Year of H.S.
Woodlake	2.8%	1.6%	Not reported
Palisades	3.6	2.1	6.0%
Manchester	4.2	2.6	8.0
Euclid	4.7	4.7	0
Newport	4.8	3.2	Not reported
Rosemont	5.1	4.1	7.8
Atwater	5.4	3.5	8.0 (10th grade)
Vista	5.4	1.7	4.0
Bradford	7.3	4.2	12.0 (10th grade)
Crestview	7.7	4.7	9.0
Fairfield	8.1	4.4	10.6
Laurel	13.3	3.7	11.0

We asked the administration at all schools to estimate the percentage of dropouts at each school. At all grade levels during junior high these estimates were negligible. However, when we looked at the estimates for the first year of high school the figures were a good deal higher. At Euclid (0%) and Vista (4%), they were low. At the other eight schools which reported, the range of estimated dropouts after junior high school (first year of high school) was from 6% (Palisades) to 12% (Bradford).

There was a strong relationship between student responses to "I would like to quit" and administrator estimates of dropout rates on the one hand and estimated parent median income levels on the other. That is, dropout rates were usually lower and fewer students responded "I would like to quit" in schools where the median parent income was higher. There were two noticeable exceptions: Bradford and Rosemont.

Bradford Junior High had the third highest parent median income ($17,900) but it had a comparatively high estimated dropout rate (12% at 10th grade - the first year of high school) and the fourth greatest percentage of student response to "I would like to quit" (7.3%). Looking further, we can see that Bradford parents had a comparatively low level of educational attainment combined with their high level of income. Bradford was a highly industrialized, union community where parents worked at fairly well paid jobs. Thus, probably they and their junior high children saw less value to schooling than did parents and students in the other communities where the Study was conducted.

On the other hand, Rosemont parents had the lowest median income by a wide margin ($4,000) but a fairly low estimated dropout rate (7.8%) and a relatively low percentage of student response to "I would like to quit" (5.1%). Parents in this stable (little migration), Mexican-American community also had the lowest educational attainment of all the schools. However, they and their junior high children obviously valued educational attainment.

Table 2.5 reports junior high student responses to questions about future college attendance. At all schools, somewhat lower percentages of students said they would like to attend a four-year college than thought they would actually do so. Thus, we see again the impact of parental expectations upon student views of their future educational plans.

B. Tye found no great differences in future educational plans of girls as compared to boys, with one exception: somewhat larger percentages of boys both responded would like to and probably will go to trade or technical school (boys, 8.5% - girls, 3.9%).

B. Tye also examined correlations between data on self-concept and educational future plans. She found a pattern which suggested that students who planned on some form of higher education had higher self-concepts (SC-Acad, SC-Peers, SC-Gen) than those who planned to quit school, finish high school, or who didn't know.

Further, students whose future plans did not include some form of higher education were more likely to <u>agree</u> with the statement, "If you don't want to go to college, this school doesn't think you're very important."

Table 2.5

Junior High Student Desire To Attend
A 4-Year College - Percentages

School	"I would like to go a 4-year college	"I will probably go to a 4-year college
Laurel	17.4%	18.6%
Rosemont	17.8	23.4
Crestview	20.5	25.1
Bradford	22.8	25.7
Atwater	24.7	29.0
Fairfield	25.3	31.9
Euclid	27.6	29.9
Manchester	30.9	40.4
Vista	33.2	40.4
Palisades	37.7	46.8
Newport	38.2	41.1
Woodlake	39.3	46.3

These patterns, well established by junior high and taken together, suggest that most junior high schools still are places where the obviously college bound students are most valued. And the students know it.

Scheirer and Kraut, in a review of the self-concept literature, point out that improved self-concept is a <u>result</u> of success, rather than a precondition for success.[26] Thus, it is conceivable that the school contributes to a lowered self-concept for non-college bound students. This would seem to be particularly critical at the junior high school level where early adolescents are so sensitive to criticism and so concerned with being accepted and successful.

School Organization

Today, one can find any number of grade levels included in the junior high school (e.g., 6-8, 7-8, 7-9); and, in fact, there are several labels for schools which serve early adolescents--junior high school, intermediate school, middle school. Regardless of the grade span or the label, one fact is clear: the junior high school is an urban phenomenon. While you can find junior high schools or intermediate schools or middle schools in most suburban areas and in many rural areas, there are junior high schools of some description in <u>all</u> urban centers. This, too, has its roots in our history.

By 1900, approximately 40% of the population lived in urban areas and more and more people were leaving rural areas and moving to the cities. In the cities the family was not as strong a force for the education and/or socialization of children and youth as it had been in the rural areas. Also, immigrants were arriving literally by the millions and settling in the cities. By 1910, every third person in the United States was either foreign-born or of foreign-born parentage.

City residents, including those who had migrated from rural areas and those who had immigrated from foreign lands, depended almost totally upon an income from industrial work. Labor organizations and corporations grew in size and often came into conflict. Government activities expanded and the United States became more active internationally. The early twentieth century in the United States was a time of growth and optimism.

All of these forces influenced education. Industrial skills required were new and often complex. That fact, combined with the high dropout rate, caused many people both in education and out to call for a junior high which would stress vocational education for young people who would soon join the work force.

Because of the large number of children of immigrants, citizenship education was added to the curriculum so that they could "...understand and appreciate the American heritage...."[27]

Thus, as the family and other institutions began to have less and less influence upon the early adolescent, the junior high was expected to perform more and more functions for the society. By the mid-1920s, the junior high was an established reality, at least in urban America.

One seemingly unintended effect of the emergence of the junior high was that because it was removed from the pressure of preparing all students for college admission, it could be more experimental. During the 1930s, 1940s, and early 1950s, efforts were made to develop block-time, core classes, homeroom programs, exploratory and elective courses, student involvement in course planning, and socially and personally relevant course content.

Because few school people had the necessary skills or resources to implement these worthwhile innovations, many of them pursued the more simplistic notion of "academic excellence." The result was that many junior highs came to pattern their curricula after the senior high school, particularly with regard to academic studies. Tanner and Tanner describe this movement as follows:

> ...Grouping pupils by ability in all academic subjects became a widespread practice. The priority given the academic studies was accompanied by a neglect of the general education function--not to mention the exploratory and enrichment function. In many respects, the junior high school assumed a function of sifting and sorting youngsters in preparation for the senior high school. In accommodating itself to the pressures of the times, the junior high school curriculum was showing signs of losing the small but recognizable curriculum authenticity it had managed to gain during its earlier years of existence.[28]

During the 1960s and 1970s many educators began to advocate the "middle school" as the organizational plan which could best serve to bridge the gap between the elementary and secondary phases of schooling.

The middle school usually includes grades 6-7-8 or 5-6-7-8, with the ninth grade incorporated in the high school. Proponents claim that this removes the pressure to design the program for college preparatory work. Supposedly, the middle school can make available a wide range of learning options and organizational options such as team teaching, non-grading, and flexible scheduling. Physical facilities with laboratories, industrial arts and homemaking spaces, libraries, gymnasia and the like offer learning opportunities not found in typical elementary schools.

The intent of the middle school is to provide

...a curriculum which includes provision for a planned sequence of concepts in the general education areas; major emphasis on the interests and skills for continued learning; a balanced program of exploratory experiences and other activities and services for personal development; and appropriate attention to the development of values.[29]

Eichorn reports that the middle-school concept rapidly gained acceptance. He cites a survey from 1965 which identified only 499 middle schools and one in 1976 which identified 4,060.[30] On the surface, then, it would seem that Americans supported the idea that the special needs of early adolescents required a kind of intermediate schooling that was distinctly different from the high school.

Unfortunately, growth in numbers of schools called "middle-school" indicates very little in terms of what really goes on in those schools. While Eichorn says that "The middle-school movement erupted as a protest against the program...of the junior high school...",[31] there is evidence that middle schools are coming into being for economic reasons because of the overall decline in public school enrollments. For example, at a curriculum conference of the Association of California School Administrators (ACSA) in 1979, my wife and I "ran into" an old acquaintance, then an assistant superintendent for instruction in a prestigious California school district. After exchanging the usual pleasantries, he launched into an enthusiastic description of how his district had "moved into" middle schools, placing grades 5-8 together instead of grades 7-9. Barbara kept pestering him with the question, "Why?"

At first, he gave us some of the typical responses which usually accompany such innovations. After he was pressed, he finally admitted that because of declining enrollments it was "expedient" to move ninth graders to the high schools, upper elementary students to middle schools and close whatever elementary schools it was necessary to close. In the final analysis, I would guess that there was little difference in the experience of pre- or early adolescents attending a middle-school in that district from those who earlier had attended a junior high. Likewise, and beyond the age of the students and some superficial organizational things, our Study found no important differences between junior highs and middle schools.

Now, in the 1980s, we are perhaps inevitably confused as to what the proper role of the intermediate school should be. We are torn between a tradition of academic preparation for the few and the social reality of a hetergeneous population. We are torn, also, between our vision of a truly appropriate educational experience for pre- and early adolescents and our inability to achieve this in day-to-day practice. And finally, we are eternally on the horns of the fiscal dilemma: how to provide the best and most appropriate schooling for youngsters with the meager funding allowed by our society for the purpose.

In attempting to sort out these conflicting issues, we must first address two basic questions: (1) what are the functions that the junior high should serve? and (2) what are the needs of the students served by the junior high?

The Functions of the Junior High

Study of Schooling Data. Because of the continual debate over the functions of schools, the following four questions were asked of junior high teachers, parents and students by A Study of Schooling:

Schools usually provide education in a variety of areas. However, some areas may be more important at one school than at another.

As far as as you can tell, how important does THIS SCHOOL think each of the following areas is for the education of students at this school?

a. SOCIAL DEVELOPMENT (Instruction which helps students learn to get along with other students and adults, prepares students for social and civic responsibility, develops students' awareness and appreciation of our own and other cultures)

O Very   O Somewhat   O Somewhat   O Very
  Important   Important   Unimportant   Unimportant

b. INTELLECTUAL DEVELOPMENT (Instruction in basic skills in mathematics, reading, and written and verbal communication; and in critical thinking and problem-solving abilities)

O   O   O   O

c. PERSONAL DEVELOPMENT (Instruction which builds self-confidence, creativity, ability to think independently, and self-discipline)

O   O   O   O

d. VOCATIONAL DEVELOPMENT (Instruction which prepares students for employment, development of skills necessary for getting a job, development of awareness about career choices and alternatives)

O   O   O   O

Which one do you think receives the most emphasis at this school? (Please mark ONLY ONE.)
   O Social development
   O Intellectual development
   O Personal development
   O Vocational development

Regardless of how you answered the previous questions, how important do YOU THINK each of these areas should be at this school?

a. Social development

O Very   O Somewhat   O Somewhat   O Very
  Important   Important   Unimportant   Unimportant

b. Intellectual development

O   O   O   O

c. Personal development

O   O   O   O

d. Vocational development

O   O   O   O

If you had to choose only one, which do YOU THINK this school should emphasize? (Please mark ONLY ONE.)
O Social development
O Intellectual development
O Personal development
O Vocational development

Table 2.6 shows the responses of junior high teachers, parents and students to the question, "How important does this school think each function is?"

Table 2.6

Junior High Teacher, Parent and Student Perceptions of the Importance Placed Upon Functions by the School

	Teachers			Parents			Students		
	x̄*	sd	N	x̄	sd	N	x̄	sd	N
Functions									
Social	3.23	0.74	393	3.21	0.76	2624	3.33	0.75	4875
Intel-lectual	3.66	0.56	395	3.50	0.68	2607	3.66	0.63	4861
Person-al	3.18	0.76	392	3.17	0.83	2587	3.28	0.82	4849
Voca-tional	2.98	0.83	395	3.00	0.90	2598	3.36	0.88	4860

* 1.00-2.89 = Very Unimportant
  1.50-2.49 = Somewhat Unimportant
  2.50-3.49 = Somewhat Unimportant
  3.50-4.00 = Very Important

All groups (teachers, parents, students) felt that the intellectual function was very important at the school and that all other functions were felt only to be somewhat important by the school. Teachers' and parents' mean scores showed that they thought the second most importance was placed upon the social function, followed by personal and then vocational.

58

Interestingly, students perceived that the second most importance was placed by the schools on the vocational function followed by social and then personal. All groups saw schools as intellectually oriented and students saw them also as quite vocationally oriented. All groups perceived that all four functions were important to the schools.

Teachers, parents and students were also asked which <u>one</u> function received the most emphasis at the school. Table 2.7 reports these responses.

Table 2.7

Junior High School Teacher, Parent and Student Perceptions
of the One Function Which Receives the Most Emphasis at School--
Percentages

Data Source	Social	Intellectual	Personal	Vocational	N
Teachers	16.3%	64.4%	8.7%	10.7%	393
Parents	19.5	56.3	11.2	13.0	2494
Students	11.7	64.1	11.2	13.1	4733

Clearly, the greatest percentage of all groups perceived that the intellectual function received the most emphasis at the school. Also, the smallest percentage of all groups thought that the personal function received the most emphasis at the school.

Table 2.8 shows the responses of junior high teachers, parents and students to the question, "How important do <u>you</u> think each of these functions should be at this school?" Previously they were asked their perceptions of what existed at the school. Now they were asked what they thought <u>should</u> exist.

Parents thought all functions should be very important; teachers said all functions except the vocational function should be very important; students said that only the intellectual and vocational functions should be very important.

Overman attempted to answer the question, "To what extent are schools meeting the expectations of

59

teachers, parents, and students in regard to these various functions?"[32] She did this by comparing responses to two questions: "How important does this school think each function is?" (Table 2.6) and "How important do you think each function should be at this school?" (Table 2.8). She arbitrarily selected the value of a difference score equal to or less than .25 as evidence of satisfaction with what the school was doing relative to expectations and a score equal to or greater than .50 as evidence of dissatisfaction. Scores between .25 and .50 were not recorded either as satisfaction or dissatisfaction. Results were placed in a "Satisfaction Index" which is included here as Table 2.9.

Table 2.8

Junior High School Teacher, Parent and Student Views
of What the Functions of Their School Should Be

	Teachers			Parents			Students		
Functions	$\bar{x}$*	sd	N	$\bar{x}$	sd	N	$\bar{x}$	sd	N
Social	3.68	0.55	388	3.63	0.55	2512	3.46	0.68	4785
Intel-lectual	3.83	0.41	390	3.89	0.34	2527	3.63	0.65	4782
Person-al	3.81	0.45	390	3.79	0.45	2506	3.48	0.73	4751
Voca-tional	3.46	0.68	389	3.61	0.66	2514	3.62	0.73	4773

```
* 1.00-2.89 = Very unimportant
  1.50-2.49 = Somewhat unimportant
  2.50-3.49 = Somewhat unimportant
  3.50-4.00 = Very important
```

There was an outstanding array of student "satis-faction" entries. At all schools there was evidence of student satisfaction with the Social function; at all except Fairfield satisfaction with the Intellectual function; and at all except Crestview, Woodlake and Palisades satisfaction with the Personal function. However, only at five schools were there indicators of satisfaction with the Vocational function.

Teachers at all schools except Fairfield appeared to be satisfied with the Intellectual function. For parents, however, there were very few indicators of satisfaction (five). Three of these were for the Intellectual function and two were at one school (Rosemont--Intellectual, Personal).

Table 2.9

Junior High Student, Teacher, Parent Satisfaction
With School Performance of Functions (Satisfaction Index)

	Satisfaction ($\Delta\overline{<}.25$)				Dissatisfaction ($\Delta\overline{>}.50$)			
	Soc	Int	Per	Voc	Soc	Int	Per	Voc
Vista	S	T S	S		T		TP	TP
Crestview	S	T S			T		TP	TP
Fairfield	S		S	TS	TP	P	TP	P
Rosemont	S	TPS	PS	S	T		T	T
Newport	TPS	T S	S				TP	T
Woodlake	T S	T S					P	T
Atwater	S	T S	S				P	TP
Palisades	T S	T S	T				P	
Laurel	S	PS	S	S	T		TP	
Manchester	S	T S	S	S			TP	P
Bradford	S	T S	S	S	P	P	TP	TP
Euclid	S	TPS	S	T	T		TP	P

The most striking observation when looking at the dissatisfaction side of this table was that there were no students represented. Parents at all schools except Rosemont evidenced dissatisfaction with the Personal function. Fairfield and Bradford were noteworthy in that there was evidence of parent dissatisfaction with all four functions.

Several notes of caution are called for here. The satisfaction-dissatisfaction scale reported related only to the gap between what groups saw as functions

61

performed by a particular school and some idealized version of the functions to be performed by that school. The seeming high level of parent dissatisfaction was limited to that one variable. That could have been attributed to the skewed nature of the parent sample (described under "limitations" in Chapter 1) or by the fact that parents held extremely high expectations for those schools which their children attended. Other data reported in later chapters seems to suggest parent satisfaction with local schools but a dissatisfaction with the more general concept "schooling." Suffice it to say, parents in this sample wanted the schools to perform all functions and were not sure that this was being done well enough.

Table 2.10 reports the response of junior high teachers, parents and students to the question, "Which one function do you think this school should emphasize?"

Table 2.10

Junior High School Teacher, Parent and Student Perceptions of the One Function Which the School Should Emphasize

Function-Percentage Responding

Data Source	Social	Intellectual	Personal	Vocational	N
Teachers	13.9%	46.7%	29.3%	10.1%	396
Parents	9.5	51.1	21.1	18.2	2605
Students	13.4	38.0	18.3	30.3	4733

Parent responses showed somewhat higher percentages than teachers on the Intellectual and Vocational functions and somewhat lower percentages on the Social and Personal functions. Students' scores differed considerably from parents' and teachers' scores, particularly in the lower percentage of students who thought the Intellectual function should be emphasized and the larger percentage who thought the Vocational function should be emphasized.

Overman, in addition to attempting to derive a functions "satisfaction" score, also attempted to put together a functions "congruence" score for each school.[33] An individual functions congruence measure was generated by comparing each individual's responses to the two questions: " Which function receives the most emphasis at this school?" and "Which function do you think this school should emphasize?" When the individual selected the same function in response to both questions, a code was assigned which indicated congruence. If different functions were selected for the two questions, a code was assigned which indicated incongruence. Having done this, it was possible to determine the percentage of teachers, parents and students at each school who thought the school was emphasizing what it should have been emphasizing.

Table 2.11 shows the congruence scores for teachers, parents and students at all junior high schools. The overall pattern on junior high responses was for student congruence scores to be highest, followed by parents and then teachers. However, there were only slight differences overall and the pattern varied at many schools. The important finding was that half of the junior high students and slightly more than half of the teachers and parents thought that the schools emphasized one function but that they should emphasize another. You will recall that most teachers, parents and students thought that the school did emphasize the Intellectual function.

As with the satisfaction-dissatisfaction scores, the congruence scores need to be viewed with caution. They speak to the function of the school only--what it is perceived to be and what is thought it should be. However, since our findings reveal so much dissatisfaction and so much perception of incongruence, it seems legitimate to suggest that perhaps the function question is not yet answered for the junior high school. It is, indeed, "a school in search of a mission."

Table 2.11

Junior High Function Congruence--
% Seeing Congruence

Teachers		Parents		Students	
Rosemont	61.0%	Palisades	52.7%	Euclid	62.4%
Vista	58.3	Vista	52.6	Manchester	58.0
Atwater	56.5	Woodlake)	52.6	Rosemont	57.5
Woodlake	53.8	Atwater	52.0	Atwater	52.6
Palisades	52.6	Rosemont	50.0	Woodlake	52.0
Crestview	43.8	Euclid	48.6	Newport	51.6
Bradford	40.7	Manchester	47.1	Palisades	47.4
Laurel	38.1	Laurel	44.8	Bradford	47.4
Newport	36.2	Newport	43.1	Fairfield	46.2
Manchester	35.5	Bradford	42.3	Laurel	44.3
Euclid	33.3	Crestview	41.0	Crestview	44.1
Fairfield	31.4	Fairfield	37.4	Vista	43.3
Range	29.6	Range	15.3	Range	19.1

An Historical View of Aims of Junior Highs. The
junior high was a reality in American schooling by
1920. It was new and it came about for a variety of
reasons. Some of the reasons were diametrically
opposed to each other--improved academic preparation
for college and vocational training for early dropouts.

Because of its newness and because of the differences in views about its justification, there was much
interest in the aims of junior high schooling and there
were many attempts to bring together various conflicting viewpoints.

Van Til, et al., summarized the many aims proposed
for the junior high school in the 1920s. "...as viewed
in the 1920s, the junior high school was a separately
organized and administered school which sought to:

I. Effect economy in time through a downward extension
    of secondary education

64

a. by placing college preparatory subjects in the seventh and eighth grades, making possible earlier completion of college requirements,

b. by eliminating the duplication and repetition in the seventh and eighth grade programs and substituting new and worthwhile content,

c. by promoting by subjects rather than by grade level, thereby making possible acceleration,

d. by introducing departmental teaching with specially trained teachers who are able to advance pupils further and encourage superior scholarship;

II. Improve the holding power of the schools by providing for enriched activities, guidance, and a program built around the needs of the group;

III. Improve articulation between elementary and secondary education

a. by introducing an intermediate step between the two,

b. by gradually introducing the elective system,

c. by continuing common education while at the same time providing varied individual educational experiences;

IV. Make possible a program suited to the nature of early adolescents

a. by providing experiences in sharing, the acceptance of responsibilities, and self-direction,

b. by providing shops, laboratories, and other special features,

c. by providing a guidance and counseling program to assist pupils with the many social, emotional, and educational problems that accompany this age level,

d. by providing for the socializing experiences needed by these maturing youngsters,

e. by segregating the early adolescents from the younger children and older adolescents, to the benefit of all three groups,

f. by homogeneously grouping the pupils to help care for their individual differences,

g. by providing vocational training for those who leave school early,

h. by providing for early differentiation in pupils' programs through electives suited to the needs and interests of individual pupils,

i. by providing special classes for retarded and advanced pupils,

j. by providing opportunities for seventh and eighth graders to participate in extracurricular and similar enriching activities;

V. Provide for exploration

a. by offering short-term or try-out courses which will acquaint pupils with various subjects and interest areas,

b. by testing, counseling, and exploratory work to discover the interests, abilities, and capacities of individual pupils,

c. by offering prevocational, exploratory and orientation experiences."[34]

Given the conflicting nature of these original aims, it is no wonder that they have markedly changed over the years. Additionally, changes in the surrounding society caused changes in the perceived aims of the junior high. For example, the passage of child labor and compulsory attendance laws affected the junior high by reducing dropouts.

As the junior high began to serve large numbers of non-college bound children, the economy of time argument was heard less and less. Likewise, retention of pupils and vocational education disappeared as aims of junior high education. During the 1920s, recognition of individual differences became a very strong emphasis

66

along with exploration and guidance as aims of the junior high.

It should be noted that the junior high never took on the vocational education aim that some early advocates hoped for. Clearly, by 1940, vocational choice-making as an aim of schooling was transferred to the high school. In fact, most of the original aims identified for the junior high school had been transferred to the high school by 1940.

In the 1940s, a classic statement on the aims of the junior high school was developed by William T. Gruhn and Harl R. Douglass. Although it is now nearly forty years old, it is probably still the most influential and oft quoted statement on the subject.

Van Til, et al., summarize the statement as follows:

AIM I. Integration

To provide learning experiences in which pupils may use the skills, attitudes, interests, ideals and understandings previously acquired in such a way that these will become coordinated and integrated into effective and wholesome pupil behavior.

To provide for all pupils a broad, general, and common education in the basic knowledge and skills which will lead to wholesome, well-integrated behavior, attitudes, interests, ideals and understandings.

AIM II. Exploration

To lead pupils to discover and explore their specialized interests, aptitudes and abilities as a basis for decisions regarding educational opportunities.

To lead pupils to discover and explore their specialized interests, aptitudes and abilities as a basis for present and future vocational decisions.

To stimulate pupils and provide opportunities for them to develop a continually widening range of cultural, social, civic, avocational, and recreational interests.

AIM III. Guidance

To assist pupils to make intelligent decisions regarding present educational activities and opportunities and to prepare them to make future educational decisions.

To assist pupils to make intelligent decisions regarding present vocational opportunities and to prepare them to make future vocational decisions.

To assist pupils to make satisfactory mental, emotional, and social adjustments in their growth toward wholesome, well-adjusted personalities.

To stimulate and prepare pupils to participate as effectively as possible in learning activities so that they may reach the maximum development of their personal powers and qualities.

AIM IV. Differentiation

To provide differentiated educational facilities and opportunities suited to the varying backgrounds, interests, aptitudes, abilities, personalities, and needs of pupils in order that each pupil may realize most economically and completely the ultimate aims of education.

AIM V. Socialization

To provide increasingly for learning experiences designed to prepare pupils for effective and satisfying participation in the present complex social order.

To provide increasingly for learning experiences designed to prepare pupils to adjust themselves and contribute to future developments and changes in that social order.

AIM VI. Articulation

To provide a gradual transition from pre-adolescent education to an educational program suited to the needs and interests of adolescent boys and girls.[35]

This statement contains no mention of economy of time; there is no direct reference to retaining students in school; and vocational training is de-emphasized and replaced with the idea of exploration of interests, aptitudes and abilities. There are new emphases upon guidance, individualization of instruction and integration as aims of the junior high school.

In general, these six aims have remained as the guiding principles for junior high school education up to the present time. For this reason, they are used as the organizing framework for the next section of this book. In that section, one chapter is devoted to each aim and to pertinent data from A Study of Schooling.

From the analysis of these data, I hope to determine the degree to which, in reality, these are the current aims of the junior high. Further, and based upon normative judgment and the characteristics of early adolescents described at the beginning of this chapter, I hope to determine the degree to which they are appropriate for today's junior high school. As a result of these discussions, a revised set of aims will be proposed for junior highs which is thought to be more appropriate for today's early adolescents. Finally, a set of appropriate practices directed at achieving these aims will be described.

Chapter II, Notes and References

1. Donald H. Eichorn, "The School" in Toward Adolescence: The Middle School Years, Seventy-Ninth yearbook of the National Society for the Study of Education, Part I (Chicago: University of Chicago Press, 1980), p. 73.

2. William Van Til, Gordon, F. Vars, John H. Lounsbury, Modern Education for the Junior High School Years. (Indianapolis: The Bobbs-Merrill Company, Inc., 1967, 2nd Edition), pp. 5-6.

3. N.C. Heironomous, "Is This the Earliest Known Junior High School?" The Clearing House (May, 1940), p. 518.

4. Van Til, et al., op. cit., pp. 7-8.

5. National Education Association, Report of the Committee of Ten on Secondary School Studies (New York: American Book Company, 1894), p. 45.

6. Van Til, et al., op. cit., p. 7.

7. Commission on the Reorganization of Secondary Education, Cardinal Principles of Secondary Education, Bulletin 1918, No. 35 (Washington: U.S. Department of the Interior, Bureau of Education, 1918), pp. 12-13.

8. E.L. Thorndike, The Elimination of Pupils from School, Bulletin 1907, No. 4 (Washington: U.S. Department of the Interior, Bureau of Education, 1907).

9. Leonard P. Ayers, Laggards in Our Schools (New York: Russell Sage Foundation, Survey Associates, Inc., 1909).

10. George D. Strayer, Age and Grade Census of Schools and Colleges, Bulletin 1911, No. 5 (Washington: U.S. Department of Interior, Bureau of Education, 1911).

11. Van Til, et al., op. cit., p. 13.

12. G. Stanley Hall, Adolescence (New York: D. Appelton-Century Company, 1905).

13. R.A. Mackie, Education During Adolescence (New York: E.P. Dutton & Company, 1920), p. 32.

14. Joan Scheff Lipsitz, "The Age Group," in Toward Adolescence: The Middle School Years, Seventy-Ninth Yearbook of the National Society for the Study of Education, Part I (Chicago: University of Chicago Press, 1980), p. 12.

15. Robert J. Havighurst, Developmental Tasks and Education, 3rd ed. (New York: David McKay Company, Inc., 1972), p. 2.

16. Condensed from Developmental Tasks in Education, by Daniel Tanner and Laurel N. Tanner, Curriculum Development: Theory into Practice (New York: Macmillan Publishing Co., 1975), p. 135.

17. William T. Gruhn, "Reaffirming the Role of the Junior High School in the American School System," in Lawrence J. Barnett, Gerald Handel, Helen Weser, The School in the Middle: Divided Opinion on Dividing Schools (New York: Center for Urban Education, 1968), p. 33.

18. James S. Coleman, The Adolescent Society (Glencoe, Illinois: The Free Press, 1961).

19. Gertrude Noar, The Junior High School Today and Tomorrow (New York: Prentice-Hall, Inc., 1953), p. 42.

20. M. Ann Grooms, Perspectives on the Middle School (Columbus, Ohio: Charles E. Merrill Books, Inc., 1967), p. 18.

21. Erik Erikson, Identity: Youth and Crisis (New York: W.W. Norton, 1968), p. 23.

22. Jean Piaget, The Psychology of Intelligence (New York: Harcourt Brace Jovanovich, Inc., 1950), pp. 87-158.

23. Jean Piaget, Science of Education and the Psychology of the Child (New York: Orion Press, 1970).

24. Conrad F. Toepfer, "Brain Growth Periodization Data: Some Suggestions for Reorganizing Middle Grades Education," The High School Journal, 63 (March, 1980):224-226.

25. Barbara Benham Tye, Student Life, Chapter 2, "Student and Self: The Personal Domain," an unpublished I/D/E/A report, August, 1979, p. 2.

26. Scheirer and Kraut, "Increasing Educational Achievement Via Self-Concept Change," Review of Educational Research, 49, No. 1, Winter, 1979, pp. 131-149.

71

27. Van Til, et al., op. cit., p. 18.

28. Tanner and Tanner, op. cit., p. 460.

29. William M. Alexander, et al., The Emerging Middle School, 2nd ed. (New York: Holt, Rinehart and Winston, Inc., 1969), p. 19.

30. Eichorn, op. cit., p. 58. The two surveys cited were: (1) William A. Cuff, "Middle Schools on the March," Bulletin of the National Association of Secondary School Principals 51 (February, 1967): 82-86; and (2) Kenneth Brooks, "The Middle School: A National Survey," Middle School Journal 8 (February, 1978): 6-7.

31. Ibid., p. 57.

32. Bette C. Overman, Functions of Schooling: Perceptions and Preferences of Teachers, Parents and Students, Study of Schooling, Technical Report 10 (Arlington, Va.: ERIC Document Reproduction Service, 1980).

33. Ibid., p. 84.

34. Van Til, et al., op. cit., pp. 26-27. Four sources were quoted for functions: (1) Thomas H. Briggs, The Junior High School (Boston: Houghton Mifflin Company, 1920) pp. 162-174; (2) Leonard V. Koos, The Junior High School (New York: Harcourt, Brace and Howe, 1920), p. 18; (3) Calvin O. Davis, Junior High School Education (Yonkers-on-Hudson, N.Y.: World Book Company, 1924. p. 7; (4) NEA Department of Superintendence, The Junior High School Curriculum, Fifth Yearbook (Washington: The Department, 1927), p. 20.

35. Ibid., p. 30-31. This was summarized from: William T. Gruhn and Harl R. Douglass, The Modern Junior High School (New York: The Ronald Press Company, 1947), op. 59-60. (See also 2nd ed., 1956, pp. 31-32.)

CHAPTER III

INTEGRATION

Introduction

One of the most common criticisms of schooling has been that it involves too much passive learning. Over sixty years ago, Whitehead observed "...I have been much struck by the paralysis of thought induced in pupils by the aimless accumulation of precise knowledge, inert and unutilized."[1] Nearly thirty years later, Dressel added "The student reads, listens, fills out workbooks, occasionally writes; and always he prepares for the day when he must repeat on an examination the material which he has learned...."[2]

The authors of the 1958 NSSE Yearbook, The Integration of Educational Experiences, from which the second quote was taken, perceived that the problem of passive learning was, in fact, a problem of the integration of learning. However, they made a clear distinction between learning experiences which are "integrated" and those which are "integrating" or "integrative."

The distinction between integrated and integrating learning experiences is far more than an exercise in semantics. In the main, both concepts have been ignored by practitioners. Worse, the advocates of reform of junior high education generally have chosen to emphasize the wrong concept, integrated experiences.

Integrated experiences are those which are planned by curriculumists and teachers so that related concepts, generalizations, contents and/or processes are brought together and organized ahead of time for learners. Core, block, and interdisciplinary courses are the main organizational plans which purport to promote integration.

Such plans are usually advocated by the current proponents of the middle school. For example, John H. Lounsbury and Gordon F. Vars make a case for a core design in middle schools as follows:

73

A major portion of the common learnings should be provided through a core program, most simply described as a problem-centered block-time program. At its best, core provides students with a direct and continuing opportunity to examine in depth both personal and social problems that have meaning to them. It also provides a situation in which a teacher can know a limited number of students well enough to offer the advisement or counseling most of them need so badly during the transition years, and in the process they can learn essential human relations and communication skills.

Most, but not all, of the content and skills traditionally taught in English, social studies, and science classes may be taught in core, where they become tools to be utilized in the process of inquiry. Art and music, so often relegated to a peripheral role, also become important sources and tools in an inquiry process which knows no subject matter limitations.[3]

Integrating experiences, on the other hand, are those which cause the individual learner to make his or her own organization, or to actively utilize information. The focus is not upon how the curriculum is organized. Rather, it is upon the teaching and learning, upon developing a flexible individual who is self-reliant and who is seeking relationships between past and present experiences and learnings. Dressel metaphorically states the difference between integration and integrating as follows: "The father may build his son a house from a set of blocks or he may encourage the child to build his own house."[4]

This chapter explores the degree to which integrated and integrating experiences were provided in the twelve junior high and middle schools sampled by A Study of Schooling. It was relatively easy to document attempts to provide integrated experiences. Schedules and curriculum guides were examined. The results of that examination are reported in the next section of this chapter.

It was not such a simple task to get at integrating experiences, for in the final analysis those take place

74

in the thinking and behavior of the learners. However, it was possible, from student and teacher report and from classroom observation, to make some estimate of the degree to which students were actively involved in learning. These data also are reported in this chapter.

Finally, in this chapter, I try to synthesize these data and to suggest some conclusions and hypotheses about the ability of junior high schools to provide experiences for early adolescents which will cause them to practice integrative behaviors.

School Schedules

There were almost no examples of interdisciplinary integration at the twelve schools we studied. There was a course called "Unified Arts" at both Crestview Middle School and Vista Junior High. However, this was nothing more than a scheduling euphemism for certain non-academic courses. At Vista, it included home economics and industrial arts, and all students were assigned to one semester of each during 7th grade. At nearby Crestview, it included music, art, industrial arts and homemaking. Except for those in performing music classes (e.g., band, chorus), all students had "Unified Arts" two or three days a week during 6th, 7th, and 8th grades. However, the four subject areas were taught separately. They were not integrated.

There were a few other isolated instances of subject integration. Health was taught as part of P.E. at Atwater Junior High, there was an integrated domestic arts course at Laurel Middle School (home economics and shop for boys and girls together), one 8th grade teacher at Vista Junior High taught both English and history to three classes, and the remedial reading program at Newport Junior High utilized learning centers extensively. There was a two-period language arts block at Crestview Middle School for all students in all three grades; it was planned by teams of teachers at each grade level, but taught by individual teachers.

The overwhelming organizational plan at all twelve schools was to have separate subjects, with each student having six or seven of these each day.

As stated previously, we were not able to determine directly the degree to which <u>integrating</u> experiences actually took place for students. However, we did gather a good deal of data about the learning activities in which students were engaged.

We asked students whether or not they listened to or watched their teachers demonstrate how to do something. Teachers reported the frequency with which their students listened to or watched them. And observers recorded, in two ways, the frequency of teachers' explaining, lecturing, or instructing. In short, we had four measures of the degree to which students were the recipients of "frontal" teaching.

Over 90% of the junior high students reported that they listened to or watched their teachers in each of the subject areas. School scores differed little from this overall percentage. Obviously, then, lectures and demonstrations were a major part of students' experiences. However, these data did not tell us how frequently students listened to lectures and observed demonstrations, nor did it actually tell us whether this activity occurred more than others.

Teachers' self-reports about this activity gave us a little more information, in that teachers rated the frequency with which their students listened to or watched them. In all subjects, teachers rated this activity as occurring "often" (Table 3.1).

Observation data showed that the percentage of teacher time spent on lecturing, explanation and demonstration was more than that for any other activity. <u>On the average, junior high teachers in our sample spent slightly more than one-fourth of their time lecturing, explaining, or demonstrating</u>. And, on the average, about three-fourths of this time was spent before the entire class.

There was some variation in this activity across subject areas, according to teacher reports. P.E. and foreign language teachers reported the most student listening, while teachers of science reported the least.

Table 3.1

Teacher Report of Classroom Activities Frequently Used (By Subjects)

	X Freq.	sd	N
ENGLISH			
Listen to teacher	3.27	.65	66
Read for fun or interest	3.10	.65	67
Write answers to questions	2.96	.71	67
Take tests or quizzes	2.91	.74	66
Have class discussions	2.79	.66	67
Do reports or research	2.73	.83	67
SOCIAL STUDIES			
Listen to teacher	3.23	.52	44
Have class discussions	3.05	.61	44
Write answers to questions	3.00	.49	43
Take tests or quizzes	2.98	.46	44
Do reports or research	2.60	.49	43
MATH			
Write answers to questions	3.68	.50	66
Listen to teacher	3.36	.57	66
Take tests or quizzes	3.17	.55	64
SCIENCE			
Listen to teacher	3.18	.76	39
Watch teacher demonstrate	3.00	.75	40
Write answers to questions	2.95	.68	40
Do preplanned projects/ experiments	2.95	.72	39
Have class discussions	2.78	.58	40
Build or draw things	2.65	.66	40
Take tests or quizzes	2.62	.59	40

	X Freq.	sd	N
FINE ARTS			
Practice skills learned	3.51	.75	41
Perform or make art works	3.44	.98	41
Watch teacher demonstrate	3.29	.67	42
Listen to teacher	3.26	.59	42
Look at art works or performances	2.76	.73	41
Have class discussions	2.57	.63	42
FOREIGN LANGUAGES			
Practice skills learned	3.50	.53	10
Listen to teacher	3.40	.52	10
Take tests or quizzes	3.20	.42	10
Write answers to questions	3.00	.47	10
Act things out	2.50	.71	10
VOCATIONAL EDUCATION			
Listen to teacher	3.32	.47	44
Use machines, equipment	3.00	1.01	44
Build or draw things	2.95	.99	44
Have class discussions	2.52	.76	44
Take tests or quizzes	2.51	.63	43
Write answers to questions	2.50	.66	44
PHYSICAL EDUCATION			
Listen to teacher	3.50	.51	18
Practice skills learned	3.33	.69	18
Play team games	3.33	.59	18
Do exercises	3.22	.81	18
Play individual sports	2.72	.83	18

Response categories: 2.50-3.49   Often
3.50-4.00   Always or most of the time

Each teacher in our study was presented with a list of activities (which was slightly different for each subject area) and asked to tell how often students did each in their classroom. Response choices and their respective code values were: always or most of the time (4) often (3) not very often (2) and never (1).

We also asked teachers how useful they thought those activities were. Response choices for these items were: very useful (4) somewhat useful (3) somewhat useless (2) very useless (1).

We gave these same lists of activities to the students in our study and asked them whether or not they did them (yes or no) and how much they liked or would like doing each (like very much, like somewhat, dislike somewhat, or dislike very much).

English. Across all junior high school English classes, there were no activities which teachers thought occurred "always or most of the time," but there were six which they said occurred "often." Listening to the teacher was the activity with the highest mean score, followed by five other traditional activities: Read for fun or interest, write answers to questions, take tests or quizzes, have class discussions, and do reports or research.

There was some variability both across and within schools for all six activities. The variability within schools for "Do reports" was quite high at most schools. That is, while some English teachers at a school said that they had students do a lot of writing of reports, others said they had them do very little. That was true at two-thirds of the schools, including Crestview Middle School where teachers reported that they did a lot of planning together.

English teachers in the sample found all of these activities to be at least "somewhat useful." Not surprisingly, they found the six which they said occurred "often" to be "very useful." There was general agreement that listening to the teacher and reading for fun and information were "very useful" (sd of .38 and .39). Also, there tended to be agreement that class discussions and writing answers to questions were also "very useful." However, there was a good deal of variance from school to school and from teacher

78

to teacher regarding the usefulness of all other activities.

Student data cast a different perspective on these activities in English classes. The activities preferred by most students were not necessarily the same ones as those that the teachers said occurred "often." The most-liked activities were: Go on field trips (93%), read for fun or interest (86%), build or draw things (84%), make films and recordings (81%), and listen to the teacher (78%). However, aside from listening to the teacher, students very seldom participated in such activities.

Three major ideas emerge from this body of data. First, although there was a good deal of variance in activities from English classroom to English classroom, there was a general sameness about what junior high school students did in English classes throughout the schools. Basically, they listened, read, wrote, and recalled what they had learned. Also, they had some class discussions.

Second, the activities most used were "traditional" ones, in that they were the same ones which have been found in junior high English classes ever since there have been junior highs. This was true in spite of the fact that students expressed a preference for other activities and teachers themselves indicated that alternative activities were also useful in the classroom.

Third, while it is not possible to make judgments from the data presented here about the degree to which English students practiced integrative behavior, we <u>can</u> say that junior high school English classes in <u>our</u> sample were teacher-dominated and that students, by and large, were involved in relatively passive learning activities rather than active ones.

In an attempt to determine the degree to which critical thinking skills were taught, we also asked students and teachers in a sample of English classes some questions about critical thinking activities (Table 3.2). We asked teachers how often these things were done by students in their classrooms, and how useful they were as activities. We asked students how often they did these activities, and how much they like or would like doing each one. Responses to these items

79

were somewhat contradictory. (The response category mean ranges for Tables 3.2 through 3.8 are: 1.00-1.49 = Never; 1.50-2.49 = Not very often; 2.50-3.49 = Often; and 3.50 - 4.00 = Always or most of the time.)

Students in the sample said that they "often" remembered facts, dates, words, names, or rules, but that they didn't often do the other things. Teachers, on the other hand, said that all four activities occurred "often." In fact, they indicated that, on the average, remembering facts, etc., occurred <u>less</u> often than did the other three activities.[6]

Table 3.2

Teacher and Student Report of the Frequency of
Critical Thinking Activities in 67 <u>English</u> Classes

	STUDENTS			TEACHERS		
Activity	X	Rank	sd	X	Rank	sd
Remember facts, dates, words, names, or rules	2.71	(1)	.39	2.73	(4)	.77
Tell in own words what has been read, seen, or heard	2.40	(2)	.37	3.21	(1)	.69
Write own stories, plays, or poems	2.23	(3)	.57	2.79	(3)	.83
Tell how stories, people and ideas are the same or different	2.10	(4)	.40	2.87	(2)	.72

Teachers said that remembering facts, etc., and writing own stories, etc., were "somewhat useful," but that the other two activities were "very useful." Students said they somewhat disliked remembering facts, dates, and so on, but that they somewhat liked all the other activities.

80

Social Studies. There were no activities which teachers thought occurred "always or most of the time," but there were five which they said occurred "often" in social studies: listen to the teacher had the highest mean score, followed by have class discussions, write answers to questions, take tests or quizzes, and do reports or research (Table 3.1).

In social studies, there was very little variability across schools or within schools. Thus, the pattern above was not only an average pattern but, also, it existed in most social studies classrooms sampled in the Study.

Social studies teachers thought that only three activities were "very useful:" listening to the teacher, having class discussions, and doing reports or research. They said that all other activities were "somewhat useful." For the most part, there was little variability in these responses--very few teachers disagreed.

Seventy-five percent or more of the students sampled in social studies classes said that they liked seven of the classroom activities: go on field trips (93%), build or draw things (81%), read for fun or interest (81%), listen to the teacher (80%), listen to speakers (76%), and make films or recordings (75%). Thus, as in English classes, students in social studies classes reported that they liked many activities which they did not do very often. The five activities the greatest percentage of students reported doing in social studies were the same five reported by teachers as most often used.

Data on critical thinking in sampled social studies classes are reported in Table 3.3. Teachers and students had different perceptions of the situation. Teachers said that students were "often" asked to tell in their own words what they had read, seen, or heard. Students said that they were "not very often" involved in that activity.

Students said that they were "often" asked to remember facts, dates, names, or places, and reported this as the most frequent activity in their social studies classes. Teachers said "often," but reported it as the most infrequent of all the possible critical thinking activities in their classrooms.

Teachers said that remembering facts, etc., was "somewhat useful," but that the other three activities were all "very useful." Students reported that they somewhat liked all of the activities.

Table 3.3

Teacher and Student Report of the Frequency of
Critical Thinking Activities in 44 Social Studies Classes

Activity	STUDENTS			TEACHERS		
	X	Rank	sd	X	Rank	sd
Remember facts, dates, names, or places	2.91	(1)	.36	2.73	(4)	.66
Tell in own words what has been read, seen, or heard	2.30	(4)	.37	3.18	(1)	.62
Write own stories, plays, or poems	2.59	(2)	.32	2.91	(3)	.68
Tell how stories, people and ideas are the same or different	2.48	(3)	.43	3.14	(2)	.64

There appeared to be even more of a "sameness" in our sampled social studies classes than in our sampled English classes. Very few teachers varied from the norm in terms of the frequency of activities or critical thinking abilities required of students. Basically, students listened to the teacher, had whole class discussions, wrote answers to questions, took tests and quizzes and wrote reports.

It seemed that the social studies curriculum was really a language arts curriculum, dominated by listening, reading, writing, and talking. The investigative methods of social scientists which would help students to become critical thinkers and to develop integrative behavior were not in evidence.

Mathematics. In our sample of math classes, teachers reported that students wrote answers to questions "always or most of the time". They also "often" listened to the teacher and took tests or quizzes. That was all that occurred with any regularity and it was the same for most if not all of the math classes in the junior highs which we sampled. There was very little variability; only a rare teacher reported any different pattern. Apparently, one thing that students could count on was what they were going to do in math classes--answer questions, listen to the teacher, and take tests. (Table 3.1).

Mathematics teachers in our sample said that these three commonly occurring activities were "very useful." They also thought that field trips, guest speakers, class discussions, and building or drawing things were "somewhat useful" activities. However, except for the three commonly occurring activities, math teachers differed greatly in their perceptions of the usefulness of activities. It was as if a large number of math teachers thought it might be good to vary their activities somewhat, even though they didn't do so.

Student perceptions of what they did in their math classes were amazingly consistent with teacher perceptions. That is, by far the greatest percentages reported that they answered questions, listened to the teacher, and took tests.

Seventy-five percent or more of the students sampled in math classes said that they liked the following activities: field trips (90%), listening to the teacher (81%), building or drawing things (80%), and having class discussions (77%).

Data on critical thinking in sampled mathematics classes are reported in table 3.4. The data were very different from that found in both English and social studies classes, in that students' and teachers' perceptions in math were in agreement on what occurred in their classrooms; this was not the case in English and social studies. In math, students and teachers both thought that doing number problems happened most often, followed in order of frequency by remembering facts, rules, or operations; telling how rules, operations, and problems are the same or different; doing word problems; and telling in your own words what you have learned. Teachers said that number problems were done "always or most of the time," and the other activities were done "often." Students said that they did not often tell in their own words what they had learned, but that they did the other activities "often".

Table 3.4

Teacher and Student Report of the Frequency of
Critical Thinking Activities in 66 <u>Mathematics</u> Classes

Activity	STUDENTS			TEACHERS		
	X	Rank	sd	X	Rank	sd
Remember facts, rules, or operations	3.06	(2)	.27	3.39	(2)	.65
Do number problems	3.39	(1)	.26	3.66	(1)	.54
Tell in own words what has been learned	2.15	(5)	.40	2.82	(5)	.74
Do word problems	2.53	(4)	.36	2.85	(4)	.64
Tell how rules, operations, and problems are the same or different	2.55	(3)	.26	2.91	(3)	.76

Teachers found all cognitive activities to be "very useful," with number problems and remembering facts and operations being rated very high by almost every math teacher in our sample. Students said they somewhat liked all five of the cognitive activities.

As with English and social studies, this seemed a rather passive curriculum: listen and write. There was little opportunity to practice higher cognitive or integrative behaviors. This seems an incredibly wasted opportunity since the discipline of mathematics offers so much opportunity for cognitive development. Students liked their math activities—somewhat. Teachers, however, perhaps sensed that something was wrong, since they so strongly saw the value of alternative activities. They didn't use them in their classrooms, though.

Maybe here we really have a theme for the improvement of schooling, and a simple one at that. Rather than designing grand curriculum plans or reorganizations of our schools, perhaps we simply ought to make it possible for teachers to learn how to teach better (i.e., to broaden their repertoire of activities, and learn to teach for critical thinking and integrative abilities).

Science. According to teacher report, the science classes appeared to have the most variety of classroom activities for students, at least among the academic subjects in our sample. Teachers of science reported that seven different activities occurred "often" in their classes (Table 3.1). These were listen to the teacher, watch the teacher demonstrate, write answers to questions, do preplanned experiments/projects, have class discussions, build or draw things, and take tests or quizzes.

Variability across schools and within schools was evident in most reported activities. Whereas our data suggest that activities in mathematics and social studies classes were quite predictable, they suggest just the opposite in science classes.

Science teachers in the sample thought that three activities were "very useful:" listening to the teacher, doing preplanned experiments or projects, and watching the teacher demonstrate. They thought that making films or recordings was "somewhat useless," but that all the other activities were "somewhat useful."

Student perceptions of the occurrence of activities in sampled science classes were slightly at odds with those of the teachers. Over 90% of the students said they did listen to the teacher, watch the teacher demonstrate, write answers to questions, and take tests or quizzes. However, only 79% said that they had class discussions, and fewer than 70% said they did preplanned projects and experiments or built and drew things. Teachers said that these all occurred "often."

As with all previous subjects, students indicated a liking for the less passive activities (e.g., field

85

trips--92%), as well as more traditional activities (e.g., watch the teacher demonstrate--83%).

Data on critical thinking in science classes are reported in Table 3.5. Once again we find a subject where student and teacher perceptions differed somewhat regarding what occurred in the classroom. Teachers indicated that all cognitive activities occurred "often": tell how facts, things, and rules are the same or different; tell in your own words what you have read, seen, or heard; and do experiments, take things apart, or create new things. Both students and teachers said that remember facts, names, or rules occurred "often." However, students ranked it first in frequency and teachers ranked it last.

Teachers said that remember facts, names, or rules and tell how facts, things, and rules are the same or different were both "somewhat useful." They found all other cognitive activities "very useful." Students responded that they "somewhat liked" all of the critical thinking activities.

We asked teachers and students about the use of materials and equipment. Only slightly more than half of the sampled science students said they used things like models, charts, and pulleys or animals and plants. Over 70% said they used lab equipment and materials. Teacher reports were similar.

In summary, the science curriculum appeared to be more varied and active than English, social studies, and math curricula. Even so, it seemed to be dominated by listening, watching, reading, and writing rather than "doing."

There seemed to be a good deal of difference in what happened from one science class to the next. Teachers seemed quite free to design their own programs. An amazingly large number appeared to have students involved in preplanned experiments or projects. Few had students plan their own experiments or projects, though.

Thus, it seems fair to say that science teachers in our sample of junior highs were developing some integrative behavior, even though more probably could have been done. Interestingly, however, science at the time of the Study was not much more than an elective at many of the junior highs.

Table 3.5

Teacher and Student Report of the Frequency of
Critical Thinking Activities in 39 Science Classes

	STUDENTS			TEACHERS		
Activity	X	Rank	sd	X	Rank	sd
Remember facts, names, or rules	2.82	(1)	.27	2.59	(5)	.64
Tell in own words what has been read, seen, or heard	2.35	(4)	.29	2.95	(3)	.60
Use what you have learned to solve science problems	2.74	(2)	.36	3.03	(1)	.55
Tell how facts, things, and rules, are the same or different	2.46	(3)	.27	2.63	(4)	.63
Do experiments, take things apart, or create new things	2.31	(5)	.63	2.97	(2)	.83

The Arts. Classes in the arts seemed to contain an approximately even balance between passive and active student activities. According to the teachers in the classes we sampled, activities which occurred "always or most of the time" or "often" were: practice skills learned, perform or make art works, watch the teacher demonstrate, listen to the teacher, look at art works or performances, and have class discussions (Table 3.1).

There was a good deal of variability in the responses of teachers in our arts sample to the question of classroom activities. The fact of variability and the fact of a balance between active and passive activities were not surprising when our sample of junior high school arts classes were examined--it was pretty accurately reflective of the total offerings at our twelve schools. The courses ranged from music appreciation to chorus to band and orchestra in music. There were art classes and crafts classes, drama and courses labelled "Humanities." Lest the reader get the impression that the arts offerings were rich at the junior high school level, however, let him/her be reminded that this range was across twelve schools. At any one school, offerings in the arts were quite limited. The variability shown here was suggestive only of the facts that arts offerings were not standardized across junior highs and that they depended only upon the preferences of local administrators and teachers, or upon local tradition.

Teachers responded to the question about the usefulness of activities almost exactly as they did to the question about frequency. That is, those activities which they reported as occurring most of the time or "often" were the ones they said were the most useful.

Student perceptions of the occurrence of activities in sampled arts classes were very close to those of the teachers. The six activities which the teachers said occurred the most frequently were the ones which the greatest percentages of the students said they did.

Over three-fourths of the student sample indicated a liking for a fairly large array of activities: field trips (89%); looking at art works or performances (86%); watching the teacher demonstrate (85%); looking at films, filmstrips, or slides (83%); practicing skills learned (82%); performing or making art works (76%); and listening to the teacher (76%).

Data on critical thinking in sampled arts classes are reported in Table 3.6. Student and teacher perceptions were very similar. They both said that all but one of the critical thinking activities occurred "often." Students said that telling what is seen, heard, or felt when looking at art works or performances didn't occur often, while the teachers said they thought it did occur "often." Responses were quite varied from teacher to teacher, probably due to the range of classes covered under the heading "the arts."

Teachers of the arts in our sample said that all critical thinking activities were "very useful" except for remember names, rules, or ways to do things, which they considered only "somewhat useful." There was strong agreement among the teachers on these items. Students responded that they liked all activities <u>somewhat</u>. They said "like very much" to none of them.

It is difficult to generalize about activities in classes in the arts in the schools we studied, because those classes were quite varied when all schools were considered. However, we can say that offerings were limited at any one of the schools and that they varied greatly from one school to another. Across all twelve schools, activities reported used in arts classes were about half active and half passive. That is, about half were performance activities and half were appreciation, or "learning about" activities.

While we do not know for sure about the development of integrative behavior, the data we did examine seemed to suggest that the arts offered a good deal of potential for such development, at least where performance and appreciation were blended together. It would seem, however, that more opportunity for students to be involved in a wide range of the arts should be developed. Perhaps our schools should be less concerned about the academics and should utilize the potential of the arts more fully in the development of integrative behavior.

<u>Foreign Language</u>. In our sample of foreign language classes, teachers reported that students "always or most of the time" practice speaking the language they are studying. They also "often" listen to the teacher, take tests or quizzes, write answers to questions, and act things out (Table 3.1). The first four activities were common across all schools and classes in the sample, while the last one, acting things out, varied in occurrence from class to class. Thus, as with math classes and except for act things out, students in our sample of junior high schools could count on what they were going to do in foreign language classes: practice what they learned, listen to the teacher, take tests or quizzes and answer questions.

The activities which teachers in these classes said occurred "often" were also the ones they said were the most valuable. In fact, every teacher in the small sample of ten said that practice speaking the language and listen to the teacher were both "very useful."

Table 3.6

Teacher and Student Report of the Frequency of
Critical Thinking Activities in 42 Arts Classes

Activity	STUDENTS			TEACHERS		
	X	Rank	sd	X	Rank	sd
Remember names, rules, or ways to do things	3.01	(2)	.28	2.93	(5)	.74
Do things the way the teachers shows or tells	3.21	(1)	.26	3.41	(1)	.55
Finish each project started	2.95	(3)	.40	3.22	(3)	.70
Tell what is seen, heard, or felt when looking at art works or performances	2.46	(7)	.40	2.60	(7)	.73
Use what is learned in doing other projects or performances	2.72	(5)	.40	3.00	(4)	.71
Make projects or performances express feelings or thoughts	2.53	(6)	.35	2.86	(6)	.72
Decide what is good about projects or performances	2.81	(4)	.31	3.24	(2)	.73

Student perceptions of what the activities were in the sampled foreign language classes were similar to those of the teachers except that only 22% of the students said that they acted things out in class, while teachers said that this was done "often." Over

90% of the students said that they did the other four activities which teachers had said occurred "often" or "always or most of the time."

Except for practice speaking the language, the activities which the greatest percentage of sampled students said they liked were four of the six which teachers said least often occurred: field trips (96%), guest speakers (80%), making films or recordings (78%) and having class discussions (75%). Eighty-four percent said they liked to practice speaking the language they were learning.

Data on critical thinking activities in sampled foreign language classes are reported in Table 3.7. Students and teachers in our sample both perceived that remembering vocabulary, translating, reading, writing, and speaking activities all occurred "often." However, where teachers said that tell how places, people, and ideas are the same or different occurred "often," students said it happened "not very often." There was little variability in teacher responses from school to school or class to class about any of these activities.

Teachers thought that remembering vocabulary, reading, speaking, and writing were all "very useful," but that translating and telling about similarities and differences were only "somewhat useful." Students said that they liked all the activities somewhat, with speaking ranked first.

I have lived and travelled extensively outside of the United States and I value highly the mastery of languages. Additionally, I see mastery of more than one language as a partial remedy for a worldwide, as well as particularly American, condition--ethnocentrism. I believe that foreign language instruction should be far more wide-spread at the junior high level than it now is. However, if our data are any indication of the state of junior high school foreign language instruction in general, then I must raise some questions before advocating its increase.

Our data suggested a heavy reliance upon commercially prepared programs. Such programs included texts, workbooks, games, films and records and seemed to balance reading, writing, speaking, and vocabulary development. Only in a few cases was there a special emphasis upon speaking, even though teachers recognized its singular usefulness and students ranked it as most liked. Also, there were few classes where comparing and contrasting cultures and ideas were in evidence, and teachers indicated this to be the least useful of the critical thinking activities. Such activities have great potential for developing integrative behavior-- foreign language teaching has that potential. I would hope to see that potential realized, through improvement of foreign language instruction first and then through broadening of that instruction to include all junior high students.

Table 3.7

Teacher and Student Report of the Frequency of
Critical Thinking Activities in 10 Foreign Language Classes

Activity	STUDENTS			TEACHERS		
	X	Rank	sd	X	Rank	sd
Remember words, names, sentences, places	3.38	(1)	.36	3.30	(1.5)	.48
Translate from one language to another	3.28	(3.5)	.38	3.00	(4)	.67
Read in the language being studied	3.18	(5)	.47	3.10	(3)	.57
Speak in the language being studied	3.28	(3.5)	.28	3.30	(1.5)	.48
Write in the language being studied	3.29	(2)	.34	2.90	(5)	.48
Tell how places, people and ideas are the same or different	2.18	(6)	.40	2.50	(6)	.71

Vocational/career education. In our sample of vocational/career education classes, teachers said that six activities occurred "often": listening to the teacher, using machines and equipment, building or drawing things, having class discussions, taking tests or quizzes, and writing answers to questions (Table 3.1).

There was a good deal of variability in several of these activities, probably reflective of the fact that, like the arts, there were many kinds of classes represented (e.g., industrial arts, home economics, typing, agriculture, office training, mechanical drawing). As with the arts, this did not imply a rich curriculum. At most junior highs, students had one semester or maybe two in which to sample these courses. At one school, Fairfield, some students—tracked already by grade seven—had many vocational/career courses. Neither option, very few vocational/career courses for all students or many courses for some students, seems reasonable.

Teachers responded to the usefulness of activities almost exactly as they did to the occurrence of them. That is, those activities which they reported as occurring "often" or "always or most of the time" were the ones they considered most useful.

Student perceptions of the occurrence of activities in sampled vocational/career education classes were quite similar to teacher perceptions. The six activities which teachers said occurred the most frequently were the same ones the students said they did.

The greatest percentage of students said that they liked to go on field trips (87%). However, large numbers also liked the activities which occurred most often: listen to the teacher (86%), build or draw things (85%), and use machines or equipment (81%). There seemed to be a very good match between teacher and student perceived occurrence, teacher perceived usefulness and student liking of activities in the vocational/career education sample, despite the variability of responses due to the many types of courses in the sample.

Data on critical thinking in sampled vocational/career education classes are reported in Table 3.8. Students and teachers in the sample both responded that students "often" did the following: remember facts, names of things, or ways of doing things; show in some way that they really understand what they are learning;

use what they learn in doing other projects or assignments.

Teachers in the sample said that all of these critical thinking activities were "very useful," and students said that they somewhat liked them.

Table 3.8

Teacher and Student Report of the Frequency of
Critical Thinking Activities in 44
Vocational/Career Education Classes

	STUDENTS			TEACHERS		
Activity	X	Rank	sd	X	Rank	sd
Remember facts, names, of things, or ways of doing things	2.92	(2)	.34	3.25	(2)	.69
Show in some way that they really understand what they are learning	2.91	(3)	.32	3.34	(1)	.61
Use what they learn in doing other projects or assignments	2.94	(1)	.38	3.23	(3)	.77

Vocational/career education classes have been thought of as active classes, places where students "do things." This was more true of vocational/career education classes in our sample than of the academic subjects in our sample. Even so, about half of the students' time was taken up with passive activities--listening and writing.

In our vocational educational sample, critical thinking activities other than recall took up a greater amount of time than they did in academic courses. These data do not speak to the quality of such activities, but at least they were present. Thus, the potential for the development of integrative behavior in vocational/career education courses seemed high for students. And yet, the opportunity to take such

94

courses was limited to one or two semesters in three years.

It is my contention that all junior high students should have more vocational/career education courses than the curriculum presently allows. If they are well taught, such courses have a high potential for the development of the intellectual abilities and integrative behavior of students.

Physical Education. The one activity which teachers of physical education in our sample reported as occurring "always or most of the time" was listen to the teacher. Those activities which were perceived as occurring "often" were practicing skills learned, playing team games, doing exercises, and playing individual sports (Table 3.1). There was a good deal of variability associated with the responses to the last two activities.

The activities which P.E. teachers in our sample reported as occurring most often were also the ones they said were the most useful and, in this view, there was little variability--that is, there were no P.E. teachers who did not think these activities were useful.

A great percentage of students indicated that they did four of the five activities listed above. However, only 52% said that they played individual sports, while 69% said that they did take tests for skills. Large percentages of students in the sample reported that they liked the five activities listed above as well as taking skills tests.

There were no questions asked in P.E. classes about critical thinking activities.

Even though there was a great deal of listening to the teacher in our sample of P.E. classes, students by and large were very active. However, major emphasis seemed to be upon competition and team sports rather than upon the development of skills in life-long individual sports. Thus, in terms of integrative behavior, much of the P.E. in our sample contributed, in the long run, to the development of spectators of competition rather than to lifelong participation in sports activity.

95

Observation data were collected in 362 classrooms in the twelve junior high schools which participated in A Study of Schooling. Classes were randomly sampled to represent each of the eight major subject areas.

Each class was usually observed by one assigned observer for three separate periods spread over a two-week block of time. These data were accumulated into a single observational protocol for each classroom. Inter-observer reliability of the data was assessed for a subsample of classes and was found to be generally adequate.[9]

The nature of the observation system was quite complex, and it is thoroughly described elsewhere.[10] The data presented in this chapter came from two of the four major sections of the instrument: the classroom snapshot (CS) and the five minute interaction (FMI).

The CS provides information about what each adult (usually a teacher) and student in the classroom was doing, the size of the student group, and the nature of the activities in progress. One CS was filled out by the observer prior to filling out an FMI.

Table 3.9 gives a summary, by subject, of classroom activities as recorded by observers using the Classroom Snapshot (CS). Observers pinpointed the activities which were in progress in the classrooms and how the students and teachers were involved in these activities. They did this four times per period for a total of twelve snapshots per class.

Most of the percentages in Table 3.9 were derived by weighting each configuration by the number of students involved. When divided by the total number of students present in all snapshots for each class, the resultant figures represented the likelihood of students being found in each configuration.

Looking at Table 3.9, we can see that the two activities which involved the most students, overall, were (1) being lectured to (22.2%) and (2) working on written assignments (20.9%). Relatively large numbers of students were also involved in routine activities preparatory to or following instruction (15.7%) and in taking tests or quizzes (5.6%). When these four

96

activities were taken together, they accounted for approximately 65% of students observed. The only other activity which had noticeably high percentages (14.4%) was that defining the psychomotor form of practicing skills. This was represented almost totally by the kinds of skills taught in the nonacademic subjects (the arts, vocational education and physical education), although there was a relatively high percentage in science classes, probably because of students involved in various types of laboratory work.

While the activities observed were not exactly parallel to those teachers and students were questioned about, these data do seem to verify the findings reported previously from those sources. That is, classroom activity, particularly in the academic subjects, was predominantly teacher-dominated, passive and traditional.

There were a number of differences from subject to subject which were notable. The high level of active practice in the nonacademic subjects has already been mentioned. Also, there was considerably less working on written assignments and taking of tests or quizzes in nonacademic classes. There was even less teacher talk.

Foreign language classes had a profile unique from all other subjects. They were somewhat low by comparison on teacher lecturing and explaining, very low on doing written assignments and quite high by comparison on verbal practice and taking tests or quizzes. These data tended to confirm the conclusions drawn from teacher and student reports, that activity in foreign language classes did not emphasize speaking; they were not "conversational" courses. Instead, there was a balanced mixture of listening, writing, and speaking.

Fewer than 5% of the students were found in discussion, simulations, or role playing, activities which are generally considered to require students to more actively participate in the learning process. There was a very large discrepancy in data about class discussions. Teachers and students both reported that class discussions occurred "often," but observers found students involved in class discussions only about 5% of the time. The interpretation I give this discrepancy is that students and teachers included any form of verbal interaction, and a certain amount of "teacher

97

Table 3.9

Summary by Subject of Snapshot Activities Percentage of Students Involved

Activity	English	Math	Social Studies	Science	Foreign Language	Fine Arts	Voc/Car. Educ	P.E.	Overall Classes
Preparation for assignments/ instructions/clean-up	14.8	14.4	16.7	14.7	15.0	18.0	16.4	24.7	15.7
Explain, lecture, or read aloud	22.6	28.1	28.0	23.6	14.9	13.9	19.8	10.2	22.2
Demonstration	0.4	1.9	0.3	1.3	0.0	0.7	3.9	3.8	1.5
Discussion	5.6	3.4	7.8	4.8	4.2	2.2	2.7	0.0	4.6
Simulation/role playing	0.0	0.0	0.1	0.1	0.0	1.1	0.3	0.0	0.2
Reading	8.4	0.0	4.8	1.4	3.4	0.0	1.7	0.0	2.9
Work on written assignments	30.5	35.3	21.7	20.1	8.9	4.5	8.5	0.9	20.9
Practice or perform (psychomotor)	1.2	1.5	0.3	15.6	0.6	39.2	35.0	49.6	14.4
Practice or perform (verbal)	2.9	0.7	1.0	0.8	31.0	11.8	2.9	4.2	4.0
Take tests or quizzes	7.5	8.0	6.4	6.5	13.0	1.8	1.3	0.8	5.6
Using audiovisual materials	2.3	1.5	9.0	8.0	6.7	3.0	3.0	0.0	4.3
Social interaction (non-task)	3.2	4.7	3.5	3.0	0.8	3.3	4.0	6.1	3.5
Adult discipline of student(s)	0.2	0.2	0.0	0.0	1.0	0.1	0.1	0.5	0.3
Sample size (number of classrooms)	73	68	53	41	11	44	48	24	362

talk," in their definition of "discussion." I recall teachers who often said to their students, "We will discuss chapter three when you finish reading it." Translated, that meant "Be prepared to orally give the correct answers to the recall questions at the end of the chapter."

A similar discrepancy appeared regarding teacher demonstration in science and arts classes. Students and teachers reported that this activity occurred "often," while observers reported that almost no teacher demonstration took place.

I was surprised by the observation data on two other variables. Only about 4% of the students were observed using audiovisual materials and/or equipment. Given the emphasis on audiovisuals--not to mention their instructional potential--in the past nearly 30 years, I would have expected this percentage to be higher. Second, I was surprised and pleased to note that the percentage of "teacher disciplining student" was almost nonexistent (0.3%).

Finally, the greatest puzzle presented by the CS data had to do with the activity "reading." Although seventeen (23.3%) of the 73 sampled classes that were classified as English were, in fact, actually reading classes, only 8.4% of the students in these 73 classes were observed reading. Over all classes observed in all subjects, only 2.9% of the students were observed reading. Over and over, regardless of the subject, the pattern was listen to the teacher and then either work on a written assignment, in the case of academic subjects, or practice skills, in the case of nonacademic subjects. Before the "back-to-the-basics" movement, with its simple solutions, has its way and we get even more reading classes, or more time spent on reading as it is presently taught, we need to determine what good reading teaching is. Certainly, it is not only teacher talk and written assignments.

Table 3.10 gives a summary, by subject, of related classroom activities as recorded by observers using the FMI. The FMI portion of the observation instrument was a more continuous accounting of how time was spent in the classroom, focusing upon the teacher and upon the interactive process between the teacher and the students. These data yielded estimates of the percentage of class time various teacher-student interaction configurations occurred--that is, who (teacher or student) is doing what (questioning, lecturing, correcting, responding, etc.) to whom (teacher or student), and how (verbally, non-verbally, with positive affect, with guidance, etc.) and in what context (instruction, behavioral control, routines, social). In this chapter, only data on the what and whom of classroom life is reported. Other aspects of these data will be reported later, as appropriate, in other chapters.

Four equally-spaced FMIs were completed for each class period observed, for a total of twelve FMIs in all.

Approximately one-half of the time in every subject except P.E. was occupied with teacher talk, and in P.E. it was over 40%. The frequency of student talk ranged from just over 22% in foreign language to under 10% in P.E. with slightly more of it evidenced in the academic subjects (foreign language, English, math, science, social studies) than in non-academic subjects (P.E., arts, vocational/career education).

Approximately 10% of teacher time was spent working alone, except in P.E. and foreign language where it was only about 5%. Also, except for P.E., teachers were observed spending about 10% of their time monitoring or observing students. P.E. teachers in our sample spent nearly one-third of their time doing this.

A closer examination of what teacher talk consisted of shows that only about 6% of it on the average across all subjects was spent asking questions, and most of that was direct questioning requiring simple recall answers from students--"What is the capital of Missouri?" While commands accounted for about 5% of teacher talk, on the average (12% in the arts and about 10% in foreign language), praise and encouragement accounted for only about 1% in all subjects. This was particularly interesting in light of the fact that all teachers, regardless of what subject they taught, vigorously agreed with the questionnaire item that stated, "Learning is enhanced when teachers praise generously the accomplishments of individual students." This item had the second highest mean score of all of the 21 "educational beliefs" items asked of teachers.

Teachers corrected students rarely, and when they did it was almost never with guidance or an explanation

Table 3.10

Summary by Subject of Selected Classroom Activities Recorded by the FMI--Percentage of Time Observed

Activity	English	Math	Social Studies	Science	Foreign Language	Fine Arts	Voc/Car. Educ	P.E.	Overall Classes
				Subject Areas					
Adult talk	50.7	54.8	47.0	52.7	50.8	47.2	50.7	41.5	49.8
Student talk	17.6	16.5	14.1	15.1	22.3	10.1	12.7	9.3	14.6
Adult working alone	11.0	9.2	10.4	10.0	5.4	8.4	13.4	6.4	10.3
Adult monitoring/ observing	9.7	8.6	12.6	10.9	12.2	7.0	10.0	30.5	11.1
Adult to Student "Whats"									
Direct questions	7.4	8.4	5.5	6.3	6.4	3.9	4.1	2.6	5.9
Open-ended questions	0.6	0.3	0.6	0.3	0.1	0.3	0.3	0.1	0.6
Responses to (student(s))	4.4	4.3	3.8	4.4	4.1	2.8	4.9	2.2	3.8
Praise/encourage	1.0	0.9	0.8	0.7	1.1	1.2	0.7	1.2	0.9
Imperative commands	4.9	3.4	4.1	3.8	10.3	11.8	4.0	8.1	5.3
Simple correction	2.4	2.7	2.0	3.6	4.4	2.8	1.8	2.0	2.5
Correction with guidance	1.0	0.7	0.7	0.8	0.8	0.8	0.6	0.5	0.8
Instruction/ explanation	24.1	29.5	25.9	28.5	20.3	28.7	32.8	21.9	27.5

as to what the student might do as an alternative. What teachers did do a lot of was explain or instruct.

Conclusions

According to student and teacher reports and according to observation data, junior high students in classes in all subjects in our sampled schools spent large amounts of time listening to the teacher. In addition to this, the most common activity, they also wrote answers to questions a lot and often took tests or quizzes. Less often, they wrote reports, read, or were involved in discussion. In short, they were almost always involved in passive and traditional activities. Activities such as simulation and role play were nearly non-existent.

There were differences among the subjects. In the non-academic subjects and to a lesser degree in science, students were involved more actively in learning. However, with the exception of P.E., students had less access to these courses because they were electives or were offered on a limited basis at any single school.

When student and teacher reports of critical thinking activities were examined, they showed that recall of facts, dates, names, words and the like was the most common activity and that any activities that called for more complex behaviors were not so common. With this data, too, it was more often that teacher and student perceptions were at variance. Teachers tended to perceive more occurrence of higher cognitive activity than did students.

Our observation data tended to support student perceptions. For example, we saw almost no questioning of students and when we did it was direct questioning which called for simple recall answers.

My colleague, Ken Sirotnik, in reporting our observation data, likened life in a classroom to the series of Andy Warhol films which portrayed a number of life events. Sirotnik said:

Some years ago, Andy Warhol made a series of films portraying life events in the actual time frame they occurred, for example, six and one-half hours of a person sleeping. In the

102

film, "The Haircut", we see what seems like hours of interminable sameness--a closeup of a man's face and head with little or no expression and the hands and tools of a barber at work. At one point the man twitches--not a big twitch--but, relative to what has been going on, a noticeable momentary change in countenance. The audience cheers in a nearly hysterical relief from the accumulated boredom and strain of rationalizing their stay in the theatre.

If Warhol were to have made a film of the typical American classroom, the data we have just reviewed might have easily been the script. We would watch the secondary classroom scene unfold, fifty-five minutes during which a hint of affect would be cause for celebration--positive affect would be nice, but even negative would suffice, as a welcome change from the flat affective neutrality pervading the screen. It if were a physical education class, we would break out in applause were the teacher to actually spend time helping a student (or group of students) perfect their baseball swing instead of monitoring whatever physical activities were in progress. If it were a science class, we would cheer wildly were the teacher to actually demonstrate the effects of air pressure and vacuums instead of only explaining them and/or monitoring the total class as students worked independently on their written assignments. Similar scenarios and positive audience response could be laid out in the other subject areas--small group poetry reading and discussion sessions in an English class; role play simulations of civil liberty suits in a social studies class; etc.

What if we were forced to view the movie from the standpoint of the student? Depending upon the time frame you wished, the film could run 330 minutes for the typical 6-period day, 495 hours for the typical 90-day semester, over 40 continuous 24-hour days for the typical school year. In all, typical secondary students play out their 6-year role involuntarily, subordinately and in a physical setting that usually translates to no more than a four foot square of space per person <u>not</u> taking into account desks, tables, etc. The scenario and time frame for elementary classes and students is nearly the same, if not more uneventful, considering how little variety is offered in course content beyond the three R's.

These observations are not new. They were made, far more eloquently, almost twenty years ago by Philip Jackson (1965).[11] His commentary on classroom life was based on over 1000 hours of observation in a few elementary classrooms. As it turns out, he was also accurately portraying a few hours of observation on over 1000 elementary and secondary classrooms nearly two decades later.[12]

The data discussed in this chapter did not speak directly to the presence of "integrating" experiences, those which not only caused the learner to memorize information but which also required that that information be organized and/or utilized by the learner in some way. However, the data did suggest that opportunity for such behavior was very limited, at best.

Our data on "integration," that is, the organization of curriculum prior to involving students with it, suggests that it, too, was nearly non-existent in our sample of schools. Further, there was absolutely no difference found between the five middle schools in our sample and the seven junior high schools with regard to "integration," even though this is one of the main tenets of the advocates of middle schools. As a matter of fact, there were no differences between the two types of schools with regard to any data reported in this chapter.

In an attempt to understand the predominant "didactics/practice/test" pattern found in junior high school classrooms, I turned to data about educational beliefs. Of the 21 items and four subscales in the instrument, data from three items appeared to be particularly relevant to this discussion.[13]

Teachers were asked to respond on a six-point agree-disagree scale to the following item about teacher control: "Good teacher-student relations are enhanced when it is clear that the teacher, not the students, is in charge of classroom activities." The mean score for the 392 responding junior high school teachers was 5.44, which indicated a high level of agreement. Thus, the fact that "frontal" teaching dominated our sample of schools seemed to be consistent with the teacher belief that the teacher should be "in charge."

Further, teachers in our sample agreed with three items which stated that imparting basic knowledge was of paramount importance in teaching. For example, one such item said: "Before students are encouraged to exercise independent thoughts, they should be thoroughly grounded in facts and knowledge of basic subjects." The mean response to this item was 3.97, indicating "mild" agreement on a six-point scale.

An interesting contradiction appeared in our data on teachers' educational beliefs. Teachers were also asked to respond to an item that said: "The learning of basic facts is less important in schooling than acquiring the ability to synthesize facts and ideas into a broader perspective" (integrative behavior). The mean score for this item was 3.94, indicating "mild" agreement. However, the large standard deviation (1.67) indicated a lot of disagreement among teachers about this item. And the response seemed to be consistent with earlier data which suggested that some teachers, at least, recognized the desirability of classroom activities other than telling, writing, and testing.

If our teachers sensed that they should have been doing some things differently, why did they continue to use didactic, traditional methods? I suggest at least three reasons.

To begin with, I hypothesize that teachers perceived that didactic, traditional ways of teaching are what is expected of them by the society as a whole. And they are correct. Despite much of the public criticism of schooling over the past two decades and in spite of the many lofty goal statements of school districts and of state departments of education,[14] there is a basic societal satisfaction with schooling as it is. We asked parents at our schools how satisfied they were with what the schools were providing for their children in each of the subject areas discussed earlier. At all schools, for all subjects, parents, on the average, reported that they were satisfied.

The reformers among us can criticize our schools for teaching such things as dependence upon authority, linear thinking, social apathy, materialism, competition, and the like. We refer to these things as the "hidden curriculum," but they are not hidden. They are very much in the open, they are very much supported by society, and they will continue to be unless societal values themselves begin to change.

Indeed, the national response to the report of the Commission on Excellence in Education suggests that pressure will be placed upon schools to do more of the same for some time to come.[15] The discussions of "excellence" do not refer to helping teachers enlarge their repertoires of classroom activities. No mention is made of providing teachers with richer banks of materials to use in teaching. Instead, the focus is on more "academic" learning of the type we have traditionally had, as unproductive of integrative behavior for students as it may be.

I also hypothesize that teachers continue to use didactic and traditional methods of teaching because they don't know how to use any other methods. While they may have read about other methods or heard them described or seen them in a film during their pre-service training or during some in-service course, they have not had the opportunity to practice them. They fall back on the classroom activities they experienced when they were junior high students themselves.

Finally, and not unrelated to the hypotheses stated above, I suggest that teachers use the methods and activities they do because of the circumstances which surround their daily work. They find themselves in a room, approximately 30 feet by 30 feet, with 25-40 students and they are given bits of time called periods during which they are to plan and carry out some teaching-learning activities. They have materials to use, but even these usually dictate that the activities will be didactic and traditional.

Thus, we come full circle to Dressel's observation: "The student reads, listens, fills out workbooks, occasionally writes; and always he prepares for the day when he must repeat on an examination the materials he has learned..."[16] Now, a quarter-century later, the same description seems appropriate for our junior high

schools. Can we change the situation? Maybe we don't
really want to.

1. Alfred N. Whitehead, <u>The Aims of Education</u>, (New York: Mac-millan Co., 1929), p. 58.

2. Paul L. Dressel, "The Meaning and Significance of Integra-tion," <u>The Integration of Educational Experiences</u>, the Fifty-Seventh Yearbook of the National Society for the Study of Education, Part III. (Chicago: The University of Chicago Press, 1958), p. 3.

3. John H. Lounsbury and Gordon F. Vars, <u>A Curriculum for the Middle School Years.</u> (New York: Harper and Row, 1978), p. 46.

4. Paul L. Dressel, op. cit., p. 7.

5. This section of the chapter draws heavily from Joyce Wright, <u>Teaching and Learning.</u> I/D/E/A Study of Schooling Technical Report 18. Arlington, Va.: ERIC Document Reproduction Ser-vice, 1980.

6. It was disappointing to note that at Crestview Middle School, where there was a 2-hour language arts block, student scoring of the occurrence of activities other than "remembering facts, etc." was the lowest of all the junior highs. Teachers there also indicated that "Writing of stories, plays, or poems" and "Telling how stories, people and ideas were different" did not happen often.

7. It should be noted that there were foreign language classes at only six of the twelve junior high schools in the Study, and it was an elective at all of these. This includes Spanish at Rosemont but not English as a second language (ESL), which was taught to many students there but was sampled as part of English rather than foreign language.

8. This section of the chapter draws heavily from Kenneth A. Sirotnik, <u>What You See is What You Get: A Summary of Observa-tions in Over 1,000 Elementary and Secondary Classrooms,</u> Technical Report 29. Arlington, Va.: ERIC Document Reproduc-tion Service, 1981.

9. Kenneth A. Sirotnik, <u>An Inter-Observer Reliability Study of the SRI Observation System as Modified for Use in a Study of Schooling.</u> I/D/E/A Study of Schooling Technical Report No. 27. Arlington, Va.: ERIC Document Reproduction Service, 1981.

10. Phillip Giesen and Kenneth A. Sirotnik, The Methodology of Classroom Observation in A Study of Schooling, I/D/E/A Study of Schooling Technical Report 5. Arlington, Va.: ERIC Document Reproduction Service, 1979.

11. Philip W. Jackson, Life in Classrooms. (New York: Holt, Rinehart, and Winston, Inc.), 1968.

12. Kenneth A. Sirotnik, What You See Is What You Get, op. cit., pp. 17-19.

13. For a full discussion of teacher educational beliefs, see David P. Wright, Teachers' Educational Beliefs. I/D/E/A Study of Schooling Technical Report 14. Arlington, Va.: ERIC Document Reproduction Service, 1980.

14. M. Frances Klein, State and District Curriculum Guides: One Aspect of the Formal Curriculum. I/D/E/A Study of Schooling Technical Report No. 9. Arlington, Va.: ERIC Document Reproduction Service, 1980.

15. National Commission on Excellence in Education, A Nation at Risk: the Imperative for Educational Reform. (Washington, D.C.: U.S. Government Printing Office), 1983.

16. Paul L. Dressel, 1958, op. cit.

CHAPTER IV

EXPLORATION

Introduction

Currently, the most widely accepted definition of the aim of the junior high known as "exploration" is probably still the one presented by Van Til and his colleagues initially in 1961:

> "...To lead pupils to discover and explore their specialized interests, aptitudes, and abilities as a basis for present and future vocational decisions. To stimulate pupils and provide opportunities for them to develop a continually widening range of cultural, social, civic, avocational, and recreational interests."[1]

The history of the concept is consistent with the history of the junior high school, itself, described in Chapter 2. That is, in early junior highs, exploration meant the testing by students of academic areas that might later be elected in the senior high; or, similarly, sampling vocational areas.

In actuality, this form of exploration was more likely a narrowing experience rather than a broadening one because the early "exploratory" courses were the beginning of the sorting out of academic and vocational students. The question before us now is, of course, have things really changed or improved since the early days of the junior high?

Commonly, in today's junior highs, all students are enrolled in a set of academic courses: English, math, and social studies. They have P.E. and, to varying degrees, they experience "exploratory" courses in science, foreign language, the arts, and a variety of vocational subjects. However, the balance between academic and exploratory courses and the degree to which all students have common or segregated (tracked) experiences varies from locality to locality and is an issue which is examined in this chapter.

111

Regardless of the variety of practices from school to school, the concept, "exploration," has come to be identified specifically with the junior high. However, there are those who have brought a somewhat more balanced view to this notion. Gelford said:

I wonder if we are not guilty of gross conceit if we believe that educational exploration for any purpose is uniquely confined to a junior high school, even for the most part. It strikes me that an eleventh grade course in chemistry may serve a very practical purpose insofar as exploration is concerned. I wonder if the athletic lad who tries out for track even in the eleventh grade may not be serving the cause of exploration. I wonder further if the whole program of reading in the elementary school may not well be the most important exploratory of all...[2]

The remainder of this chapter sets forth the data from A Study of Schooling which seem to shed light upon the exploration function of the American junior high school. After examining the way in which the Study junior highs were organized to facilitate exploration, I look more closely at the arts as a particular example of an exploratory curriculum, and at student participation in extracurricular activities. The data on student attitudes toward school subjects are then examined for their relevance to the exploration function of junior highs.

The second half of the chapter concerns itself with exploration at the classroom level. Data on student decision-making, various perceptions of the use of instructional materials and equipment, and teacher estimates of the appropriateness of class content and materials are set forth and discussed. The chapter ends with conclusions and hypotheses about the exploration function of junior high schools.

Organization for Exploration

I agree with Gelford's principle that most school experiences at all levels are really exploratory experiences and that exploration is not a concept limited to junior high school. Even so, junior highs are supposed to be organized to facilitate student

112

opportunities to explore a variety of subjects. The degree to which they actually do this as a function of school organization is the subject of this section.

To begin with, the schools with the richest offerings, at least in terms of the numbers of choices available, were easily the traditional three-year junior highs (grades 7-9). The three-year middle schools (grades 6-8) had the second greatest number of options followed by the two-year intermediate schools (grades 7-8).

The course offerings of four schools are examined here in more depth. First, Woodlake's program is presented as an example of the traditional grade 7-9 schools. Second, I look at Palisades since it is exemplary of our middle schools. Also, Crestview Middle School is explored because it is so unique. Finally, Euclid is examined in some depth since it is representative of the two-year intermediate schools.

There were four traditional grade 7-9 junior high schools--Atwater, Bradford, Newport, and Woodlake. All of them offered English, math, social studies, and P.E. as required courses in all grades.

At Woodlake Junior High, there appeared to be many exploratory options for students at each successive grade level (see Figure 4.1). However, that was not totally true since there were certain patterns that persisted at the school and limited choices for many students. Such patterns were common at most junior highs. For example, performing music students were often enrolled in their specialty (e.g., chorus, band, orchestra) for three full years with the result that they had fewer exploratory courses than other students.

Second, students were required to have at least one semester of art and either shop (boys) or home economics (girls) as well as one exploratory science course. Although it was not true at Woodlake, many schools enrolled non-performing music students in an exploratory semester of general music appreciation.

Finally, we noted that students were often placed in exploratory courses on the basis of the school's judgment of their ability rather than on the basis of the student's (or parent's) interest. For example, at Woodlake, students with low reading achievement were

113

GRADE 7

ENGLISH
MATH
READING
WORLD HISTORY
P.E.
EXPLORATORY: CHOOSE 4 SEMESTERS
  2 SEM.: PERFORMING MUSIC
          (INSTR. OR VOCAL)
          EXPLORATORY FRENCH
  1 SEM.: SCIENCE 7
          ART 7
          SPEECH 7
          EXPLORATORY SHOP
          CRAFTS

GRADE 8

ENGLISH
MATH
U.S. HISTORY
P.E.
SCIENCE
EXPLORATORY: CHOOSE 4 SEMESTERS
  2 SEM.: PERFORMING MUSIC
          (INSTR. OR VOCAL)
          EXPLORATORY FRENCH II
          SPANISH I
  1 SEM.: HOME EC. 8
          SHOP (EXPLOR. OR ADV.)
          ART I
          ART II
          SPEECH
          JOURNALISM
          EX. CRAFTS
          READING
          ENGINES
          MAR. BIO./SPACE SCI.
          DRAMA

GRADE 9

ENGLISH
MATH OR PRE-ALGEBRA OR GEOMETRY
REGIONAL HISTORY/CIVICS
P.E.
EXPLORATORY: CHOOSE 6 SEMESTERS
  2 SEM.: HOME EC. 9
          FRENCH I
          SPANISH I
  1 SEM.: HOME EC. 9
          ADV. SHOP
          ART II
          ART III
          SPEECH
          JOURNALISM
          CRAFTS
          READING
          ENGINES
          MAR. BIO/SPACE SCI.
          APPLIED SCIENCE
          DRAMA

Figure 4.1 Course Offerings at Woodlake Junior High

114

certainly "placed" in exploratory reading with the consequence that their elective options were limited.

Newport Junior High had more courses for students to choose from than did Woodlake. However, it also had one less period and, thus, students had fewer exploratory options. Performing music students could choose only three semester-long exploratory courses in their three years. Bradford and Atwater Junior Highs both had fewer exploratory offerings than Woodlake although they allowed each student a number of choices (11 and 12 semester choices respectively).

There was one unique twist at Bradford. There was no exploratory music course except band. However, the school, with its pool, offered swimming at all grade levels. Was that a fair trade-off?

There were five three-year middle schools (grades 6-8): Crestview, Laurel, Manchester, Palisades, and Rosemont. They all required math, social studies, P.E. and some combination of English, language arts and reading at all grade levels. Also required was an uneven amount of science. For example, a student at Rosemont had three times the exposure to instruction in science than did a student at Laurel.

Figure 4.2 presents course offerings at Palisades Middle School at the time of the Study. Students appeared to be informally "tracked" into exploratory options at the middle schools.

Palisades served as a good example of this informal tracking. First, there were the performing music students. That was their sole exploratory option. Next were the foreign language students. They could also have two other semesters of choice--I would wager that they "chose" one semester of art and another of either homemaking (girls) or woodshop (boys). Finally, there were the non-performing music and non-foreign language students. Their options more often than not were a semester each of art and general music in grade 6, science and either home economics or woodshop in grade 7, and then two semester courses of their choice in grade 8. There was one other variation. Very able students were allowed to substitute exploratories for the required reading course. Obviously, those who could not read quite so well needed to "explore" reading a bit more.

GRADE 6

LANGUAGE ARTS
READING
MATH
SOCIAL STUDIES (CAREERS)
P.E.
EXPLORATORY: CHOOSE 2 SEMESTERS
  2 SEM.: PERFORMING MUSIC
          (INSTR. OR VOCAL)
          FRENCH 7-8
          SPANISH 7-8
  1 SEM.: FOODS 8
          WOODSHOP 8
          ART 8
          GUITAR
          DRAMA 8
          TYPING

GRADE 7

LANGUAGE ARTS
READING
MATH
SOCIAL STUDIES
P.E.
EXPLORATORY: CHOOSE 2 SEMESTERS
  2 SEM.: PERFORMING MUSIC
          (INSTR. OR VOCAL)
          FRENCH 7-8
          SPANISH 7-8
  1 SEM.: SCIENCE 7
          HOME EC. 7
          WOODSHOP 7

GRADE 8

LANGUAGE ARTS/READING
MATH
STATE HISTORY & CULTURE
SCIENCE
P.E./HEALTH
EXPLORATORY: CHOOSE 2 SEMESTERS
  2 SEM.: PERFORMING MUSIC
          (INSTR. OR VOCAL)
          FRENCH 7-8
          SPANISH 7-8
  1 SEM.: FOODS 8
          WOODSHOP 8
          ART 8
          GUITAR
          DRAMA 8
          TYPING

Figure 4.2 Course Offerings At Palisades Middle School

Manchester and Rosemont Middle Schools had a few more options than Palisades but the same patterns existed. Laurel really gave no options in the 6th or 7th grades, assigning all students to various combinations of art, general music, shop, home economics and science at both grade levels which accounted for four semesters in total. At the 8th grade level, students did choose two one-semester courses.

116

Crestview was even more limited in that students had no choices at any grade level. The schedule at the school was quite unique and is presented in Figure 4.3. Students had one full period of math, science and social studies each day for three years and two full periods of language arts. In addition, they alternated P.E. with a course entitled unified arts which consisted of art, music, home economics and shop (they could substitute band for unified arts).

GRADES 6-8

MATH
LANGUAGE ARTS
SCIENCE
SOCIAL STUDIES
P.E. (M-W & alt. F)
UNIFIED ARTS OR BAND (T-Th & alt. F)

Figure 4.3 Course Offerings at Crestview Middle School

There were three two-year intermediate schools (grades 7 and 8)--Euclid, Fairfield, and Vista. They all required math, language arts, social studies, science all year long for two years and P.E. for one or two semesters each year. Figure 4.4 presents course offerings at Euclid Junior High at the time of the Study.

GRADE 7

LANGUAGE ARTS
MATH
SOCIAL STUDIES
SCIENCE
STUDY HALL
P.E./EXPLORATORY: CHOOSE 3
  SEMESTERS
  2 SEM.: BAND
  1 SEM.: ART
          VOCAL MUSIC
          STUDY HALL
          HOME EC.
          IND. ARTS

GRADE 8

LANGUAGE ARTS
MATH
AMERICAN HISTORY
SCIENCE
STUDY HALL
P.E./EXPLORATORY: CHOOSE 3
  SEMESTERS
  2 SEM.: BAND
          SPANISH
  1 SEM.: ART
          VOCAL MUSIC
          STUDY HALL
          HOME EC.
          IND. ARTS

Figure 4.4 Course Offerings at Euclid Junior High School

117

Euclid had seven periods per day rather than six. Language arts, math, social studies, science and study hall were required for one period per day both years. P.E. was required for one period for one semester each year. Once again, we see that performing music students were separated from others.

The Vista program was very similar except that it offered no foreign language, had performing vocal music, and offered typing, journalism and yearbook as semester electives.

Fairfield was very different from the other schools. There was band, otherwise no other music. There was one craft course, otherwise no art. English, social studies, math, science and P.E. were required. There was a one-semester reading elective at both grade levels. Otherwise, students chose from a semester of office assistance for one period or two-period-long semester courses entitled: Home and Community, General Mechanical Repair, Duplicating Skills, Horticulture, Building Maintenance, and General Construction Trades.

There was no doubt about the practical vocational orientation to the exploration opportunities offered students at Fairfield Junior High, nor was there any doubt about the separation of the college bound and non-college bound students into separate tracks. At least at Fairfield, the exploratory offerings were not balanced in favor of the academically oriented students as they were in the other eleven schools in the Study.

A constant theme unearthed by A Study of Schooling is that of sameness and yet difference. We found that teacher talk dominated all subjects at all levels of schooling in most classrooms in all schools. At the junior high level, we found that what students do in any math class is pretty much what they do in all math classes--sameness. And, yet, we found that each school was unique in many ways. While all junior highs required math, English or language arts, social studies, and P.E. of every student, they were greatly different with regard to their offerings of science and the so-called exploratory courses.

The differences in exploratory offerings seemed attributable to four factors. To begin with, school size played a role. Large schools had more course offerings. In that sense, the comprehensive school lives up to the claims of its proponents. Second, local tradition played an important part. If a school had a good band and the community was proud of it, you could bet that there would be a strong instrumental music program at the school. The same could be said for drama and other subjects, too. Third, teacher interest seemed to be involved both in determining what was offered and, perhaps, in determining what wasn't offered. Finally, we saw evidence of general societal pressure and/or direction by school administration in that new options had crept into the offerings--i.e., foreign language added in the early 60s, reading in the late 60s and even "careers" at some schools during the 70s.

I have very mixed feelings about performing music as an exploratory option (e.g., band, orchestra, guitar, chorus, glee club). I applaud the fact that students have the option. I recognize the satisfaction inherent in performance and I recognize the potential for the development of integrative behavior. On the other hand, my experience teaches me that performing music students are often segregated from other students, treated as elites, and miss out on other options. The answer probably rests with all students having many performance opportunities of all kinds (e.g., music, dance, art, drama, sports) and in assuring that students are not segregated on this basis.

Social studies was another interesting subject area with regard to exploration. I could not help but be struck by the ethnocentric nature of what was offered. U.S. history was at every school for a year. That's fine. In addition, state or regional history usually occupied a second year. Very little time was left for other areas of the world or, for that matter, for any discipline other than history or geography. There was not one social science elective offered in our sample.

Earlier in this section I pointed out that there was a great variation in student exposure to science from school to school. It was also clear that science in 1977, had not yet reached the "required" status of English, math, social studies, or even P.E. A rekindling of interest in both math and science education in the mid 1980s seems likely to raise the status of science at the junior high level, however. In Chapter 3 we saw that, in general, integrative behavior seemed to be slightly more attended to in science than in other academic areas. Increased emphasis on science, therefore, may be beneficial to students in more ways than one.

Finally, let us turn to the issue of the expanded curriculum. If anything is clear from the examination of schedules in this section, it is that the curricula of most of the junior highs, at least in our sample, were "cluttered." We have tried modular scheduling, mini-courses and numerous other ways of organizing for exploration. However, none of those innovations have seemed to be sustained. Perhaps Gelford was onto something when he stated that all courses have an element of exploration and perhaps the people at Crestview were, too. Perhaps the schedule should be kept simple (and common for all students) and exploration should be a matter of what is done within the classrooms. Our faith in school organization as a way of solving education problems may be overrated.

The Arts As An Exploratory Curriculum

Every junior high in our sample offered courses in the arts for purposes of exploration. With a special grant from the Rockefeller Foundation and the JDR 3rd Fund, we examined this and other aspects of arts education in some detail. We asked both students and teachers about the importance to them of eight of the commonly stated goals of arts education. These data, reported in Table 4.1, gave interesting insights into how students and teachers viewed the concept of exploration as well as how they viewed the arts.

The 46 arts teachers thought that four of the goals were very important. The greatest percentage of teachers chose the personal goal "Feel good about what can be done in the arts." The second greatest percentage chose the intellectual goal "Learn how to look at, listen to and understand art works." Two other general goals were chosen as very important: "Earn class credits," and "Improve art skills." Teachers indicated that all other goals were somewhat important, and students thought that all goals for the arts were only somewhat important.

On the average, the teachers rated all goals except one as more important than did the students, "Prepare

120

Table 4.1

Student and Teacher Perceptions of the Importance of Goals of Art Education

	Students (N=1172)			Teachers (N=46)		
	$\overline{X}$	Rank	S.D.	$\overline{X}$	Rank	S.D.
1. Learn to do and make new and different things in one's own way	3.21	(5)	.83	3.46	(5)	.81
2. Learn about artists, performers, writers and their work	2.80	(8)	.95	3.26	(7)	.68
3. Improve art skills	3.48	(1)	.81	3.59	(3.5)	.78
4. Learn how to look at, listen to and understand art works	3.20	(6)	.86	3.74	(2)	.44
5. Prepare for a career in the arts	2.82	(7)	1.02	2.51	(8)	.92
6. Have fun	3.36	(4)	.85	3.39	(6)	.68
7. Feel good about what can be done in the arts	3.43	(2)	.76	3.87	(1)	.40
8. Earn class credits	3.38	(3)	.88	3.59	(3.5)	.80

Response categories: 1.00-1.49 Very unimportant
1.50-2.49 Somewhat unimportant
2.50-3.49 Somewhat important
3.50-4.00 Very important

for a career in the arts." It was barely rated as somewhat important by the teachers. Over and over, students expressed the view that schooling had a functional value to them vis-a-vis preparation for the world of work. Teachers may have been more realistic about the amount of talent necessary to have a career in the arts or they may have seen more of an intrinsic value in the arts. Whatever, students were more career oriented even though they, too, rated the vocational goal lower than most other goals.

There was great variability in responses to all statements from school to school and within schools from both students and teachers. One possible explanation was that so many subjects were included in the arts: performing music, music appreciation, visual arts, crafts, drama, humanities. Many goals were no doubt emphasized differently from subject to subject and even class to class.

Teachers of the arts were also asked to agree or disagree with twelve statements of belief about the arts. Their responses are reported in Table 4.2 and some were quite surprising. For example, there was general agreement that a solid foundation of basic skills should be taught before students are encouraged to use the arts for personal expression. Likewise, there was overall disagreement with the statement, "Students can learn more by experimenting freely with art materials, musical sounds, and word combinations than they can through formal instruction." In short, the teachers of exploratory arts courses, as a rule, opted for the formal aspects of their disciplines rather than the exploratory aspects. It might be hypothesized that teachers of the arts were trying to make their subjects more "academic." Given that the academic subjects have the highest priority in schooling, this was not surprising.

Teachers of the arts had good reason to respond the way they did. We asked parents and all teachers whether or not the school should spend more time teaching things like art, music, and drama. The overall response of both groups was no. In fact, over two-thirds of the parents said no. Obviously, the arts were still considered "a frill" in our sample. Such data suggests that parents and teachers--including teachers of the arts--may not be all that committed to the exploratory role of the junior high school.

Table 4.2

Selected Beliefs of Arts Teachers (N=46)

Beliefs	$\overline{X}$	S.D.
Skills are learned best in the context of a real experience, such as putting on a play.	3.70	.51
The teacher should emphasize great art, music, and theater because students have access to the mediocre.	3.46	.78
The quality of student experiences is more important than the quality of their products or performances.	3.41	.71
A carefully sequenced set of experiences is essential for learning in the arts.	3.27	.72
Student satisfaction is a more reliable measure of learning than an impressive product.	3.07	.80
A solid foundation of basic skills should be taught before students are encouraged to use the arts for personal expression.	2.89	1.17
Learning the rules of the game is the most effective route to having successful arts experiences.	2.87	.88
Students can learn more by experimenting freely with art materials, musical sounds, and word combinations than they can through formal instruction.	2.13	.94
Children's natural feelings for acting, drawing, and using words can be destroyed by attention to skill development.	2.09	1.05
Students should be allowed to stop working on a project if they dislike it.	2.05	1.04
The content of art classes should be confined to the best examples of traditional arts.	1.85	.99
Arts education should not be concerned with popular arts such as rock and roll, television, billboard paintings, or clothing decoration.	1.61	.90

Response categories: 1.00-1.49 = Strongly disagree
1.50-2.49 = Mildly disagree
2.50-3.49 = Mildly agree
3.50-4.00 = Strongly agree

123

Student Participation in Extracurricular Activities

In addition to the so-called exploratory and/or elective courses, junior high students are frequently given opportunities to explore their academic, vocational, and avocational interests and aptitudes through what are called extracurricular activities. Such activities take place before or after school, at lunch time or in some block of time set aside for them within the regular school day. There were extracurricular activities at all of the junior highs in our sample. Table 4.3 reports the percentages of students who participated in six kinds of extracurricular activities across all of the twelve junior highs.

Table 4.3

Percentage of Students Participating
in Extracurricular Activities (N=5,311)

Activity	%	School-by-School Range
Sports teams	52.7	44.5 - 79.4
Music, drama, acting groups	40.2	18.7 - 64.3
Special interest clubs	35.0	12.8 - 71.7
Honor society	21.5	13.1 - 36.5
School or community service activities	31.1	23.6 - 56.3
Student government	15.2	9.3 - 22.5

More than half of the responding students said that they participated in sport teams, the greatest percentage for any extracurricular activity. At all schools except two, a greater percentage of students participated in sport teams than in any other activity. At Manchester, more students participated in special interest clubs and at Palisades more participated in music, drama, and acting groups.

Approximately 40% of the students said that they participated in music, drama, or acting groups, the second greatest percentage for any extracurricular activity. However, some of the responses may have been by students who were enrolled in regular rather than in extracurricular classes.

There were three schools where more than half of the students indicated that they participated in special interest clubs (Manchester, Euclid, Atwater). Fewer than 20% indicated participation at three schools (Palisades, Crestview, Woodlake). Across all schools, it was 35%. There appeared to be no relationship between participation in special interest clubs and any other factor (e.g., school size, transportation, student ethnicity).

Slightly more than 30% of the sampled students across all junior highs indicated participation in school or community service activities. This item reminded me of the few exciting but short-run experiments such as the Parkway Plan in Philadelphia and the Metro Plan in Chicago wherein an attempt was made to move outside of the walls of the school and utilize the community as a laboratory. We asked our sample of parents, teachers and students to respond to the following statement: "There are other places in this community where students could be taught, but this school does not make use of them." Across all schools, almost half of the students agreed with the item. Only about one-third of the teachers and fewer than 30% of the parents agreed. The idea that schooling belongs inside the walls of the school was a very powerful one in our sample.

Only about 20% of the junior high students in our sample participated in some type of honor society and only about 15% were involved in student government. Over one-third of our total sample of students agreed with the item, "Student government is a waste of time."

About 12% of the junior high students did not answer the question about extracurricular activities. Of the 5,311 who did respond, an average of only 19% reported that they did not participate in any of the six activities listed. For those students who did participate, the average across all junior highs was 2.3 activities per student.

In addition to asking about extracurricular activities, we also asked students to agree or disagree on a four point scale with the following item, "Assemblies and other special events are usually interesting at this school." While the range of responses within schools was quite wide, the mean response at all schools indicated overall agreement with the statement. Thus, assemblies and other special events were generally viewed positively by junior high students in our sample.

Extracurricular activities, then, appeared to be serving fairly well the exploratory function in our sample of schools. There were students who did not participate, however, and it did seem that schools should look closely at those students and their interests with the objective of expanding offerings.

Student Attitudes Toward Subjects[3]

The amount of exploration carried out in the various school subjects, at least in part, was thought to be a function of students' attitudes toward these subjects. For that reason, we asked them a series of questions which gave us information about these attitudes.

To begin with, students were asked to indicate how much they liked each school subject. They were given four response choices: Like very much, Like somewhat, Dislike somewhat, Dislike very much. Table 4.4 reports this data by combining the percentages of students who selected the first two responses, Like very much and Like somewhat.

A large majority of students reported that they liked all subjects. The greatest percentages were reported for the two exploratory subjects, the arts and vocational education, followed by the other non-academic subject, P.E. Of the academic subjects, the greatest percentage reported liking math, and the least percentage foreign language.

Students were also asked to indicate their perceptions of the importance of the eight subjects. Four choices were again available: Very important, Somewhat important, Somewhat unimportant, and Very unimportant. The percentages of students who selected the two positive responses were combined in Table 4.5. The greatest percentage of students said that math and English were important. As might be expected, vocational education was also selected by a large percentage as being important. The arts had the lowest percentages, followed by foreign language and P.E. Even so, over 70% of the junior high students in the sample said that all subjects were important.

Table 4.4

Student Liking of Subjects

Subject	% Like	N
Arts	85.9	5130
Voc. Ed.	81.0	4912
P.E.	80.1	5177
Math	74.8	5160
Science	66.1	5068
Social Studies	66.0	5184
Foreign Language	62.0	4734

Table 4.5

Student Perception of Subject Importance

Subject	% Important	N
Math	95.0	5154
English	91.5	5220
Voc. Ed.	85.1	4972
Social Studies	83.1	5146
Science	78.8	5046
P.E.	75.3	5174
Foreign Language	73.5	4842
Arts	70.4	5103

The perceived value of school vis-a-vis preparation for work was also demonstrated in many of the responses of students to the one open-ended question in the

student questionnaire, "What is the most important thing that you have learned so far in this class?" For example, students said such things as:
-- Everything because it will help me when I grow up and find a job. (language arts)
-- It will help me when I grow up so I can find a good job. (science)
-- It is very important 'cause when you grow up and go out to find a job they really ask you if you know how to type. (typing)
-- For my career it is very important to me. Thank you. (math)
-- This class for some is to prepare for later business but for me it is to have fun. (band)
-- If I didn't want to go to college I would have gotten out of this class. (Spanish)
-- I have learned the elements. Because when I grow up I want to become a photographer. So I have to know about color and contrast. (art)
-- When I came into this class I wanted to know what it would be like to work on a newspaper. Now I know. (journalism)

All sampled junior high students were asked to tell how they liked all subjects and were asked how important they thought each was. However, only those students in the classes sampled were asked about the difficulty and interest of the class itself. Five responses were available to students in rating difficulty: Too easy, Sort of easy, Not too easy, Not too hard, Too hard. Table 4.6 contains the percentage of students who reported the subject of that class to be hard (Sort of hard and Too hard), easy (Sort of easy and Too easy), and just right (Not too easy, Not too hard).

Generally, only a small percentage of students reported their work to be too hard. P.E., the arts, and vocational education were reported to be hard by the smallest percentage of students and easiest by the largest percentage. Approximately one-half of the students in each subject reported that it was just right (Not too easy, Not too hard).

Students were also asked to rate the extent of their interest in the work in the present class. Four response choices were available: Very interesting, Sort of interesting, Sort of boring, Very boring. Table 4.7 reports the percentage of students who indicated that they found the class interesting (combination of Very interesting and Somewhat interesting). Over 60% of the students rated all subjects as interesting. Vocational education, P.E., and the arts classes were rated as interesting by the largest percentage of students while nearly 40% of the students in English classes did not find them interesting. It is worth noting that while only a small percentage of students in general reported liking of foreign language, a quite higher percentage of students enrolled in foreign language classes found the subject interesting.

Table 4.6

Student Perception of Subject Difficulty

Subject	% Hard	% Easy	% Just Right	N
Foreign Language	23.3	29.2	47.5	219
Social Studies	17.9	27.5	54.6	1420
Science	17.1	29.0	53.9	1056
Math	14.0	32.2	53.8	1670
English	12.5	31.6	55.9	1644
Voc. Ed.	8.2	42.0	49.8	1023
Arts	7.6	45.7	46.7	1176
P.E.	5.0	45.8	49.2	754

On the average, all subjects were liked and thought to be important. Also, students enrolled in specific classes generally thought that all subjects were about right in difficulty and were interesting. Vocational education was generally among the most liked and most important and was perceived to be easy and interesting by many students enrolled in vocational education classes. The arts had a similar profile except that a smaller percentage of students said they were important. The other exploratory subject, foreign language, while seen as interesting by a large percentage who were enrolled, was liked and seen as important by a smaller percentage of students compared to other subjects. Student attitudes toward the exploratory subjects were different than attitudes toward the academic subjects. The academic subjects (English, math, science, social studies) were generally liked less but seen as more important. They were seen as more difficult and less interesting by students enrolled in them.

Table 4.7

Student Perception of Subject Interest

Subject	% Interesting	N
Voc. Ed.	84.1	1022
P.E.	83.6	752
Arts	77.6	1176
Foreign Language	74.7	217
Math	69.6	1666
Social Studies	69.2	1416
Science	66.1	1060
English	62.6	1645

Student Decision-Making

It would seem logical that the amount and kinds of decision-making by students would be some measure of the degree to which they were allowed to "explore" at their schools. If that assumption is logical, then it can be concluded that students in our sample of junior high schools did not "explore." For sure, they did not "decide."

There were three interesting measures of student decision-making in the Study. First, we asked observers to note decisions made by teachers and students during the course of their classroom observations. Subject by subject results are reported for six classroom decision-making loci in Table 4.8. Teachers made more than nine of every ten decisions in every subject except vocational education and that was almost 90%. The only thing students were at all allowed to decide about was where they sat. Not one student was observed making a decision about whom he/she should work with in a group and almost no students were observed deciding about content or materials of instruction.

Table 4.8

Observed Locus of Classroom Decision-making:
Percentage of Decisions Made by Teachers
Subject by Subject

LOCI	English %	Math %	Social Studies %	Science %	Arts %	For. Lang. %	Voc. Ed. %	P.E. %
Seats	62.9	76.4	67.4	80.6	77.5	57.1	57.6	-
Groups	100.0	100.0	100.0	100.0	100.0	100.0	100.0	100.0
Content	98.6	98.5	98.1	97.6	95.3	100.0	93.6	100.0
Materials	91.2	100.0	94.1	92.1	87.8	100.0	87.5	95.5
Space	88.4	93.4	95.7	91.4	89.7	90.9	85.7	86.4
Time	97.2	97.0	100.0	97.6	100.0	100.0	87.2	100.0
Learning Activities	97.2	97.0	100.0	97.6	100.0	100.0	97.9	100.0
Overall	90.5	94.7	93.5	93.7	92.8	94.2	87.2	96.8

There were eight questions on the student questionnaire which constituted a student decision-making scale. Those items were:
-- We are free to talk in this class about anything we want.
-- Students help make the rules for this class.
-- We are free to work with anyone we want to in this class.
-- We can decide what we want to learn in this class.
-- Students help decide what we do in this class.
-- Different students can do different things in this class.

131

-- Sometimes I can study or do things I am interested in even if they are different from what
other students are studying or doing.
-- I help decide what I do in this class.

Table 4.9 reports the composite scale scores for
these items by subject. It can be seen that, on the
average, students in every subject felt that they were
not much involved in classroom decision-making.
Further, the very low standard deviations indicated
that the response was consistent across classes within
subjects. In other words, students in almost all
classes perceived that they did not make decisions.
They said they made more decisions in the non-academic
subjects: vocational education, P.E., and the arts, and
the least in foreign language, math, and social studies.

Table 4.9

Student Participation in Decision-Making by Subject

Subject	$\overline{X}$	S.D.	Classroom N
Voc. Ed.	2.43	0.33	49
P.E.	2.42	0.21	25
Art	2.33	0.31	45
English	2.19	0.28	72
Science	2.18	0.33	42
Social Studies	2.10	0.20	53
Math	2.09	0.26	70
Foreign Lang.	2.03	0.24	11
Overall	2.22	0.30	367

Response Categories: 1.0 - 1.50 No Participation
1.51 - 2.50 Little Participation
2.51 - 3.50 Some Participation
3.51 - 4.00 Much Participation

We also asked students what their wishes were
regarding involvement in decision-making: "I would like
to be able to make more decisions about what goes on in
this class." Slightly over 60% of the 8,301 students
agreed with the item. The range of responses from

132

school to school was not very great, 70% at Laurel as a high and 53% at Woodlake as a low. More interesting perhaps was the fact that nearly 40% of the student sample did not agree with the statement. Did they not really want to decide? Did they not care about deciding at school? Or were they so used to having their decisions made for them that they saw no reason to decide for themselves?

Classroom Materials and Equipment

Another way of finding out the degree to which exploration was allowed and encouraged on the part of junior high students was to examine the availability, use, adequacy, content of, and attitudes toward instructional materials and equipment in the classrooms. We did that in a number of ways.

Teachers in sampled classes in five academic subject areas (English/language arts, math, social studies, science, foreign language) were presented with a list of materials and asked to tell how often students used each one in their classrooms. Response choices were: Always or most of the time, Often, Not very often, and Never. Materials which were used always or most of the time or often are listed in Table 4.10 for each of the five subjects.

We also asked teachers how useful they thought those materials were. Response choices for there items were: Very useful, Somewhat useful, Somewhat useless, Very useless.

We gave the same lists of materials to students in sampled classes and asked them whether they used them and how much they liked using them. The response modes for using them was Yes or No. For liking it was: Like very much, Like somewhat, Dislike somewhat, and Dislike very much.

As far as the actual content of instruction was concerned, we asked each participating teacher to provide us with a package of "curriculum materials" used in the sampled class. These were to contain (1) a list of topics taught in that class, (2) a list of skills taught in that class, (3) a list of textbooks and major supplementary materials used in that class, (4) samples of tests and quizzes used, and (5) samples

133

of worksheets used in that class. In all, we received
366 such packages from junior high teachers.[4]

Table 4.10

Teacher Report of Materials Frequently Used
in the Classroom (Academic Subjects Only)

ENGLISH (N=67)

Materials	$\overline{X}$ Freq.	S.D.
Worksheets	2.97	.78
Other books	2.81	.66
Textbooks	2.78	.96

MATH (N=66)

Materials	$\overline{X}$ Freq.	S.D.
Textbooks	3.32	.88
Worksheets	2.92	.56

SOCIAL STUDIES (N=44)

Materials	$\overline{X}$ Freq.	S.D.
Textbooks	3.36	.75
Things like globes, maps charts	3.32	.56
Films, film-strips, slides	2.82	.50
Worksheets	2.77	.80
Other books	2.68	.64

SCIENCE (N=40)

Materials	$\overline{X}$ Freq.	S.D.
Textbooks	3.13	.76
Lab equipment and materials	3.05	.76
Worksheets	2.82	.72
Films, film-strips, slides	2.73	.41
Things like models, charts, pulleys	2.64	.58

FOREIGN LANGUAGE (N=10)

Materials	$\overline{X}$ Freq.	S.D.
Textbooks	3.60	.97
Worksheets	3.00	.82
Other books	3.00	.67
Games, simulations	2.56	.53

Response categories: 2.50 - 3.49 Often
3.50 - 4.00 Always or most of the time

Finally, we observed in 362 classes and, among many other things, specifically noted what instructional materials and equipment were available. We also estimated its adequacy and restrictions placed upon student use.

English. Worksheets, other books and textbooks were reported by English teachers to be used often. Although they also considered newspapers and magazines, learning kits, films, filmstrips, or slides, tape recordings or records, games or simulations, and television all to be somewhat useful, teachers reported that they did not use them often. They also said that teaching machines or equipment for computer assisted instruction was somewhat useless and at most schools, teachers indicated that they were never used. At one school, Fairfield, teaching machines were used often in the fairly large Title I reading program and they also were reported to have modest use in reading programs at Newport, Palisades, Rosemont, and Bradford.

There was variability both across and within schools with regard to use of classroom instructional materials and equipment. There were some teachers at a few schools (Crestview, Newport, Atwater, Laurel) who indicated that they did not use textbooks very often. Likewise, a few teachers at many schools stated that they used learning kits a good deal.

Students in our sampled English classes reported that they liked television very much but only about 16% said they ever used it. They reported that they somewhat liked all of the other materials and equipment discussed above. However, fewer than half of them indicated that they used anything but textbooks, worksheets and other books. Over three-quarters of the students said they used each of these three things.

Books and worksheets dominated the English classrooms in our sample and the use of technology (e.g., teaching machines, television) was almost totally non-existent. Our observers did report that about one-third of the English classes had audio-visual equipment, about one-quarter had tapes, records and overhead projectors (to support teacher lectures, no doubt). Also, they reported that there were teaching machines in over 20% of the classes (probably mostly in reading classes). "Other books" appeared to be quite important to English teachers, even more important than textbooks. They considered textbooks somewhat useful, but other books, they said, were very useful--and they reported using them often. This is probably a result of the effort to have books of high interest and low reading ability for poorer readers. Unfortunately, school budgets are often tight so that opportunity for teachers to purchase "other books," hardback or paperback, is often limited. Requiring students to pay for such books is self-defeating because it is often those students who can't afford them who need them the most.

There were 53 English curriculum packages submitted for analysis. By far most of these emphasized grammar, mechanics, composition, and literature study. Less attention was given to creative writing, research techniques, study skills, critical thinking, speaking or listening. Book reports and the traditional Friday spelling test were very common. There certainly was no need to "go back to the basics" in our sample of English classes. That's where they were.

Basic English textbooks varied greatly from school to school except for one grammar series and one spelling series. However, there was a good bit of overlap in some of the supplementary worksheet materials. To the extent that junior high students encountered major American and European authors, it was evidently through anthologies--this means primarily in the form of short stories, poetry, and other short forms. Virtually never were students expected to read a major work that required substantial time and/or effort.

One of the reasons for variability in many of these responses was that many English/language arts classes at the junior high level, in fact, were reading classes.

On the basis of the materials we received from 59 reading classes, we can say that most of those classes were remedial, geared to students reading anywhere from one and one-half years below grade level to non-readers. Teaching in these classes was purported to be individualized.[5]

Decoding skills predominated in these classes. Comprehension, interpretation, application, and other higher cognitive abilities were less emphasized. In fact, after decoding, the most common skill development emphases had to do with mechanics of writing (e.g., punctuation, abbreviation, handwriting) and information locating rather than reading skills (e.g., vocabulary building, comprehension).

There were what appeared to be some quite outstanding reading programs in our sample of schools. For example at Laurel there were 156 students in the Title I reading program (there was a total of 276 students at the school--56.5% were Title I students). Each student was tested in auditory vocabulary, reading comprehension, phonetic analysis and reading rate. Students then worked only in areas where they were below grade level. A highly structured and sequenced commercial program in which students moved at their own rates was central to the program. The main stated goal of the program was to "motivate students to read and enjoy it."

Math. Only textbooks and worksheets were reported by math teachers as being used often. They also said that other books, games or simulations, things like counters, slide rules, calculators and computers, learning kits, teaching machines, and films, filmstrips or slides were all somewhat useful. However, they said that they never used teaching machines and the other materials were not used very often.

There was little variability in these responses from school to school or among teachers at any given school. A few teachers at Rosemont said they did not often use tests and some teachers at different schools said they often used learning kits, games or simulations, or things like counters, slide rules, calculators or computers. There were almost no teachers who said that they did not use worksheets.

Approximately 85% of the students in our sampled math classes said that they used textbooks and worksheets, only about 35% said they used games or simulations and approximately 20% or fewer reported used any other materials. However, on the average, math students reported that they liked all materials and equipment.

In Chapter 3, we found that math activities from school to school and from class to class in our sample were almost identical. The same can be said of the materials of instruction. Students almost always used worksheets and/or textbooks.

Observers did report that nearly one-third of the sampled math classes had games and puzzles and that one-quarter had teaching aids. Also, about 35% had overhead projectors. But fewer than 10% had teaching machines. Observers reported that an adequate amount of instructional materials and equipment appeared to be available.

There were 61 math curriculum packages submitted for analysis. The one strong generalization which can be made from these analyses is that aside from algebra and geometry content, math at the junior high level was a review of basic mathematics. For example, metrics was mentioned in only 18 packages.

One teacher at Bradford Junior High listed as one of 37 skills to be developed, "Recognizing unsolvable problems." In a subject dominated by dry textbooks, worksheets and teacher talk this truly seemed a welcome change. The potential for both integrative behavior and exploration is so great in mathematics and, yet, neither seemed in evidence. This situation is described quite well by Marshall Gordon as follows:

. . . When we consider a second level--teaching for understanding--the emphasis on relational knowledge in the sense that the student comes to see why things are the way they are . . . While in the control stage one fills in blanks, in the understanding stage one solves problems . . .

. . . At a third level, however, in teaching for liberation it is necessary to establish that the particular mathematics is interesting and important for the student. In this situation the concern is for the personal construction of knowledge. Here, rather than being a problem solver, one is a problem power/chooser . . .

We found no evidence of this third level of mathematics teaching in our sampled math classes. There was a good deal of first level teaching, however.

Social Studies. More of a variety of instructional materials was reported to be used often by social studies teachers than by teachers of English, reading, or math. In addition to textbooks, worksheets and other books, the social studies teachers in our sample reported that they often used things like globes, maps, and charts, as well as films, filmstrips, and slides.

On the average, these teachers said that all of the above except textbooks were _very_ useful. Texts were said to be somewhat useful. Of the choices offered, only teaching machines were thought not to be useful by our sample of the social studies teachers.

There was not much variability from school to school or among teachers at any given school with regard to these responses. A few teachers at Bradford said they did not often use texts; some teachers at Crestview indicated a good deal of use of films, filmstrips, and slides; worksheets were reported to be used infrequently by a small number of teachers at Rosemont, Newport, and Woodlake; and a scattering of teachers at various schools used games, simulations, newspapers and magazines.

Social studies teachers appeared to use audio-visual materials more than teachers of other subjects in our sample. This seemed to fit nicely with the fact that students indicated a strong liking for them. It also seemed logical since the content of social studies lends itself to presentation through a variety of media.

We really did not find out how effectively films, slides, and filmstrips were used. However, over the years, I have observed a good deal of misuse of audio-visual materials in schools. For example, in more than one school social studies teachers automatically sent students to the auditorium every Friday to see whatever films were available. This was nothing more than babysitting. Audio-visual materials can be very valuable tools for the student to use in exploring ideas. However, students need to be prepared for what they are to see and they need to have follow-up if maximum learning is to take place.

A major problem is access. For audio-visual materials to be used appropriately they must be readily available to classrooms. Having teachers order such materials months in advance of actual use is silly. Such a practice encourages the "Friday film fair."

Student report of the use of instructional materials in our sample of social studies classes was very similar to the teacher report. While students indicated that they liked all materials suggested to them, they said that they very much liked television and films, filmstrips, and slides. Fewer than 10% reported using television.

Observers reported that nearly 90% of observed social studies classes had maps and globes, over half had audio-visual equipment, over one-third had overhead projectors, and about one-fifth had games and puzzles. Nearly all observed classes were judged to be adequately supplied with instructional materials.

There were 45 curriculum packages available for analysis from social studies teachers in the sample. United States history was taught in all schools at the 8th grade level except in one state where it was taught in the 7th grade. Six of the twelve schools also had required courses in state history.

Note taking, research and study skills, map reading, and how to take tests were the most commonly mentioned skills to be developed. In our analysis, we rarely encountered any testing which involved anything other than recall of specific information (e.g., names, dates, places, events).

There were a very few teachers who specified a desire for students to develop critical thinking or higher level cognitive abilities. We found MACOS in only one school and geography and/or history of other than the United States, the Western Hemisphere, or Europe was rare. The social studies curriculum in our sample of classrooms was very ethnocentric. That is, it was narrowly focused on the United States and did little or nothing to build an awareness of global interdependence.

The major proposed innovation in the social studies of the past two decades has been the move to concept-oriented teaching. However, almost none of the teaching packets we received reflected such a position. We did find the following United States history outline at Palisades:

-- scientific revolution
-- disciplines of social and natural sciences
-- nationalism
-- business cycles
-- family patterns
-- wars

Far more typical were the following traditional topic outlines:

U.S. History	State History	World Geography
Indian societies	early inhabitants	prehistoric man
explorations	revolution and early government	ancient civilizations
colonization		Middle Ages, Renaissance, Industrial Revolution
revolution	Indians, Civil War, Reconstruction	
forming the government	social and economic changes	WWII, comparing communism and capitalism
westward expansion		
	duties of the three branches of state and federal government	Africa, Asia, Australia

Note that the U.S. history "coverage" stopped at the period of Reconstruction. I can almost hear the discussion at the department meeting when the social studies teachers dealt with the problems that they weren't "getting all the way through to the present." They did a very logical thing. They cut the curriculum in half by stopping at the period of Reconstruction. This was at Woodlake. At Rosemont, they stopped after the Revolution. I checked to see what the high schools did in U.S. history in those districts. They started over again, beginning with colonization and often ending with Reconstruction. The preoccupation with coverage dominated the social studies in our schools. Focus on concept learning and exploration was only moderately evident. Perhaps this was why such a potentially interesting subject was among the least liked subjects by the junior high students in our sample.

Science. A wider variety of instructional materials and equipment were reported to be used by science

141

teachers than by teachers of other academic subjects. In addition to textbooks and worksheets, the science teachers in our sample reported that they often used things like lab equipment, models, charts, and pulleys, as well as films, filmstrips, and slides.

On the average, these teachers said that all of the above except textbooks were very useful. Texts were said to be somewhat useful. While they thought that other books, learning kits, simulations, magazines, television, tape recordings, teaching machines, and other materials and equipment were somewhat useful, they reported that they used them never or not very often.

There was some variability from school to school in these responses. Some teachers at Rosemont, and to a lesser degree at Fairfield and Bradford, reported extensive use of learning kits, newspapers or magazines, games or simulations. At Newport some science was taught without lab equipment and materials.

Large percentages of students in our sampled junior high science classes reported that they used textbooks, lab equipment and materials, worksheets, and audio-visuals. Only slightly more than half of the sample indicated that they used things like models, charts, and pulleys. They liked textbooks, other books, worksheets, and teaching machines least.

Observers did not report on how many of the science classes were actually laboratories. However, they did report that approximately 60% of the students sat at desks with chairs attached and which were in rows. With this data and from my own observations, I believe it safe to say that there were few, if any, science laboratories at the junior high level. Rather, students sat at conventional seating and the teacher perhaps had a lab table at which he or she could demonstrate. Such arrangements were far from conducive to exploration and pursuit of inquiry in a subject supposedly made to order for such activity.

Observers noted audio-visual equipment in about one-third of the science classes, but overhead projectors in fewer than one-fourth of them. Over half of the classes in this sample had a variety of teaching aids but fewer than 3% had any live animals and only about 40% had live plants.

142

There were 36 curriculum packages submitted for analysis by junior high science teachers. As was shown in the previous chapter, the amount and kind of science teaching varied greatly from school to school. Our curriculum analysis did reveal some similarity in topics within the two basic groups, life science and earth science. The following examples were fairly typical:

Life Science	Earth Science
cells, organisms	geology
plant and animal diversity	astronomy
populations and communications	oceanography
food producers, food chain	meteorology
nature cycles	map reading
human body systems	metrics
flowering plants	states of matter
plant and animal reproduction	atoms, molecules
genetics	crystals, rocks, minerals, and weathering
	erosion, volcanoes, earthquakes, fossils
	atmosphere, water cycle

Contrary to the situation in social studies, the science curricula were not trapped by the perceived need to "cover" a whole time series, from the earliest history of humankind to the present. However, as can be noted from the two lists above, there was an attempt to "cover" as much as possible. Concept learning was little emphasized in the science classes in our sample. The emphasis, as with the other academic subjects, seemed mostly to be upon teaching as many facts as possible.

Testing appeared to contain the usual objective techniques: multiple choice, fill-in, matching, true-false. However, there occasionally was problem solving and calculation (e.g., doing chemistry formulas and physics problems).

Several publishers were represented in the listings of the texts in the teacher packages which were reviewed. However, there were not as many as for social studies. We did examine quite closely one of the sets of materials of the so-called "modern" science developed in the 60s. As with many of these curricula, teachers referred to it as highly "individualized."

143

However, an examination of the materials indicated that all students did the same readings, worksheets, and experiments, and were expected to come to the same conclusions, only at different times.

There was little evidence found in any materials to suggest either a concern for the environment or career awareness in science. In no topic list did the name of a single figure outside of the United States from the world of science appear.

Use of lab equipment was frequently listed in the packages of one of the skills to be developed by students. The abilities to use scientific method and to develop good study techniques were also frequently stated. It was difficult to tell from the materials about the quality of the actual lab experiences. As was stated earlier, most science classes were not held in well-equipped labs. Many teachers referred to experiments and projects, but sample tests and worksheets gave little indication of their quality. Also, in Chapter 3 we saw that teachers and students disagreed somewhat about both the frequency of working on experiments and on whether they were planned by teachers or students. Teachers said that there were more experiments than did students and they also perceived that more were student planned than did students. Also, in Chapter 3 we saw that students often watched teachers perform experiments in front of the class. Thus, while science had the potential of being a highly exploratory subject for students, the lack of equipment and the presence of didactic instructional traditions seemed to limit the actual amount of exploring students did in our sample of junior high science classes.

Foreign Language. We had questionnaire responses from ten foreign language teachers about their materials of instruction. On the average, they said that they always or most of the time used textbooks and that they often used worksheets, other books, games, and simulations.

These teachers said that the books and the worksheets, as well as audio-visuals and tapes and records, were very useful. While they thought that learning kits, television, and newspapers or magazines were somewhat useful, they never or not very often used them. The story of foreign language and television is an interesting one. I can remember the big push in the early 60s to have foreign language instruction for all students beginning in grade five or so. There were not enough qualified teachers, of course. The answer seemed to be TV. In some places we even had airplanes aloft prepared to broadcast foreign language instruction to anyone prepared to receive it. Not one of the junior highs in A Study of Schooling reported the use of TV for foreign language instruction. Few, if any, of the innovations of the past two decades accurately assessed what it would take to overcome the overwhelming strength of tradition as represented by the teacher using his or her usual tools of the trade: lecture, textbooks, and worksheets.

There was almost no variability from school to school or class to class regarding teacher report of the use of materials of instruction in foreign language. Student data supported this finding. About three-fourths of the students sampled said they used worksheets and about 85% said textbooks. Only about half indicated the use of other books, audio-visuals, games or simulations, tape recordings or records. There was little evidence of the so-called oral-aural approach.

There were observations in only eleven junior high foreign language classes. Observers saw a.v. equipment in four classes, tapes and/or records in three, overhead projectors in two, maps and/or globes in two, and there were displays having to do with countries where the language was spoken in only six of the classes.

There were only eight foreign language curriculum packages submitted for analysis. The skills to be developed in these classes seemed to represent a balance between reading and comprehension, vocabulary building, speaking and writing with a somewhat larger proportion of emphasis on speaking. There was scant evidence of time spent upon current events or study of the culture or other aspects of life in the countries where the language was spoken.

We got no sense of what, if any, textbook series dominated the field. We did note a tendency for some publishers to use a similar format for all languages. That is, they published the same program translated into various languages.

145

Spanish was offered in seven schools, French in four, and German in one. Five schools offered two languages. They were all electives and, by and large, were restricted to the college bound. All in all, opportunities for junior high students in our sample to explore foreign languages was very, very limited.

The Arts. We did not ask students or teachers in arts, vocational education, or P.E. questions about the use of materials or equipment in their classes. However, we did make observations in a sample of classes and we did collect curriculum packages from teachers of each subject.

Observers judged that the availability of materials was adequate in all of the 44 arts classroom observed. They judged that space was adequate in over half and "spacious" in about 40% of these classes. About 65% of the classrooms had some kind of adjacent room also available (e.g., storage, teacher office). In nearly 60% of these classes, art work on bulletin boards was primarily student made. In all other subjects, it was always primarily commercially or teacher made.

Thirty-five curriculum packages were submitted by junior high teachers of the arts. In the visual arts, some teachers listed media as topics to be taught while others listed concepts such as "line," "texture," "pattern." Choral music topics clustered around sight-reading skills and band topics included "proper playing habits," "sight-reading" and different styles of music. General music courses listed musical concepts as topics: rhythm, melody, harmony, form, etc. The one drama teacher who submitted a package listed theater history, terminology, acting techniques, and elements of technical theater as topics.

Skills lists as well as procedures of evaluation seemed to suggest a predominant emphasis upon performance rather than "learning about" the arts. Texts did not play an important part except in music and one publisher seemed to dominate that field.

Teachers were asked whether or not they had people from outside the school who were connected with the arts come to work with their students. Very few did. Musicians or singers were the most common but the average number of visits across all the junior highs was about one per class per semester. Palisades Middle School, among all the junior highs, appeared to utilize the greatest number of resource people in the arts.

Vocational Education. Observers judged that the availability of materials was adequate in all of the 48 vocational education classrooms which were observed. They judged that space was more than adequate in about 60% of the classrooms and adequate in almost all the rest. Almost half of the classrooms had some kind of adjacent room also available. Student use of equipment was usually restricted because of safety needs. Our analysis of 41 curriculum packages certainly showed a concern for safety in shop and home economics classes.

Most home economics and shop classes were sex-segregated, with boys taking shop and girls home economics. There were exceptions. Vista, for example, had a completely co-ed unified arts program for all students which included both home economics and shop.

Curriculum content varied greatly among courses referred to as homemaking. There often were high-carbohydrate recipes used in cooking classes. There was infrequent mention of the various influences brought to bear on consumer decision-making (e.g., packaging, advertising). There was almost no metric measurement being taught in our sample of homemaking or shop classes. On the other hand, at Laurel there was a nicely articulated 3-year course with some unusual topics such as "emerging roles of men and women," "food and the social process," "aesthetic values, labelling and legislation," and "influences on consumer practices." Also, at Atwater there were such interesting topics listed as "conservation of electricity, heat, water and materials," "money management and consumer education," "teenage pregnancy," "the elderly," and "ethnic heritage."

Texts were not common in shop classes. There were some in homemaking and two publishers seemed to dominate in the typing classes. Evaluation seemed to focus mostly on performance. Where there were tests available for analysis, they were mostly objective and focused upon recall of specific facts.

The overarching impressing I had of the opportunities for students to explore interests and aptitudes in vocational education in our sample was that it depended on where the student went to school. While most programs were well-equipped, what went on within them varied greatly.

P.E. We analyzed 25 curriculum packages submitted by P.E. teachers. P.E. was generally sex-segregated. The courses included a more or less standard battery of seasonal sports: football in the fall, basketball in the winter, softball in the spring. Volleyball was the most frequently mentioned. Other topics listed were: aerobic conditioning, archery, badminton, bowling, conditioning and corrective exercise, dance, dodgeball, fitness, folk dance, gymnastics, handball, hockey, kickball, ping pong, pool, raquetball, shuffleboard, skating, soccer, speedball, swimming, tennis, track and field, trampoline, tumbling, wrestling, and yoga. At Newport there was a "correctional" P.E. class for students with special physical problems.

As with vocational education, the impression gained from analysis of curriculum materials was that the opportunities available to explore the topics above depended on which school a student attended. It ranged all the way from almost nothing but a few team sports to a broad selection of the topics listed above.

Appropriateness of Content and Materials

We asked our sample of teachers to estimate the percentage of students in their classes for which the materials and content of the subject were appropriate according to three criteria: ability level of students, ethnic or cultural background of students, interest of students. Results are reported in Tables 4.11, 4.12, and 4.13. As can be seen from Table 4.11, nearly 30% of the sampled social studies and science teachers indicated that the materials and content in their classes was not appropriate because of the ability level of students. For math and vocational education it was about 20%. It was difficult to know what was in the minds of the teachers when they responded this way. However, there seem to be two possibilities. The first is that there just weren't many materials available in these subjects designed with high interest but written for below grade level readers. There weren't too many

148

published, funds were not available for their purchase, and/or teachers weren't aware of them.

Table 4.11

Teacher Estimate of Percent of Students
For Which Materials and Content of Class
Is Not Appropriate Because of Student Ability

Subject	%	S.D.	N
Social Studies	29.9	1.01	53
Science	29.1	.82	45
Math	20.1	1.03	70
Voc. Ed.	20.1	.82	47
P.E.	18.1	.73	35
Arts	17.5	.77	47
English	16.4	.77	83
Foreign Lang.	15.6	.67	12

The second possibility was more discouraging. That was that many teachers just did not take into account a wide range of student abilities in the planning and selection of content and materials to use in instruction. They chose content and materials knowing full well that they would be inappropriate for the students on the fringe. The fact that ability ranges were expected to be narrowed through tracking (ability or X-Y-Z grouping) and that such tracking was so prevalent (see Chapter 6) gives credence to this hypothesis.

It was not difficult to understand why P.E. and arts teachers indicated that the content and materials of their subjects was inappropriate for a smaller percentage of students. They have the reputation of being appropriate "for all people."

The cases for English and foreign language were different. Like science and social studies, they were academic subjects which relied heavily upon reading and writing. I hypothesize that English teachers saw less inappropriateness for two reasons. First, and most simply, in many schools in our sample, the lower ability students, at least in the earlier grades, were assigned to reading classes. Second, it has been my

149

experience that tracking in junior high begins with English classes. That is, counselors begin the process of ability grouping by assigning students to "sections" which are often synonymous with both reading ability and English classes. Only sometimes, not always, sections are regrouped for math and/or other subjects. Thus, classes in English tend to be more homogeneous than those in other subjects. There was evidence to suggest that this was true in our sample.

The response of foreign language teachers was easier to understand. Hypothetically, in most schools in our sample, any student could have chosen a foreign language class. Practically, however, lower ability students had so many requirements that they really couldn't opt for foreign language. Thus, classes mainly contained high ability, college bound students. It was no wonder that, on the average, these teachers found their subject appropriate for approximately 85% of their students.

As the standard deviations in Table 4.12 show, there was a wide range of responses to the question about the appropriateness of content and materials because of the ethnicity or cultural background of students. Frequently, in schools which served large numbers of Hispanic or black students, teachers of all subjects except the arts reported that materials and content were appropriate for only about half the students in their classes. This was more true of schools serving Hispanic students, probably because English was a second language for many students and materials were in English (Rosemont, Fairfield). Conversely, teachers in schools which served predominantly white students reported that materials and content were appropriate for almost all students in their classes. This seemed to give credence to the argument which states that not enough attention is given to the development and/or purchase of materials and content for minority group students and that the curriculum of American schools is designed largely for white, middle-class students.

Teachers of all subjects judged the materials and content in their classes as less appropriate on the criterion of student interest than on the criteria of student ability or student ethnicity and cultural background. On the average, teachers of the four main academic subjects in our sample said that the content

150

and materials in their classes were inappropriate for 30% or more of the students because of student interest. This jibes with other data in which teachers identify student interest as a problem. The question, of course, is a chicken-and-egg one. That is, what comes first, making the content and materials interesting to today's generation of students or making students understand the importance to them of what is being taught? In terms of student exploration, the schools in our sample were not doing too good a job, at least if student interest was considered a criterion of success.

Table 4.12

Teacher Estimate of Percent of Students
For Which Materials and Content of Class
Is Not Appropriate Because of Student
Ethnicity or Cultural Background

Subject	%	S.D.	N
Social Studies	27.8	.93	53
Voc. Ed.	22.2	1.29	47
Math	21.8	1.12	70
P.E.	21.7	1.19	35
Arts	20.1	1.16	46
English	19.7	1.03	83
Science	15.4	1.19	43
Foreign Lang.	12.4	.89	12

Table 4.13

Teacher Estimate of Percent of Students for Which
Materials and Content of Class Is Not
Appropriate Because of Student Interest

Subject	%	S.D.	N
Social Studies	39.1	1.00	53
Science	30.8	.76	45
Math	30.6	1.04	70
English	29.5	.94	83
Foreign Lang.	25.0	.89	11
Arts	24.2	.91	47
P.E.	22.4	.69	35
Voc. Ed.	21.8	.88	46

Conclusions

The chapter began by noting that the traditional three-year junior highs in our Study had more exploratory course offerings than did the middle schools or the two-year intermediate schools. However, it was also pointed out that exploration was more a matter of what went on in the classroom rather than of what courses were offered.

We also saw early in the chapter that students had quite different exploratory experiences. For example, foreign language was offered almost solely to students who were college bound. Also, at many of the junior highs in our sample, poorer readers were automatically scheduled into remedial reading classes and, thus, their elective choices were limited. Likewise, performing music students were always enrolled in chorus, band, or orchestra instead of electives. It was quite clear that by junior high, student opportunities for exploration were differentiated for the college bound and non-college bound. They were in different elective, by and large, as well as in different academic classes. And, at the great majority of schools in our sample, there were more elective choices for the academically oriented students.

We found that many students thought in terms of the vocational value of their classes. That is, they valued the degree to which a class might prepare them for a future job. Interestingly, on the average, students found the required academic subjects to be as important or more important than exploratory courses although they found the exploratories more interesting.

A very promising finding had to do with the degree of student participation in extracurricular activities in our sample of junior highs. For the students who did participate, the average number of activities was almost 2½ per student. The discouraging note was that nearly 20% said that they did not participate in any extracurricular activities at all.

Within classes, student opportunities to explore learning on their own seemed limited. They did not participate in decision-making in any subject area to any marked extent. Materials of instruction in the academic subjects were limited mostly to textbooks, other books, and worksheets. Television, teaching machines, and even things like calculators were almost never present and learning kits, audio-visuals, games and simulations were rare, also. Individualization of instruction, in reality, meant all students covering the same material, only at different rates. This, of course, has very little to do with students exploring their own interests, aptitudes, and the like.

The data in the chapter revealed some interesting aspects of each of the subject areas commonly found in junior high schools. For example, we did find a wide variety of instructional materials available in the social studies classes in our sample. Even so, we found a preoccupation with "coverage." That is, there appeared to be a preoccupation with getting through, for example, U.S. history from the explorations to the period of reconstruction after the Civil War. The curriculum was very ethnocentric with almost no opportunity for students to explore beyond the borders of the United States through their studies. Nor was there much evidence that they explored any of the real issues of the day (e.g., social injustice, war and peace, propaganda and media influence, the relationship between the individual and government). Finally, students were usually taught and expected to recall facts. There was little evidence of critical thinking and problem-solving. For me, and in terms of both integration and exploration, social studies in our sample of junior highs was the most disappointing of all the subject areas.

In science, too, emphasis was upon coverage of a number of topics and the retention of selected facts. However, there was some evidence of exploration through problem-solving and the conducting of experiments. What was impossible to justify was the tremendous discrepancy from school to school in the amount of science taught. We found that students in some schools had three times as much science as students in other schools. It is my feeling that all junior high students should have a maximum amount of science in well-equipped laboratories where, in fact, they are continually encouraged to experiment, solve problems, and explore.

There was no doubt about how much math junior high students had. In our sample, they had math every semester while they were in junior high. And, that math, except for some algebra, was basically a review of what had been taught in the elementary school. And that review was largely one of recalling facts and rules. Based upon our data, I have really come to question whether or not we need to take as long as we do to teach math. If we assume that all students should understand math up to and including pre-algebra, pre-geometry, and consumer mathematics, can we not do a better job in a shorter time? Growth and development literature suggest that we might start mathematics instruction later than we now do--at about 10 years of age when students are more ready to deal with abstract ideas. Others might suggest cutting back on math requirements at the junior high level, thus leaving more time for other explorations.

In the English/language arts classes in our sample, the emphasis was upon grammar, mechanics, composition, and literature study--the basics. Less attention was given creative writing, study skills, critical thinking, speaking or listening. Also, and at every school, basic reading skills were taught to a large number of students. In some schools it was all students and in other schools it was only those needing remediation. This was due, in part, I am sure, to the fact that sixth graders were included in middle schools. However, it was also due, I am afraid, to the fact that many students coming from elementary schools did not seem prepared well enough with reading skills.

Vocational education offerings varied greatly from school to school. All schools offered some kind of home economics and shop as a minimum. Others had more advanced or other kinds of shop and home economics courses. Typing was sometimes offered and at one school, Fairfield, several quite specialized courses were offered. Courses usually were sex-segregated and we could see the beginnings of what clearly marks all senior highs, the separation of academic and vocational students. However, we found the most contemporary of topics, (e.g., consumer education, conservation, teen-age pregnancy) in a few of the vocational education classes. All in all, and while there was much to criticize in the vocational education classes in our sample, student opportunities to explore their interests and abilities were probably as great as in any subject.

Opportunities for students to explore their interests and aptitudes existed in great measure in the

154

arts, too. That is because, as with vocational education, most classes were performance based. Two major
problems seemed to exist. First, we found that performing music students (i.e., chorus, band, orchestra)
were usually segregated from other students for much of
their school day and they always had their other
exploratory options limited because they were in
performing music. Such a situation has evolved because
performance has become an end in itself, rather than a
means toward assisting students to explore their own
interests and aptitudes. Perhaps all students should
have the opportunity for such exploration. Second, and
at least partly because of the attitudes of other
teachers, parents, and students, the teachers of the
arts in our sample did not seem all that committed to
the exploratory role of their subject. Perhaps as a
reaction to the claim that the arts are a "frill,"
teachers in our sample appeared to want to make the
arts like the academic subjects. The point is, our
schools did not seem to fully take advantage of the
exploratory value of the arts.

P.E., too, in many of our schools, seemed to be
locked into traditions which mitigated against personal
exploration on the part of students. Competitive team
sports often dominated rather than individual life-long
sports. There were a few schools where students had
good exposure to individual sports and at one school
(Bradford) all students had swimming.

Finally, foreign language was an elitist curriculum
in the sense that it usually was only available to the
college bound. It was only offered at seven of the
twelve junior highs in our sample and, in all cases,
was organized as an academic rather than conversational
course. This was true even in areas where there were
large numbers of Spanish speakers in the general
population. Such a condition in our schools is both a
reflection of and a reason for the fact that ours is
among the most ethnocentric and isolated nations of the
world. We are a major world power with schools which
produce students ignorant of the world. This seems
dangerous to me.

Teachers indicated that materials and content were
inappropriate for large numbers of students, particularly in academic subjects and particularly in terms of
student interest. Teachers and students in our sample
both identified lack of student interest as a serious

155

problem. We also asked students to agree or disagree with the statement, "There are things I want to learn about that this school doesn't teach." Across all schools, two-thirds of the students agreed.

What the data in this chapter suggested to me was that in our sample of schools, curriculum had generally not kept up with the changes in our society, new student needs, new student interests. There were some bright spots, of course. A good reading program here, a course in consumerism there. Essentially, however, those things were tacked on. The "basic" academic subjects still held sway with their demands for coverage of content--e.g., from the Age of Exploration (no pun intended) to the post-Civil War Reconstruction Era--and the truly exploratory subjects were viewed as "frills" causing those who taught them to justify them on grounds other than exploration (i.e., academic grounds, performance).

What is called for is nothing short of a total overhaul of the curriculum. We don't need to go "back to the basics." We need to "clean out the curriculum," getting rid of useless content and redesigning much of what remains so that it is directed at student needs and interests. I never liked the term "relevance" as it was applied to curriculum reforms in the last decade because it became the excuse for a lot of educational hucksterism and it frequently resulted in the addition of relatively meaningless courses to the curriculum. However, the call for relevance was a legitimate expression of the need for all courses to cause students to explore and broaden their interests, aptitudes, and abilities.

Chapter IV, Notes and References

1. William Van Til, et al., Modern Education for Junior High Schools. (Second Edition), op. cit., p. 30.

2. Abraham Gelford, "The Exploratory Concept in the Junior High Schools," The Bulletin of the National Association of Secondary School Principals, Vol. 44, No. 259 (November, 1960), pp. 32-34.

3. Joyce Wright, Students' Attitudes Toward Subjects. Unpublished Report. Research Division, I/D/E/A, Los Angeles, 1979.

4. Many teachers from our sampled classes did not submit packages. On the other hand, there were many teachers who were very, very thorough with this task; and there were several who submitted more than one package. Based upon: Barbara Benham Tye, Curriculum Materials Analysis, by Subject and By School. Unpublished Report. Research Division, I/D/E/A, Los Angeles, 1978.

5. Individualization is a concept which appears and reappears throughout this volume. Here it refers to students "covering materials at their own rates."

6. Marshall Gordon, "Conflict and Liberation: Personal Aspects of the Mathematics Experience," Curriculum Inquiry, Vol. 8, No. 3 (1978), pp. 251-271.

7. Science classes don't have live animals anymore because schools are afraid of being sued if a student is bitten. Of course, plants don't bite.

CHAPTER V

GUIDANCE

Introduction

There is some confusion surrounding the term "guidance." In part this is due, as we saw in Chapter 2, to the fact that the school is expected to carry out intellectual, vocational, personal and social functions, all at the same time. The Van Til, et al. definition reflects this comprehensive view of the guidance aim of junior high schools:

> "...To assist pupils to make intelligent decisions regarding present vocational opportunities and prepare them to make future vocational decisions. To assist pupils to make satisfactory mental, emotional, and social adjustments in their growth toward wholesome, well-adjusted personalities. To stimulate and prepare pupils to participate as effectively as possible in learning activities so that they may reach the maximum development of their personal powers and qualities."[1]

This definition addresses the functional role of the junior high vis-a-vis guidance. Structurally, there is also confusion. Teachers are expected to perform guidance functions as they work with students in their classrooms. Outside of the classrooms there is also a formal guidance structure at most junior highs. This formal guidance structure was initiated in 1908 at the high school level in Boston by Frank Parsons as a means of personalizing school services to students and relating school experiences to the workaday world outside.[2] Between 1920 and 1960, this movement resulted in the assignment to most junior highs of persons known as counselors or guidance counselors.

As we shall see in this chapter, the activities of counselors do not always result in programs which carry out the guidance function as envisioned by Van Til and his colleagues. However, such shortcomings are most often attributable to the way in which schools are organized and not to the counseling staffs per se.

This chapter explores the degree to which the guidance function was carried out in our sample of junior highs. It also examines some of the ways in which that was done. It looks specifically at activities of counselors through the perceptions of teachers, students, parents, and counselors themselves.

In the second section of the chapter, a number of variables which describe the overall school orientation to guidance are examined. Often, the perceptions of teachers, students, parents, and counselors are juxtaposed. The particular emphasis is upon the degree to which the school is seen as a nurturing place.

A third section is devoted to teacher and parent responses to questions about the exchange of information between the school and the parents. The assumption is that the school, as part of its guidance function, has the responsibility to adequately communicate with parents about their children.

An extensive amount of data are examined concerning teacher guidance in the classroom. First, I look at instructional guidance--teaching practices reported by students and observers as well as teacher report of diagnosis, individualization and evaluation practices. Second, I look at teacher affective behavior as perceived by students and observers. In this case, the question is, "To what degree is the junior high classroom a nurturing place?"

Finally, I attempt to pull all of this material together in order to draw conclusions about the guidance function in our sample of junior highs and in order to state hypotheses about junior high school education in general.

Counseling Services

Every junior high in our sample had at least one full-time counselor except Euclid Junior High. At that school with only 133 students, one counselor served both the junior high and the high school. Counselor-pupil ratios varied from one counselor for 258 students at Manchester Middle School to one counselor for 725 students at Crestview Middle School.

We asked students how easy they thought it was to get help from a counselor for (1) planning a school program, (2) a personal problem, and (3) planning a career (Table 5.1). The actual wording of the question was, "It is easy for me to get help from a counselor for..."

There were only slight differences at most schools regarding the student perceptions of the ease with which they could get different types of help from counselors. Also, patterns varied only slightly from school to school. On the average, students found it easiest to get help with planning a school program, then a personal problem, and finally planning a career. This was evidence of the lessening of the importance of the vocational function of junior high school education as compulsory attendance laws have caused all students to matriculate to high school.

For all three types of help, students at three schools were the most positive: Vista, Rosemont, Woodlake. At two schools they were clearly the most negative: Fairfield, Laurel. No clear explanations were evident for these rankings. It certainly did not have to do with pupil-counselor ratios since both Rosemont and Woodlake had very poor ratios, 497:1 and 437:1 respectively. It probably was a matter of attitudes, training of counselors, and duties they were expected to perform. The overarching impression gained from these data was that students felt that counseling services were o.k. but not outstanding.

Standard deviations for all responses at all schools were quite high, indicating that the range of responses at individual schools was quite wide. There was a good deal of disagreement, with many students feeling that they could get help and many feeling they couldn't. This fact alone raises serious questions about the organization of counseling services in our junior highs and about the role played by counselors.

As a way of gaining an understanding of the role of junior high school counselors, we asked them the following open-ended question, "Is there anything you would like to change about your job?" Typical responses were:

161

Table 5.1

Student Agreement That It Is Easy To Get Help From Counselors

For Planning a School Program					For a Personal Problem					For Planning a Career				
School	$\overline{X}$	sd	N	% Agree	School	$\overline{X}$	sd	N	% Agree	School	$\overline{X}$	sd	N	% Agree
Vista	3.16	.87	642	81.5	Rosemont	3.14	1.00	554	76.0	Vista	3.22	.86	645	83.0
Atwater	3.11	.92	314	76.8	Woodlake	3.08	.96	426	76.0					
Woodlake	3.10	.84	433	78.5	Vista	3.06	.96	646	76.3					
Rosemont	3.00	1.03	552	70.4	Manchester	2.97	1.03	592	72.5	Rosemont	3.04	1.04	553	73.3
					Atwater	2.94	.98	314	71.7	Woodlake	2.95	.92	428	71.5
Euclid	2.90	.91	126	69.9	Bradford	2.86	1.01	500	68.4	Euclid	2.81	1.00	126	65.9
Manchester	2.86	1.01	594	68.1						Atwater	2.80	.97	313	66.2
Newport	2.85	1.00	673	67.1						Bradford	2.78	.99	502	64.6
Bradford	2.79	.95	499	64.8						Manchester	2.77	1.04	592	61.6
Palisades	2.78	.99	435	63.7										
Crestview	2.62	.98	404	57.7	Palisades	2.72	1.01	435	58.1	Palisades	2.64	.98	431	55.7
					Newport	2.69	1.05	675	59.0	Newport	2.58	1.03	673	55.3
					Crestview	2.66	1.04	406	60.3	Laurel	2.57	1.13	240	54.6
					Euclid	2.60	1.08	126	57.9	Crestview	2.55	1.02	405	54.6
Laurel	2.48	1.05	241	53.6	Laurel	2.46	1.11	239	49.8	Fairfield	2.45	1.01	430	51.8
Fairfield	2.41	1.00	429	51.1	Fairfield	2.35	1.03	430	45.8					
TOTAL	2.86	.99	5342	67.8	TOTAL	2.83	1.04	5346	65.8	TOTAL	2.78	1.02	5338	63.9

Response categories: 2.50 - 3.49 = Mildly agree; 1.50 - 2.49 = Mildly disagree

162

I would like to not be responsible at all for record keeping, including handling of permanent records and scheduling of students. I would like to not be responsible for individual psychological testing of students. I feel I do not do enough of it for me to be good at it. I would like to not have to coordinate the special education program. I am responsible for all the folders, seeing that the teachers turn in various reports, etc.; must do all 3 year re-evaluations, hold annual reviews, etc. I feel that the counselor is supposed to do a great number of different jobs at this school, i.e., programming, discipline, attendance, record keeping, etc. The result is that he is able to do none of these tasks well. There needs to be some type of reorganization and a clearer definition of responsibilities.

We asked both teachers and parents to agree or disagree that counseling services were adequately meeting students' needs (see Table 5.2). On the average, parents at all schools except Euclid and Fairfield mildly agreed that they were. However, teachers at only five schools mildly disagreed that counseling services were adequately meeting student needs. At all schools except Atwater, parent responses were more positive than teacher responses. Clearly, teachers would like to see a reorganization and/or upgrading of the functions of counselors.

Probably, if you were to ask teachers, or parents for that matter, about how they would like to see the role of counselors changed (we did not ask such a question), they would respond much as counselors did. That is, they would suggest cutting back on administrative and clerical work and, thus, by implication they would call for an increase in counselor time for individual and small group problem solving with students.

I agree that such a redefinition of the counseling role is desirable. However, I doubt that increasing counselor time for individual and group counseling is enough by itself to provide adequate guidance services for pre- and early-adolescents, those young people who have so many needs for social and emotional support. In addition to direct contact with students, counselors need to have the time and skills to work with teachers,

163

developing in teachers their abilities to provide guidance for students.

Moving to this in-service training role for counselors is one of the most needed reforms in the junior high program. It also is one of the most difficult to bring about. I shall return to this topic later in this chapter.

Table 5.2

Teacher and Parent Agreement That Counseling
Services Are Adequately Meeting Student Needs

	Teachers				Parents		
School	$\overline{X}$	sd	N	School	$\overline{X}$	sd	N
Atwater	3.14	.83	22	Rosemont	3.21	.89	146
Vista	3.00	.85	48	Vista	3.01	.86	406
				Crestview	2.93	.89	250
				Bradford	2.90	.93	206
				Atwater	2.90	.95	150
				Newport	2.86	.95	242
Rosemont	2.78	.92	42	Woodlake	2.79	.81	273
Woodlake	2.63	.79	27	Manchester	2.72	.95	283
Manchester	2.56	.98	32	Laurel	2.72	.97	78
				Palisades	2.69	.95	280
Bradford	2.48	.85	27	Euclid	2.37	.94	41
Newport	2.28	.80	57	Fairfield	2.27	.97	211
Palisades	2.15	.92	40				
Euclid	2.00	.95	12				
Fairfield	1.94	.81	34				
Crestview	1.94	.88	32				
Laurel	1.76	.94	21				
TOTAL	2.42	.95	394	TOTAL	2.82	.94	2566

Response categories: 1.50 - 2.49 = Mildly disagree
2.50 - 3.49 = Mildly agree

The Caring Nature of the School

Each school has its own character, its own ambience. In terms of guidance, a school is seen either as a warm, supportive and "caring" place or a a cold, harsh and impersonal one. We asked teachers, parents, and students a number of questions which shed light on the degree to which the school was seen as a supportive and "caring" place for students. The responses to these questions were divided into three clusters.

The first cluster of variables had to do directly with the "caring" atmosphere of the school. To begin with, we asked all three groups to respond to the following statement, "Many teachers at this school don't care about students." (Table 5.3). On the average, at all schools, each group disagreed with the statement. However, teacher responses were different from those of parents and students. Teachers at four schools strongly disagreed with the statement (Woodlake, Euclid, Crestview, Bradford).

Student mean scores were generally slightly higher than those of the parents. Even so, parent and student perceptions were very close at all schools. Bradford was an interesting case. There the teachers strongly disagreed that teachers don't care about students while, at the same time, parents and students only mildly disagreed and, in fact, nearly 40% of the students agreed. The staff at Bradford was quite proud that they had established high "standards" and that student behavior had improved markedly. Obviously, "caring" means different things to the different groups.

Related to the concept of caring, we also asked both parents and teachers to indicate the degree to which students received a lot of individual attention from teachers. On the average, at all schools, the parents mildly disagreed that they did while at all schools except Fairfield, teachers mildly agreed. At Fairfield, teachers, too, mildly disagreed that students received a lot of individual attention from teachers. As with the caring item, teachers at each school tended to be more in agreement with each other while there was a good deal of disagreement among parents at any given school.

165

Table 5.3

Teacher, Parent, and Student Perceptions of the Degree to Which Teachers Care About Students*

Teachers				Parents				Students			
School	$\bar{X}$	sd	N	School	$\bar{X}$	sd	N	School	$\bar{X}$	sd	N
Woodlake	1.26	.45	27	Euclid	1.73	.91	41	Euclid	1.89	.93	124
Euclid	1.42	.67	12	Vista	1.81	.91	413	Vista	1.92	.88	638
Crestview	1.47	.67	32	Atwater	1.91	.97	154	Woodlake	1.92	.91	423
Bradford	1.48	.75	27	Woodlake	1.95	.96	281	Atwater	2.04	.97	308
Atwater	1.50	.67	22	Rosemont	1.99	1.03	153	Palisades	2.15	.99	438
Vista	1.53	.78	47	Palisades	2.09	.95	295	Rosemont	2.15	1.12	540
Rosemont	1.76	.83	41	Crestview	2.12	1.02	254	Crestview	2.16	1.02	401
Newport	1.79	.77	58	Newport	2.13	.99	252	Newport	2.26	.98	676
Laurel	1.86	.85	21	Manchester	2.17	1.03	287	Bradford	2.31	.99	523
Manchester	1.87	1.04	32	Bradford	2.35	1.03	210	Manchester	2.32	1.09	636
Fairfield	1.88	.84	34	Laurel	2.41	1.06	78	Fairfield	2.35	.98	424
Palisades	2.09	.96	39	Fairfield	2.49	1.00	214	Laurel	2.35	1.12	243
TOTAL	1.69	.82	392	TOTAL	2.09	1.00	2632	TOTAL	2.17	1.02	5374

Response categories: 1.0 - 1.49 = Strongly disagree
1.50 - 2.49 = Mildly disagree

* The item read, "Many teachers at this school don't care about students." Thus lower (disagree) scores were considered more positive.

Lest we begin to get the feeling that our junior highs were totally uncaring places, we need to examine two other pieces of student data. We asked students about being afraid to disagree with their teachers. Only students at Rosemont, on the average, agreed that they were afraid (61%). At all other schools, on the average, students said they were not afraid to disagree with teachers. Even so, the number of students who said that they were afraid to disagree was fairly large. It ranged from about 28% at Euclid to about 48% at Laurel.

Also, overall, students agreed with the statement, "People at this school can be trusted." However, there was a fair amount of disagreement within each school.

Thus, while the junior highs in our sample were not seen as ideally warm, caring places, neither were they seen as the horrible, cold, debilitating places so often portrayed in the media or in the books of the sensationalist writers of the 60s and 70s. What was most disconcerting about these data was that the teachers saw the situation so differently from students and teachers. It is such differences in perceptions which make for interesting and provocative workshop sessions involving teachers, parents, students, and administrators together.

A second set of items had to do with class placements and related matters. We asked teachers and parents to agree or disagree with a statement which said that students were usually appropriately placed in classes (Table 5.4). Parents at all schools mildly agreed that such class placement was appropriate. Teachers at all schools except Euclid and Fairfield also mildly agreed. At those two schools, they mildly disagreed.

Euclid was particularly notable in that parents agreed that placement was appropriate while teachers disagreed. There was a similar but less marked case of disagreement at Crestview. There seemed to be some relationship between school size and displeasure with student placement. There tended to be more displeasure at smaller schools. This probably was due to more limited options and less flexibility.

Another pattern seemed to emerge, also. By and large, teachers in all-white, higher-SES schools

167

Table 5.4

Teacher and Parent Agreement to the
Appropriateness of Student Placement in Classes*

	Teachers				Parents		
School	$\overline{X}$	sd	N	School	$\overline{X}$	sd	N
Vista	3.44	.65	48	Vista	3.32	.69	407
				Rosemont	3.27	.87	141
				Euclid	3.20	.69	40
				Palisades	3.10	.87	291
				Crestview	3.09	.89	249
Woodlake	2.92	.73	27	Newport	3.02	.87	240
Atwater	2.91	.53	22	Laurel	2.96	.93	78
Rosemont	2.83	.96	42	Atwater	2.92	.86	151
				Bradford	2.88	.95	204
				Woodlake	2.84	.86	273
Newport	2.75	.76	57	Fairfield	2.69	.99	210
Manchester	2.72	.85	32	Manchester	2.64	1.00	277
Laurel	2.71	.96	21				
Palisades	2.69	.86	39				
Bradford	2.63	.97	27				
Crestview	2.5	.62	32				
Euclid	2.42	.67	12				
Fairfield	1.8	.8	34				
TOTAL	2.74	.8	393	TOTAL	2.99	.90	2561

Response categories: 1.50 - 2.49 = Mildly disagree
2.50 - 3.49 = Mildly agree

* The item read, "At this school students are usually placed in the classes which are best for them." Higher scores were more positive.

thought that student placement in classes was more appropriate than teachers in minority and/or lower-SES schools. I hypothesize the existence of a kind of self-fulfilling prophecy wherein teachers expect that low SES and/or minority students will do more poorly in school, at least academically. Because of this expectation, these students are often treated as failures and, at least in part, this causes many of them to be so.

I predict that as schools respond to the pressure to raise academic standards, we will find more and more students forced into academic classes. There will then be a corresponding increase in the pre-judging of students along SES and/or ethnic lines. The end result may be higher standardized test scores for our high schools, but this will be at the expense of more failure and significantly higher drop-out rates by the end of junior high for these students.

Parents also were asked to agree or disagree with the statement, "Average students don't get enough attention at this school." At half of the schools they mildly agreed and at the other half they mildly disagreed. The overall mean for all schools was just about in the middle, too (2.54). The range of responses at each school was wide. This was truly a 50-50 item, one on which there were substantial differences of opinion at each school. Such an item would serve well as a springboard for a parent discussion meeting focused on the school program.

The third cluster of items had to do with grading. and student satisfaction with their own progress. We asked teachers and parents to agree or disagree with two statements about grades, "Students are graded too easy at this school" and "Students are graded too hard at this school." (Table 5.5). Parents at all schools and teachers at all schools except Rosemont and Palisades mildly disagreed with the "too hard" statement. At those two schools the teachers strongly disagreed. There was a good deal of agreement within most schools about this item. Adults at our sample of schools did not think students were graded too hard.

Table 5.5

Teacher and Parent Perceptions of Whether or Not
Students Are Graded Too Hard or Too Easy

Students are graded too hard...

	Teachers				Parents		
School	X̄	sd	N	School	X̄	sd	N
Vista	1.73	.71	48	Rosemont	2.03	.94	146
Newport	1.73	.52	56	Laurel	1.99	.87	79
Fairfield	1.71	.84	34	Bradford	1.98	.80	208
Crestview	1.69	.64	32	Newport	1.89	.77	244
Atwater	1.68	.48	22	Atwater	1.88	.80	150
Woodlake	1.63	.56	27	Crestview	1.83	.75	249
Bradford	1.63	.49	27	Vista	1.83	.70	408
Laurel	1.62	.67	21	Fairfield	1.83	.73	206
Euclid	1.58	.51	12	Euclid	1.82	.68	39
Manchester	1.43	.62	32	Manchester	1.81	.84	274
Palisades	1.46	.55	39	Woodlake	1.78	.69	276
Rosemont	1.45	.59	42	Palisades	1.65	.68	289
TOTAL	1.62	.61	392	TOTAL	1.84	.77	2568

Students are graded too easy...

	Teachers			Parents	
School	X̄	sd	School	X̄	sd
Rosemont	2.98	.97	Fairfield	2.09	.86
Crestview	2.87	.79	Newport	2.08	.92
Euclid	2.83	.83	Palisades	2.00	.89
Laurel	2.76	.94	Woodlake	1.98	.84
Fairfield	2.76	.94	Rosemont	1.96	.97
Newport	2.73	.88	Crestview	1.96	.91
Bradford	2.52	.89	Bradford	1.85	.81
Palisades	2.49	.93	Manchester	1.83	.88
Atwater	2.45	.89	Laurel	1.76	.91
Manchester	2.42	.92	Euclid	1.75	.63
Vista	2.28	.88	Vista	1.71	.74
Woodlake	2.22	.85	Atwater	1.70	.75
TOTAL	2.61	.92	TOTAL	1.90	.86

Response categories: 1.00 - 1.49 = Strongly disagree
1.50 - 2.49 = Mildly disagree
2.50 - 3.49 = Mildly agree

On the other hand, teachers at seven schools mildly agreed that students were graded too easy. Mean scores for teachers at the other five schools and for parents at all schools indicated mild disagreement with this item. There was a wide range of responses for teacher and parent groups at most schools, showing that there were differences of opinion.

A different response pattern occurred when teachers, parents, and students were asked to agree or disagree with the statement, "Too many students are allowed to graduate from this school without learning very much." In this case, teacher and parent responses were similar and student responses were somewhat different. Teachers at Woodlake, Palisades, and Euclid mildly disagreed, as did parents at Euclid, Vista, and Atwater. All other teachers and parent groups, on the average, mildly agreed. At five schools, students mildly disagreed. Interestingly, these were all schools which served rural/suburban, middle to low SES, white students (Vista, Crestview, Woodlake, Atwater, Euclid).

There has been a good deal written about grade inflation in schooling and about the need to "tighten up" standards. We did not collect actual grade distribution data. However, these reports on the perceptions of how easy or hard grading was suggested that many teachers in our sample thought that there was grade inflation. Parents in our sample did not think that their children were getting off too easy, though. In fact, since they disagreed with both items, one could conclude that they thought that the grades were about right.

We asked students two related questions. First, we asked them to agree or disagree with the statement, "In this school, we feel we have to get good grades all the time." (Table 5.6). Mean responses for all students indicated mild agreement with the statement. However, the high standard deviations indicated that many students also disagreed.

Agreement was highest at the six schools with total or large minority populations. It becomes obvious to hypothesize that minority students felt more pressure to succeed.

171

Table 5.6

Student Perceptions of the Pressure
on Them for Good Grades*

School	$\overline{X}$	sd	N
Rosemont	3.08	.94	556
Manchester	2.92	.97	604
Newport	2.83	.92	678
Palisades	2.79	.94	441
Laurel	2.75	1.00	243
Fairfield	2.69	.92	433
Bradford	2.69	.97	507
Euclid	2.68	.78	127
Atwater	2.62	.86	313
Vista	2.57	.84	644
Crestview	2.57	.93	406
Woodlake	2.54	.90	433
TOTAL	2.74	.94	5385

* The item read, "In this school, we feel we have
to get good grades all the time." The higher the
score, the more the agreement.

To the other item, "I am satisfied with how well I
am doing in school," students at all schools, on the
average, mildly agreed. There were no obvious school-
by-school patterns (e.g., ethnicity, size, location)
and there was considerable disagreement at every
school. Thus, we found most students feeling a modest
amount of pressure to succeed while at the same time
they felt fairly satisfied with their progress. These
feelings were matched by those of parents who, in the
main, thought that grading was satisfactory and by
those of many teachers who tended to think students
were graded too easy. Surely, this was an area for
dialogue among the various groups.

School-Parent Interaction

If the school is to perform a guidance function for
its students, it seems logical to assume that there has

172

to be much thoughtful interaction between parents and school staff members. In order to find out about such interaction, we asked a number of questions of both parents and staff members. Selected responses are reported in this section.

To begin with, we asked both teachers and parents to agree or disagree with the following statement, "The only time most parents visit schools is when their children are in trouble." (Table 5.7). To our surprise, on the average, parents at all schools mildly agreed. At all but three schools, the mean score for teacher responses was mildly agree, too. At those schools, the mean was fairly strongly agree (Fairfield, Laurel, Rosemont).

At most schools, teacher agreement was slightly higher than parent agreement and at all schools there were many parents who disagreed with the statement. The schools where agreement with the statement was greatest tended to be those which served lower SES populations. It was these populations, then, which were seen as coming to school less. That, as we shall see, should not be equated with lack of interest in their children's schooling.

The parent survey included a list of seven types of information that schools usually have about students. Parents were asked to indicate whether or not they received each type (Table 5.8).

The greatest percentage of parents said they received information about learning progress/grades (from 81.2% at Manchester to 98.7% at Atwater). Large percentages also said they received information about their children's behavior and attendance at school.

The greatest range across schools was relative to information about state or district test results. Responses ranged from a high of 59.4% at Palisades to a low of 6.9% at Bradford. At only four schools did more than half of the responding parents say that they received these results.

The lowest percentage of parents said they received information about their children's interests, from 51.1% at Rosemont to 16.3% at Bradford. Relatively low percentages also reported receipt of information about their children's physical health.

173

Table 5.7

Teacher and Parent Belief that Parents Only Visit School
When Their Children Are in Trouble

	Teachers				Parents		
School	$\overline{X}$	sd	N	School	$\overline{X}$	sd	N
Fairfield	3.70	.47	33				
Laurel	3.67	.48	21				
Rosemont	3.63	.66	41				
Bradford	3.41	.75	27	Bradford	3.44	.81	210
				Laurel	3.42	.86	79
				Fairfield	3.38	.86	215
Crestview	3.28	.77	32	Crestview	3.33	.81	253
Atwater	3.27	.83	22	Manchester	3.31	.90	285
Woodlake	3.26	.81	27				
Manchester	3.19	.82	32				
Newport	3.11	.84	57				
Palisades	3.05	.85	40	Newport	3.06	.96	244
Vista	3.02	.91	48	Rosemont	3.06	1.07	147
				Woodlake	3.05	.92	280
				Palisades	3.01	.93	293
				Atwater	2.97	1.01	153
				Vista	2.89	.96	413
				Euclid	2.83	.92	41
Euclid	2.15	.75	12				
TOTAL	3.28			TOTAL	3.14	.94	2613

Response categories: 2.50 - 3.49 = Mildly agree
3.50 - 4.00 = Strongly agree

Table 5.8

Types of Information About Children Received by Parents
Percent Yes

	Attendance	School Behavior	Physical Health	State or District Test Results	Learning Progress/ Grades	Study Skills/ Work Habits	Child's Interests
Vista	97.8	71.1	45.4	55.7	97.5	67.6	35.4
Crestview	95.2	69.0	41.8	21.2	92.3	62.4	35.0
Fairfield	91.0	80.2	42.0	17.6	88.4	45.0	25.7
Rosemont	75.4	76.3	62.0	51.5	91.0	63.7	51.1
Newport	85.8	80.2	46.5	20.2	92.7	87.3	27.9
Woodlake	66.2	61.1	34.3	28.5	92.6	56.9	24.9
Atwater	97.5	87.9	58.0	48.7	98.7	87.8	42.6
Palisades	92.2	84.7	37.5	59.4	93.2	53.6	26.9
Laurel	96.2	82.3	38.0	33.3	87.2	47.4	44.9
Manchester	88.5	88.4	31.4	25.5	81.3	45.2	30.9
Bradford	95.1	73.8	18.7	6.9	85.4	54.4	16.3
Euclid	92.7	66.7	52.5	51.2	97.4	55.0	42.5
Maximum	97.8	88.4	62.0	59.4	98.7	87.8	51.1
Minimum	66.2	61.1	18.7	6.9	81.3	45.2	16.3
Range	31.6	27.3	43.3	52.5	17.4	42.6	34.8

According to these perceptions, it was obvious that some schools did a much better job of conveying information to parents than others. Atwater, Rosemont, and Vista seemed to do the best jobs while Bradford, Woodlake, Fairfield, and Manchester did less well.

We also asked parents what their sources of information were about their children and their children's school. Across all schools, the greatest percentage said they got information from report cards (96.9%), followed by their own children (85.9%), parent-teacher conferences (79.4%), and open house (79.0%). Just less than half said they got information from PTA meetings, teachers other than at conferences, counselors, and the principal, while just over half said that they did get information from the newspaper. Almost 40% said that they got information from the "grapevine." Board meetings and advisory council meetings were poor sources of information as was radio/TV.

We asked parents about frequency of their contacts with teachers. The question was, "During the last year, about how many times have you talked to your child's (or children's) teacher(s) at this school?" The problem was that we collected data in the spring in some schools and in the fall in others. The question could have been interpreted to mean the school year in which the response was given or, in the fall, it could have been interpreted to mean the previous school year. Cross school comparisons were thought to be invalid. However, it seemed fair to say that the average number of contacts with teachers across all schools in the sample was approximately two for those parents who had contacts. It also seemed fair to say that about 20% of those who responded had no contacts at all.

Teachers were given a list of nine ways in which they might have had contacts with parents, and they were asked to tell whether they frequently, sometimes, seldom, or never had contacts in each way. We calculated the mean responses from the teachers at each school for each of the nine ways (Table 5.9). The most frequent contact with parents was through parent-teacher conferences. Teachers at all schools except Fairfield and Laurel said that they at least sometimes contacted parents in this way.

Table 5.9

Schools at Which Teachers Sometimes or Frequently Had Contacts with Parents in Various Ways

Types of Contact

Schools	Planned after School Activities (athletics, dances)	Community Activities (churches, clubs)	Social Activities	Parents Working in the school	PTA Meetings	Advisory Council Meetings	School Board Meetings	Classroom Visits	Parent-Teacher Conferences
Vista	X								X
Crestview	X			X					X
Fairfield					X				
Rosemont					X				X
Newport									X
Woodlake	X	X	X						X
Atwater	X								X
Palisades					X			X	X
Laurel					X				
Manchester	X				X			X	X
Bradford									X
Euclid	X	X	X						X

Second highest in frequency was "planned after-school activities" with teachers at half the schools indicating that contacts were made sometimes in this way. At five schools, teachers said that contacts with parents were made sometimes at PTA meetings.

There were two communities, Woodlake and Euclid, where teachers seemed to be quite integrated into the parent population, actually a part of it. These teachers indicated that they had contact with parents at community activities (churches, clubs) and social activities.

Teachers did not see advisory council or school board meetings as ways in which they made parent contacts. Only teachers at Palisades and Manchester said that they sometimes made contacts through parent classroom visits and only at Crestview did they sometimes make contacts because of "parents working in the school."

There were four schools where contacts between teachers and parents were quite infrequent (Bradford, Fairfield, Laurel, Newport). There seemed to be different reasons at each school for this infrequency. At all of the junior highs in our sample except Bradford, half or more of the responding parents said that work had prevented them from being involved. At Bradford, child care and transportation were each chosen by approximately a quarter of the parents as reasons for non-involvement, and about 30% of the parents there as well as at Newport said, "My belief that it is the job of the principal and teachers to run the school" caused them to be not involved. At Fairfield, nearly 30% said transportation was a problem and about 20% said principal/teacher attitudes hindered their involvement.

On the other hand, Rosemont presented an interesting picture. Child care, transportation, conflict with working hours, the belief that the principal and teachers should run the school, and different language spoken by the school people were all given as reasons by large percentages of parents for non-involvement in school activities. Even so, Rosemont was about at the median when compared to other schools in the sample in regard to contacts with teachers.

178

Our data suggested that home-school linkages were not very strong. Parents and teachers at all our schools, on the average, believed that parents only visit school when there are problems and teachers at many schools indicated that they only saw parents at all frequently at regularly scheduled parent-teacher conferences. There were few class visits by parents and the only information regularly received by them about their children was about grades, attendance and behavior. They indicated that sources of information were report cards, their children, and open houses. The average number of parent-teacher contacts was approximately two per year, but approximately 20% of the parents were not contacted. Advisory councils and PTA were not seen as effective communications vehicles. In several schools, large numbers of parents said "...it is the job of the principal and the teachers to run the school." However, in some schools, large numbers said that the principals' and teachers' attitudes prevented them from being involved at the school.

Data from school to school varied greatly. What was clear was that home-school communication needed to be improved and that a certain amount of self-fulfilling prophecy existed in many schools. That is, parents were perceived as disinterested, were treated as if they were, and became so.

Class visitations, special programs, home visits, increased numbers of parent-teacher conferences, and the sending of written materials home are examples of ways in which home-school communication can be improved. In the long run, it is the students who suffer when home and school do not communicate well; and this is the case for all students, not just those with problems.

Instructional Guidance

In previous chapters, we saw that the classrooms in our sample were generally dominated by teacher talk and relatively passive student activities. In fact, our observers reported seeing teachers asking questions of students only during about 7% of the observed time; and over 90% of that was direct questioning, not at all open-ended (see Table 3.10, p. 120). We also saw that classroom discussion occurred only about 5% of the observed time. (See Table 3.9, p. 116).

Within this teacher-centered, rather passive environment, teachers did a number of things to assist students to learn better. We collected several bodies of data which served to shed light upon this instructional guidance function of teachers in their classrooms.

We asked teachers to estimate the percentage of time they individualized instruction in various ways. Responses from school to school and subject to subject were very similar, but there was a wide range of responses from teacher to teacher. Overall, junior high teachers in our sample responded that they did only a moderate amount of individualizing by varying instructional methods, grouping arrangements, activities, objectives, content, and/or materials for different students. They said that they did not very often vary time schedules for different students. Large percentages of teachers said that they never used any of these ways of individualizing instruction. The impression one got from this and other data was that teachers basically relied upon the general school tracking practices and class selection to differentiate instruction for students and that within classes there was little individualization.

We also asked teachers how often they used various types of information about students if and when they individualized instruction. Again, responses from school to school and subject to subject were similar. There was a good deal of agreement among teachers that they often used their own observations of student performance and behavior and their own analysis of student classwork. Diagnostic and aptitude test results were generally not used.

We asked teachers how often they used various ways of gathering information to determine student progress (Table 5.10). Overall, having students turn in classwork or homework was the most common way of gathering information, followed by giving written tests or quizzes; then by having students perform or show how to do something; and, finally, by having students do projects or reports.

On the whole, there were differences between responses from teachers in the five academic subjects (English, math, social studies, science, and foreign language) and the two non-academic subjects (arts and

180

Table 5.10

Teacher Report of Means Used to Determine Student Progress by Subject

Subjects	Written Tests or Quizzes			Projects or Reports		Perform or Show How to Do Something		Turn in Class-work or Homework	
	$\bar{X}$	sd	N	$\bar{X}$	sd	$\bar{X}$	sd	$\bar{X}$	sd
English	3.00	.76	67	2.76	.76	2.33	.70	3.16	.73
Math	3.39	.58	65	1.69	.66	2.75	.77	3.49	.59
Social Studies	3.18	.58	44	2.75	.53	2.20	.63	3.16	.61
Science	2.83	.59	40	2.33	.69	2.45	.64	2.93	.57
Arts	2.12	.67	42	2.55	1.06	2.95	.85	2.43	1.04
Foreign Language	3.20	.63	10	1.80	.79	2.10	.88	2.90	.57
Vocational Educ.	2.48	.70	44	3.11	1.04	2.84	.78	2.75	.87
TOTAL	2.90	.77	312	2.47	.76	2.56	.78	3.04	.80

Response categories: 1.50 - 2.49 = Not very often
2.50 - 3.49 = Often
3.50 - 4.00 = Always or most of the time

181

vocational education). Not surprisingly, the teachers of academic subjects utilized written work and tests more while the non-academic teachers utilized performance and products. Proponents of more academics for all students need to recognize this fact. Our schools need to rely less on paper-and-pencil evaluation and more on performance, on active "doing." One way is to increase non-academic requirements. At a minimum, we need to help teachers in the academic courses learn better procedures of student evaluation.

Included in the student questionnaire was a comprehensive "class climate" measure. After intensive statistical analysis, a final form of this instrument was determined which contained 100 items and 18 scale dimensions. These dimensions were approximately evenly divided between those having to do with teacher behavior and those having to do with student behavior. In addition, one dimension dealt with the physical appearance of the classroom.

Data from the student decision-making scale were reported in Chapter 4 and data from the other scales having to do with student behavior will be presented in Chapter 7. At this point, we are interested in four of the scales which had to do with teaching practices: teacher clarity, knowledge of results, task difficulty, organization.³ In addition, we shall look at the results of four items about teaching practices which were in the climate measure but which were not included in any scale. These items were about appropriate practice. These data were those which told us the most about how students perceived teachers as "helpers" with their learning.

Students responded to four items which were combined to form a Teacher Clarity Scale:
-- The teacher uses words I can understand.
-- The teacher gives clear directions.
-- The students understand what the teacher is talking about.
-- I understand what the teacher is talking about.

Subject area means are shown in Table 5.11. Overall, students mildly agreed with the statement at all schools. We can say that a majority of students in the 367 classes were able to understand their teachers. However, a sizeable minority had trouble comprehending teacher directions and commands.

Table 5.11

Student Class Climate Scores Regarding Teacher Clarity--by Subject

Subject	$\overline{X}$	sd	N
Vocational Ed.	3.18	.31	49
P.E.	3.16	.22	25
Foreign Language	3.16	.28	11
Math	3.11	.28	70
Arts	3.11	.33	45
Social Studies	3.09	.30	53
English	3.08	.33	72
Science	3.01	.35	42
TOTAL	3.10	.30	367

Response categories: 2.50 - 3.49 = mildly agree
On the average, students mildly agreed that teachers of all subjects were clear.

There were only slight differences from subject to subject. Teachers of vocational education, P.E., and foreign language were viewed as most clear and teachers of science as most unclear. Perhaps this was due to the unfamiliar terms involved in the science curriculum.

Students responded to four items which were combined to form a Knowledge of Results Scale:
-- The teacher tells us how to correct the mistakes in our work.
-- The teachers tell me how to correct the mistakes in my work.
-- This teacher lets us know when we have not learned something well.
-- We know when we have learned something correctly.

Results are shown in Table 5.12. As with the Teacher Clarity Scale discussed above, students mildly agreed with these items. Results from school to school were very similar. However, teachers of foreign language were perceived as giving knowledge of results much better and teachers of science and social studies not as well.[4]   In this case, the lower ranking of science classes cannot be attributed to a complex vocabulary.

Table 5.12

Student Class Climate Scores Regarding
Knowledge of Results--by Subject

Subject	$\overline{X}$	sd	N
Foreign Language	3.35	.22	11
Math	3.20	.30	70
Vocational Education	3.17	.29	49
Arts	3.15	.29	45
English	3.13	.29	73
P.E.	3.13	.26	25
Social Studies	3.01	.35	42
Science	3.01	.35	42
TOTAL	3.13	.31	369

Response category: 2.50 - 3.49 = Mildly agree
On the average, students mildly agreed that they received feedback from teachers of all subjects.

Students responded to four items which were combined to form a Task Difficulty Scale:
-- I do not have enough time to do my work for this class.
-- Some of the things the teacher wants us to learn are just too hard.
-- I have trouble reading the books and other materials in this class.
-- The teacher gives me too much work to do in this class.

Results are shown in Table 5.13.   There were differences from school to school which were noteworthy.   Schools with large minority populations had higher mean scores (greater task difficulty) than schools with all white student bodies.   Further, Engstrom found that Hispanic and black students in ethnically and racially mixed schools had higher mean

184

scores than white students in these same schools
(Fairfield, Laurel, Palisades).[5]

Table 5.13

Student Class Climate Scores Regarding
Task Difficulty--by Subject

Subject	$\overline{X}$	sd	N
Foreign Language	2.19	.28	11
English	2.19	.30	72
Social Studies	2.18	.23	53
Science	2.17	.26	42
Math	2.16	.26	70
Vocational Education	2.09	.31	49
Art	2.08	.27	45
Physical Education	2.07	.31	25
TOTAL	2.14	.28	367

Response category: 1.50 - 2.49 = Mildly disagree.
On the average, students did not feel that
teachers in any subject made learning too difficult.

Mean scores for all subjects showed mild disagreement. Also, there was the now familiar academic vs.
non-academic dichotomy. The academic subjects had
higher mean scores than did the non-academic subjects.
Students perceived them as more difficult. This was
consistent with other data about subject difficulty
reported in Chapter 4.

Students responded to eleven items which, when
combined, formed a Class Organization Scale:
-- We know exactly what we have to get done in this
   class.
-- We know why the things we are learning in this
   class are important.
-- The grades or marks I get in this class help me
   to learn better.

185

-- We don't know what the teacher is trying to get us to learn in this class (-).*
-- Many students don't know what they're supposed to be doing during class (-).
-- This class is disorganized (-).
-- The grades or marks I get in this class have nothing to do with what I really know (-).
-- We have to learn things without knowing why (-).
-- Students know the goals of this class.
-- Things are well planned in this class.
-- Our teacher gives us good reasons for learning in this class.[6]

While students, on the average, agreed that their classes were organized, the means for this construct were a little lower than for the other measures of instructional practice.

Differences from school to school were minor. Clustering of means by subject area showed that foreign language and vocational education had relatively high scores while science was again ranked at the bottom, this time along with arts.

The four non-scaled items about appropriate practice were:

1. I have to do the work the teacher assigns, even if I already know how to do it (-).

2. We get to practice what we learn in this class.

3. We forget things we've been taught in this class because we don't practice them enough (-).

4. There are times when I have nothing to do in this class, and there are times when I have too much to do (-).

The mean scores for the first item across all students in the sample was 3.36. This meant, on the average, that students mildly agreed with the item (almost strongly agreed). This response was most pronounced at the all-white schools; the lowest mean scores were at the schools with Hispanic populations. We may be seeing a response which indicates that Hispanic students didn't perceive that they very often

---

* Items marked (-) are scored in reverse.

repeated material while many white students thought they did.

Table 5.14

Student Class Climate Scores Regarding
Class Organization--by Subject

Subject	X̄	sd	N
Foreign Language	3.03	.16	11
Vocational Education	2.98	.31	49
Math	2.96	.25	70
English	2.92	.28	72
Social Studies	2.88	.27	53
Physical Education	2.87	.22	25
Science	2.83	.26	42
Art	2.83	.27	45
TOTAL	2.90	.27	367

Response category: 2.50 - 3.49 = Mildly agree.
On the average, students mildly agreed that
classes in all subjects were organized.

On the average, students also mildly agreed with the second item. Responses were fairly similar across schools. The third item was almost the opposite of the second one and students, on the average, did what was expected, they mildly disagreed. However, at Crestview they mildly agreed; and, once again, the Hispanic schools had scores which indicated that they felt they had less appropriate practice.

A similar school by school pattern emerged for the fourth item. On the average, students mildly agreed, but Hispanic students agreed more. That Hispanic students were more negative in their perceptions of the practice of what they had been taught was not to say that their teaching was poorer. Other data, at least at one school (Rosemont), suggested that it was not poorer. It did suggest that Hispanic students saw school as more difficult and that they felt the need for more practice of what they were learning. There

187

seemed to be no difference, in these data, between schools which served black students and those which served only white students. Certainly language difference in the Hispanic schools must have played some part in the matter.

In Chapter 3 we discussed briefly some of the teacher responding behaviors. We saw that for teacher praise and correction of students with guidance, less than two percent of the FMI frames were recorded and less than one percent of the frames involved teachers rejecting or reprimanding students. When all responding behaviors were added together, the proportion of observed teacher activity spent responding to students' questions, requests, products, and behaviors amounted to only slightly more than 10% of their time.

In addition to examining level percentage of FMI frames for how frequently teachers responded to and gave feedback to students, we were also able to investigate school differences. For purposes of this analysis, we combined responding behaviors to form four variables: (1) praise, (2) correcting students, (3) reprimanding students, and (4) rejecting students. We found that three schools stood out as having distinct and interpretable scores on these variables. Bradford and Rosemont had relatively low mean scores on all four variables. In other words, it appeared that teachers at these schools gave students relatively little feedback, be it positive or negative. In contrast, Palisades had high scores on the two more positive variables--praise and feedback--and low scores on the two more negative variables--reprimand and reject. We can say, then, that Palisades teachers gave more attention to using positive versus negative forms of feedback or reinforcement to students.

Affective Guidance in the Classroom

There were five scales in the class climate measure which had to do more with student perceptions of teachers' affective behaviors than with their perceptions of teachers' instructional practices. Such behaviors were thought to be critical to the role of the teacher in classroom guidance. They were labelled: teacher concern, teacher punitiveness, teacher authoritarianism, teacher favoritism, and teacher enthusiasm.

Students responded to eight items which formed the Teacher Concern Scale:
-- The teacher makes this class enjoyable for me.
-- The teacher listens to me.
-- The teacher lets me express my feelings.
-- I like the teacher in this class.
-- I wish I had a different teacher for this class (-).
-- I feel the teacher is honest with me.
-- The teacher is friendly.
-- The teacher is fair to me.

The mean score for this scale across all 369 classes was 3.07 (mildly agree). On the average, students perceived that their teachers showed concern for them as described in the items for this scale. There were not great differences from school to school nor from subject to subject (sd = .41). Perceptions were somewhat more positive at Woodlake (3.22) and somewhat less positive at Manchester (2.87). The most positive subject was foreign language (3.20), and the least positive were science (2.99), social studies (3.03), and English (3.05).

The items for the Teacher Punitiveness Scale were:
-- The teacher makes fun of some students.
-- This teacher hurts my feelings.
-- I'm afraid of this teacher.
-- The teacher makes fun of me.
-- The teacher gets mad when I ask a question.

The mean score across all classes was 1.66 (mildly disagree) and the standard deviation was a low .29. In nearly all classes students, on the average, perceived that their teachers were not punitive. Minor differences showed that students perceived the least amount of punitiveness at Woodlake (1.48) and slightly more at Rosemont (1.86) and Manchester (1.80). As far as subject areas were concerned, the least punitiveness was perceived in foreign language (1.51) and the most in the arts and P.E. (both 1.70).

Students responded to eight items which formed a Teacher Authoritarianism Scale:
-- This teacher is too strict.
-- This teacher treats us like children.
-- This teacher will never admit when he/she is wrong.

189

-- We don't feel like we have any freedom in this class.
-- This teacher acts like he/she is better than we are.
-- This teacher "talks down" to us.
-- This teacher never changes his/her mind about anything.
-- I don't feel like I have any freedom in this class.

Even though there were slightly larger mean scores for the Teacher Authoritarianism Scale than the Teacher Punitiveness Scale, the former scores were still relatively low (2.13) and the standard deviation was a low .29. Thus, in general, students disagreed with statements which portrayed their teachers as authoritarian. Students disagreed slightly more at Woodlake (1.94) and Vista (1.97) and slightly less at Manchester (2.33) and Laurel (2.25). On the average, they disagreed the most in foreign language (1.94) and the least in P.E. (2.20).

There were three items which combined to form a Teacher Favoritism Scale:
-- The teacher likes some students in this class better than others.
-- The teacher has no favorites in this class (-).
-- The teacher treats smart students in this class better than others.

If junior high students did not view teachers as very punitive or authoritarian, they also did not perceive them to any great extent as showing favoritism. However, the mean score for Teacher Favoritism was somewhat higher than for the other two scales (2.33). So, while students did, as a group, disagree with the Teacher Favoritism items, they did perceive teachers as exhibiting more favoritism than punitive or authoritarian behavior. Students disagreed somewhat more at Woodlake (2.22) and somewhat less at Newport (2.43), Euclid (2.41), and Fairfield (2.40). On the whole, they disagreed slightly more in vocational education (2.33) and math (2.26) and slightly less in science and art (both 2.41).

In a slightly different vein, there were three items which formed a Teacher Enthusiasm Scale:
-- This teacher seems to like being a teacher.

-- This teacher seems to enjoy what he/she is teaching.
-- The teacher seems bored in this classroom (-).

It seemed to us that teachers' attitudes about teaching would influence both the instructional atmosphere and the attitudes of students about learning. Junior high students agreed that their teachers were enthusiastic about teaching (3.26). Once again, students at Woodlake were the most positive (3.41). Lower mean scores were compiled at Manchester (3.14), Fairfield (3.15), Rosemont (3.19), and Bradford (3.19). Also, means for foreign language were once again the highest (3.14). The lower means for this scale were in science (3.20), social studies (3.22), P.E. (3.22), and vocational education (3.22).

In summary, then, we can say that junior high students in our sample, on the average, saw their teachers as concerned and enthusiastic. They also saw them as not punitive, not authoritarian, and not showing favoritism.

There were slight school-to-school differences as well as slight differences across subjects. Students at Woodlake were the most positive on all five scales and students at Manchester were less positive on all scales except Teacher Favoritism. Likewise, students in foreign language perceived it most positively, of all subjects on all scales except Teacher Favoritism while the four subjects with generally lower scores were science, the arts, P.E., and social studies.

All five of the mean scores reported above from the student climate measure were either in the mildly agree range or mildly disagree range depending upon the scale construct. This seemed to jibe with observation data which showed that teachers were seen to respond to their students most often in a neutral rather than a strongly positive or negative manner. In fact, less than 3% of classroom time was characterized by observers as either positive or negative. Alternatively, the "affect" present about 80% of the time was recorded as neutral. These percentages referred only to the times when teachers and students were interacting. The balance of observed time found teachers monitoring, working alone, talking with another adult, and so forth. Thus, during actual interaction time, "affect" was neutral over 95% of the time.

191

There would be many people who might suggest that the presence in the classroom of teacher concern and enthusiasm and a minimization of teacher punitiveness, authoritarianism, and favoritism would be good in and of itself. There would be others who might say that it does not matter whether affect is positive, negative, or neutral as long as good teaching occurs. The fact is, positive teacher affect and good teaching seem to go together, at least in the eyes of students.

We examined the relationship between class climate scales which measured teaching practices on the one hand and affective behaviors on the other. These relationships were reported as Pearson correlation coefficients (r) in Table 5.15. In addition, the relationship between these affective behaviors and a measure of student satisfaction with the classroom was also reported. All correlations reported were significant at the .001 level.

Table 5.15

Pearson Correlation Coefficients
Selected Class Climate Scale Scores
Significance = .001

	Teacher Concern		Teacher Punitiveness		Teacher Authoritarianism		Teacher Favoritism		Teacher Enthusiasm	
	r	N	r	N	r	N	r	N	r	N
Teacher Clarity	.58	8035	-.34	8031	-.44	8044	-.34	8043	.49	8042
Knowledge of Results	.58	8057	-.30	8500	-.39	8290	-.31	8399	.49	8391
Task Difficulty	-.35	8232	.42	8228	.57	8241	.35	8239	-.35	8239
Organization	.64	8246	-.44	8242	-.62	8155	-.46	8152	.57	8153
Student Satisfaction	.59	7964	-.28	7960	-.47	7969	-.36	7968	.45	7967

The strongest relationships seemed to exist between Teacher Concern on the one hand and the instructional practices Organization, Teacher Clarity, and Knowledge

192

of Results. The students in our sample perceived that the teacher who showed concern was also more apt to give clear directions, let them know how they were progressing, and be well organized in teaching.

There was also a fairly strong positive relationship between Teacher Enthusiasm and the instructional behaviors labelled Teacher Clarity, Knowledge of Results, and Organization. A fairly strong negative relationship existed between Teacher Authoritarianism and the instructional behaviors listed below. Students perceived those teachers with more positive affect to be more skilled, too.

We also explored the relationship between the teacher affective measures and a measure labelled Student Satisfaction. The items which made up that scale were:
-- Students feel good about what happens in this class.
-- I don't like coming to this class (-).
-- After class, I usually have a sense of satisfaction.
-- I feel good about what happens in this class.

The strongest relationship was with Teacher Concern, followed by a fairly strong negative relationship with Teacher Authoritarianism and a positive one with Teacher Enthusiasm. Students expressed more satisfaction in classrooms with positive teacher affect.

My colleague, Gerald Engstrom, explored relationships between the class climate measures and numerous other variables from the Study.[8] In his first examination of relationships, the climate scales were intercorrelated with other class-specific items responded to by the same students. The analysis indicated that the classes the students found interesting were classes which they perceived as better organized and clearer and in which they were more satisfied. More interesting classes were seen as being easier and the boring classes were seen as more difficult. Classes where students felt they had more freedom to choose and make more decisions were also seen as easier.

In the next section of his study, Engstrom examined the relationship between individual characteristics of the student responses and their class climate scores. He found almost no relationship between student SES and the climate scores. Students from different socio-economic groups did not perceive class climate in significantly different ways. There was a relationship between race/ethnicity and the climate scores. Minority students were more positive about their classes but Hispanic students found them more difficult than did the Anglos.

The student background characteristic that most distinguished between students was gender. The group means for the two sexes were compared on a class by class basis and although the differences in the group means were not large, they were statistically different for 15 of the 18 climate scales. Of the scales we have dealt with here, only Teacher Clarity and Student Satisfaction failed to show group differences. For the remaining scales the female students scored highest on those that were positive (Knowledge of Results, Organization, Teacher Concern, Teacher Enthusiasm) and males scored highest on those that were negative (Task Difficulty, Teacher Punitiveness, Teacher Authoritarianism).

This could represent the way the two sexes were socialized into thinking about school or it could have been truly related to the way they were treated. In either case, the perceptions of school experience were different for boys and girls, with girls more positive.

In an era in which there is appropriately a good deal of focus upon discrimination against women, it seems important to point out that it is boys in early adolescence who may be having the more negative experiences in school. It is an interesting hypothesis worth further testing.

A third section of Engstrom's analysis related several groups of variables taken from the teaching questionnaire--ranging from teacher demographics to teacher descriptions of the specific class--to the climate scores for their classes.

Positive climate perceptions were related to younger teachers and to a lesser degree to female teachers. Teachers with an educational belief in teacher control had classes which were perceived more negatively by students. Teachers who felt satisfied with various aspects of their careers and school had classes which were perceived more positively by the students.

Finally, classes where students were on task and where more time was spent on instruction and less on behavior were viewed more positively on a range of climate scores.

We know that the climate of the classroom created by the teacher, in very large measure by his or her instructional and affective guidance behavior, is critical to student learning. In fact, class climate has been found to predict a significant portion of the variance in achievement independent of student background and I.Q.[9] Given that student background is so difficult to manipulate, the possibilities for manipulating classroom environment takes on special significance for those interested in the improvement of learning.

Conclusions

I began this chapter by pointing out that there is a good deal of confusion concerning the role of the junior high school vis-a-vis "guidance." Part of the confusion is attributable to the fact that the school is expected to serve such a wide array of functions simultaneously: intellectual, vocational, social, personal. However, part of the problem is also structural.

In an effort to provide a wide array of guidance services to their students, American secondary schools employ counselors who are expected to provide specialized "guidance" for students as needed. These people, counselors, have special training in such matters as group dynamics, values clarification, student assessment, conferencing, community resources, and learning theory. However, in most instances, as our data have suggested, they perform administrative tasks: scheduling, reporting, and the like.

I take the position that it is unrealistic to think that counselors can perform all, or even most, of the guidance work required in a junior high. Even if there were money enough to train and employ many more counselors, we would need to rethink the guidance function in our junior highs. Our junior highs need counselors who are well trained to organize and administer testing programs, develop and implement scheduling, counsel students with unique needs, work with parents and provide orientation to the schools and, above all, assist and train teachers in <u>their</u> counseling roles.

A critical guidance role is played by the teacher in the classroom. We found that the junior high teachers in our sample made little use of diagnostic tools as they planned instruction for students. They relied primarily on their own observations and judgment. Their methods of evaluation tended to be paper-and-pencil, highly verbal, and not particularly performance-based except in vocational education classes and the arts. Even in those classes much evaluation was carried out using written tests. Our teachers need much in-service training in the development and use of diagnostic and evaluation techniques.

We also found that there was little individualization of instruction and that students were only moderately positive in their perceptions of the degree to which teachers utilized principles of learning as tools of instructional guidance. Hispanic students tended to feel that they often had to do tasks which were too difficult or which they did not completely understand.

Overall, teachers were perceived as moderately concerned for students and enthusiastic about their work. They were not seen as authoritarian or punitive. Observers found classrooms to be neutral in regard to affect. In this chapter we saw that this affective guidance was related to instructional guidance and that it, in turn, was related to student satisfaction. Also, we learned that other researchers have shown that such classroom guidance dimensions are related to student achievement. Since these dimensions are manipulable, it would seem that they hold promise for improvement of achievement.

Given these data, it seems reasonable to suggest that schools could be diagnosed individually with a good climate measure and that in-service training programs could be designed on the basis of such diagnosis so that classroom guidance could be improved markedly. The investment in the development of the skills of teachers would seem to me to be far more profitable than redesigning organizational schemes, curriculum, or any other aspect of schooling.

A promising finding reported in this chapter was that teachers who felt satisfied with various aspects of their careers and school had classes which were perceived more positively by students. Perhaps we need to somehow "turn-around" the negativism which has come to surround teaching. We need to be concerned with once again having people see teaching as an enjoyable and worthwhile endeavor. The relationship seems fairly simple: "turned on" teachers equals "turned on" students equals better learning.

Our findings concerning home-school linkages were not so promising. Contacts were not frequent and, more importantly, a kind of self-fulfilling prophecy existed which suggested that parents were really not too interested in what went on at school. Building linkages between the home and the school is an important aspect of improved student guidance.

Even if we markedly increased home-school communication, dramatically improved teacher classroom guidance skills, and had smoothly functioning counseling offices we would still need to give more attention to the guidance function of the junior high. A comprehensive view of guidance as stated in the definition given at the beginning of this chapter addresses not only the intellectual or academic development of the students but their vocational, personal, and social development as well. And, as we saw in Chapter 2, the junior high is expected to deal with all of these aspects of student development.

What is needed is a new kind of structure which gives each student access to one adult to whom he or she can turn and with whom he or she interacts regularly throughout his or her years at the school. Such a program was developed by I/D/E/A as part of the Individually Guided Education (IGE) program. It was called the Teacher Advisor Program.

The structure of a teacher advisor program is relatively simple. Two or three blocks of time per week ranging from one-half hour to a full period are set aside for "advisory." Each qualified adult including administrators and counselors is assigned an advisee group of from 10-15 students.

The program is purposely kept flexible and includes such things as group discussions, individual conferences on school related and personal problems, values clarification activities, simulations and role plays, and group projects. It is not a study hall although some studying may be done.

Teachers are viewed as facilitators and as "advocates" for their advisees. Generally, advisees remain with the group for their entire time at the school. Thus, each group is made up of students from all grade levels at the school. The main point is that this is a special group, a place where each student has a sense of "belonging" and of support.

Implementing such a program is not easy. My experience is that students are very positive about it and that parents are generally supportive. Many teachers, however, do not like it because it is an added burden, another "prep," something to do for which they are not trained. Most teachers are not trained for such a role and this is where counselors become very important. They should coordinate such a program and must help teachers with materials, activities and the like and must provide teachers with training in necessary group and individual counseling skills.

Likewise, I have on occasion found resistance on the part of counselors. In the main, this has been because they felt teachers could not do the things that counselors were trained to do. This, of course, is true. However, the problem is one of more adequately defining guidance roles and, in the final analysis, of building structures to make sure that the guidance function of the junior high is adequately carried out.

1. William Van Til, et al., Modern Education for Junior High Schools (Second Edition, op. cit., p. 30.

2. Burton W. Gorman, Secondary Education: The High School America Needs. New York: Random House, 1971, p. 30.

3. Readers interested in the technical aspects of this class climate measure are referred to Gerald A. Engstrom. An Examination of the Viability of Class Climate As a Useful Construct in Secondary Schools. I/D/E/A Study of Schooling Technical Report 23. Arlington, Va.: ERIC Document Reproduction Service, 1981.

4. Joyce Wright, Teaching and Learning, op. cit., p. 20.

5. Gerald A. Engstrom, An Examination of the Viability of Class Climate As a Useful Construct in Secondary Schools, op. cit., pp. 18 and 23.

6. In our a priori scales, the items on perceived purpose, organization, and grading were separate. Factor analyses provided sufficient evidence to group them together into one scale. It is my opinion that the present scale score adequately measures perceived purpose or "knowledge of objectives" for those interested in the degree to which principles of learning are utilized in classrooms by teachers.

7. Some students responded in more than one class. There were 6,042 unique students in our junior high sample.

8. Gerald A. Engstrom, An Examination of the Viability of Class Climate As a Useful Construct in Secondary Schools, op. cit. The findings were reported for all secondary schools, junior highs and senior highs. There were not significant differences between the levels.

9. See for example Baruk Rosenshine, "Recent Research on Teaching Behaviors and Student Achievement," Journal of Teacher Education, Vol. 27, No. 1 (1976), pp. 61-64.

CHAPTER VI

DIFFERENTIATION

Introduction

In Chapter 3, we saw that the junior high origi-
nated as a means toward better and more economically
preparing college bound students. However, as universal attendance became a reality, it also was forced to
provide programs for the non-college bound. This
academic/non-academic dichotomy remains today.

In theory, the junior high is structured to:

...provide differentiated educational facilities and opportunities suited to the varying
backgrounds, interests, aptitudes, abilities,
personalities, and needs of pupils in order
that each pupil may realize most economically
and completely the ultimate aims of education.[1]

Frequently, teachers group students in their
classes and vary content, pace, or method of instruction for short periods of time. Such short-term,
within-class grouping seems a logical and useful way of
dealing with differing student needs and interests,
however, and particularly at the secondary levels of
schooling, differentiation has come to be synonymous
with ability grouping or tracking. This means that
students are completely separated on the basis of some
set of assumptions about their educational and/or
occupational potential. The practice of more or less
permanently separating or tracking students is ques-
tionable at best.[2]

Ability grouping is based upon a set of assumptions
widely held by educators and lay citizens which do not
hold up when examined closely. First, it is generally
believed that students differ greatly in their academic
potential and basic aptitude for schooling, and that
different educational treatments are necessary to
facilitate learning in different students. Further,
while it is often stated that learning deficiencies can
be remediated, it is generally believed that aptitude
is not likely to be altered much by schooling.

Unfortunately, it is also a widely held view that students can be accurately classified or tracked according to their learning potential.

There are many fallacies connected with this set of assumptions. First of all, learning potential is not such a definable commodity. Even when several criteria are used to "accurately" place a student in one track or another, something is bound to be overlooked. For example, rarely are a student's motivation and/or interests considered before he/she is placed in a track. Often, too, students are grouped on the basis of criteria more or less appropriate for one subject and that grouping is kept constant for many subjects where the same criteria are totally inappropriate. Math, science, or art teachers can tell you that their classes which are homogeneously grouped for English are anything but homogeneous for their own subjects.

Studies of tracking and ability grouping consistently show high correlations between race and socioeconomic status on the one hand and track on the other. Minority children and those from lower socioeconomic groups are found in large numbers in low track classes while children from upper socioeconomic levels are most often found in higher tracks.[3]

Other studies have found a relationship between class composition and achievement.[4] That is, achievement has been found to be lower in classes composed predominantly of minority and/or low SES students. Given the linkages from achievement to race and SES and then to tracking, it is no wonder that tracking and ability grouping are educational practices which have been challenged in the courts.

Another assumption connected with tracking is that students will achieve more if they are in a group with others of similar ability. However, existing research has consistently failed to demonstrate that ability grouping leads to gains in student achievement and, in fact, has shown that it can have negative effects on students placed in average and lower groups.[5] Both the content and methods of instruction vary a good deal in classes at different levels. Additionally, low track teaching assignments are less preferred by teachers. As a result, they are usually taught by the least experienced teachers in the school who lack the perquisites of seniority.

202

There is a final, insidious assumption which undergirds the practice of tracking. It is the belief that a "fast" student is, ipso facto, a "good" student and a student who learns more slowly is a "poor" student. Large numbers of students are essentially "written off" because they are slower. This writing off of slower learners, the poor, and the minorities, coupled with our firm belief in competition and the inevitability of there being losers is so wasteful of human resources that the nation risks the loss of some of its vitality. Unfortunately, we find it easier to be wasteful of the potential of our children than we do to invest in it and provide environments where it can be realized.

All in all, the evidence seems to suggest that tracking serves little, if any, educative function; its primary purpose as an organizational structure is to make life a bit easier for teachers and administrators. The fact that it cannot be convincingly justified as being demonstrably good for the students themselves may account for the common reluctance of school people to discuss openly the policies and practices which exist at their schools.

In the following statement, Oakes describes how the classification process is rarely well-defined or consistently carried out:

> ...Many districts, in fact, have no formal policy regarding the criteria for ability grouping placements; in other districts, policy exists but is not carefully followed. Decisions are often left to individual administrators, counselors, and teachers. Parents and students are often not informed as to placement criteria, about the differences in educational treatments offered to different groups, or of the restrictions on students' access to further educational or occupational opportunities which may result from various placements. Moreover, in some districts and schools, parents are not routinely informed that their children are being classified and tracked at all.[6]

Even in those rare instances where criteria for grouping may be quite explicit, they are often inappropriate or, at best, subjectively applied to students. This fact, combined with the fact that decisions once made are seldom changed (i.e., once in the "slow" or "fast" track, always in that track), suggest that many students are wrongly assigned to tracks wherein they receive inappropriate educational treatment.

In the remainder of this chapter, we shall examine the nature of tracking in our sample of junior highs. Such things as pervasiveness, flexibility, decision-making, and rationale will be described for each school. A close look will be taken at the effects of tracking practices in English, mathematics, and vocational education classes. Data from students, teachers, and parents about differentiation because of gender or race will be presented, and teacher perceptions of modes of student working in class will be examined (i.e., students working alone, in groups, as a whole class). Finally, conclusions will be drawn, including the discussion of alternatives to tracking.

The Nature of Tracking[7]

Information on the ability level of the classes we studied was gathered from the schools involved after the Study was completed. We did not originally sample classes with this criterion in mind. Data were gathered from administrators, counselors, and various school documents. The actual categorization by track of sampled classes was done by administrators and/or counselors at each school. Table 6.1 shows the estimated percentage of tracked classes at each school, the percentage of tracked classes which were sampled, and the number of sampled classes in each category: low, average, high, heterogeneous.

All schools except Euclid purposely tracked their students to some degree. The range was from 80% of the students tracked at both Bradford and Newport to 17% at Crestview. Low ability classes were slightly underrepresented at many of our schools. Because of the reluctance of school people to give us actual figures, we are not absolutely sure of our estimates as to tracking. For example, we were told that there was no ability grouping at Euclid, but six of the classes we sampled definitely were grouped homogenously.

The number of subject areas in which students were tracked varied from none at Euclid to seven at Bradford. Figure 6.1 first indicates the number of tracked subjects at each of the twelve junior highs in the Study and then shows the number of schools tracking in each subject area. Taken together, these figures show the pervasiveness of tracking in the various subject areas. The non-academic subjects were rarely tracked while English and mathematics were almost always tracked.

Table 6.1

Number of Classes Sampled at Each Track Level
at Each of the Twelve Junior Highs in the Study

Schools	Estimated % of total classes tracked*	% of sampled classes tracked	No. of classes sampled at each track level			
			low	average	high	hetero
Bradford	80	72	7	8	11	10
Newport	80	55	5	6	5	13
Laurel	76	42	3	1	6	14
Fairfield	75	70	8	11	2	9
Manchester	60	80	6	9	13	7
Vista	46	47	3	5	9	19
Palisades	40	39	7	3	4	22
Atwater	32	11	1	0	2	24
Rosemont	25	28	6	2	2	26
Woodlake	25	27	2	4	2	22
Crestview	17	19	1	2	2	22
Euclid	0	38	0	5	1	10
			49	56	59	198

* estimates provided by school and/or guidance staff

Flexibility of tracking systems varied from one school to another, also. Half of the schools placed students into tracked classes subject by subject. These tended to be the schools which tracked in the fewest subject areas. At three schools, track placements were made across subjects. For example, at Bradford students were grouped together for all their academic subjects on the basis of some overall judgment

205

of students' abilities. At Palisades and Vista both types of tracking took place. The schools are categorized as to their flexibility in tracking in Figure 6.2.

No. of subjects
tracked   Schools

0   Euclid
1   Crestview
2
3   Atwater, Palisades,
                       Rosemont, Vista,
                       Woodlake
4   Laurel
5
6   Fairfield, Manchester,
                       Newport
7   Bradford

Math   11 schools
English   10 schools
Science   6 schools
Social Studies   6 schools
Foreign Language*   5 schools
Vocational Education   4 schools
Arts   3 schools
Physical Education   0 schools

* There were foreign language classes at
  only 7 schools.

Figure 6.1 The number of tracked subjects by
school and tracked classes by subject area.

There was very little movement from track to track. One school, Palisades, reported that just over 20% of the students moved from one track level to another from year to year. At Atwater and Vista it was reported that fewer than 10% moved. We had no data from Fairfield and the question was not appropriate for Euclid. At all other schools, only between 10 and 20% of the students were reported to move from one track to another from one year to another and that movement was usually to a lower track. This is stark evidence of the self-fulfilling prophecy associated with tracking.

Less Flexible -- Tracking Across Subjects		More Flexible -- Tracking Subject by Subject	No Formal System
Bradford	Palisades	Atwater	Euclid
Manchester	Vista	Crestview	
Newport		Fairfield	
		Laurel	
		Rosemont	
		Woodlake	

Figure 6.2 Flexibility of tracking systems

Years ago, when I worked at the Office of Economic Opportunity (OEO) in the Job Corps program, I wrote that we could predict who our high school age clients would be by visiting second grade classes. My point was that by that time, when students were about seven years old, they had been "grouped" for reading instruction. There were the good readers, the "Robins," There were the average readers, the "Canaries." And there were the poor readers, called the "Orioles" but thought of as "Buzzards." You could predict from such early grouping who would succeed in school and who would not. The fact is that those junior high students who are labelled as "Y" or "low" track have probably been labelled that way since they were seven years old or earlier. It isn't any wonder that they come to believe it and behave in expected ways.

Oakes, in her study, found that the control of tracking decisions at most schools resided with the counselors and teachers together. At two schools (Atwater, Newport), counselors had the sole responsibility for placement decisions and at two other schools (Vista, Woodlake) it was solely up to teachers. At no school were parents and/or students reported to have a role in these decisions.

Interestingly, the characteristics of the tracking systems at the schools in the sample did not appear to be associated with such common variables as school size, location, teacher demographics, or curriculum content. Neither did it seem to matter whether a school was called a junior high or a middle school.

Only eight schools offered rationales for using homogeneous grouping. All of these stated the belief that individual differences of students were better accommodated in tracked settings. Only two of the schools also specifically mentioned making the teaching task easier.

The assumption that tracking yields teachably homogeneous groups is patently absurd. In most junior high classrooms, whatever the track, there are likely to be students functioning at a wide range of levels and learning in many different ways. And, yet, we pretend this isn't so. We continue to teach to the whole group using lecture, reading, and filling in worksheets as our main techniques. Even as class size goes down the teaching procedures remain pretty much the same. And so-called homogeneous grouping reinforces the situation.

Overall, the evidence seems to suggest that tracking serves little if any educative function. It does make it easier for poor teaching to be carried out and for student behavior to be "managed" because it is assumed that the homogeneous grouping has eliminated individual differences. Unfortunately, it also makes the school a major participant in the insidious practice of sorting, segregating, and wasting our most precious resource, human beings.

The Effects of Tracking

My colleague, Jeannie Oakes, used a subset of classes from A Study of Schooling to examine the effects of tracking in some detail. Because English and math were the most frequently tracked subjects, she used the 156 English and 141 math classes at the junior and senior high schools in the Study as her sample.

Oakes looked at the relationship between track level and such other factors as: time spent on instruction, content of instruction, teaching practices, classroom affect, peer relations, and student attitudes. The patterns she found were dramatic. Both the quantity and quality were markedly different for the track levels at both the junior and senior high schools.[9]

Table 6.2

Number of Classes Sampled at Each Track Level --
Secondary English and Math Classes

| | Class Level | | | | |
	low	average	high	hetero	total
HS English	12	31	18	22	83
JH English	18	15	16	24	73
HS Math	19	20	22	11	72
JH Math	17	17	19	16	69

To begin with, the topics studied in high track classes were those traditionally associated with preparation for higher education while those studied in low track classes were more likely to be related to basic literacy and computation, and "everyday life and work knowledge." Not only were low track students cut off from higher education, high track students were cut off from much very basic survival knowledge and skills.

Additionally, teachers of higher track classes tended to require higher levels of cognitive functioning more than did teachers of classes at lower track levels. They had some concern that their students learn independence and critical thinking while teachers of lower track classes seemed to emphasize conformity and obedience to rules and expectations. Thus, we gain a glimpse of a "democratic" society in which the highly educated, creative, critical-thinkers lead the law-abiding, obedient followers. It is obvious that the practice of tracking addresses far greater issues than ease of teaching.

Also, high track classes spent more time on instructional activity during class than did lower track classes. Furthermore, high track English students were expected to spend more time on homework.

209

Instructional practices were distributed among tracks in such a way that students in the lowest groups were the least likely to experience better teaching. The reader will recall the discussion of class climate from the previous chapter. Oakes clearly found meaningful differences in teacher clarity and teacher enthusiasm among tracks with the higher tracks having more positive scores. She found the greatest differences in students' perceptions of teachers as concerned or punitive and in the positive expressions teachers made toward students in their interactions with them. Students in the lower tracks were more likely to view the teachers as punitive, while students in the higher tracks tended to view their teachers as concerned and supportive. These variables are among a large number which form a constellation of teacher behaviors thought to influence student achievement.[10]

Peer relationships were reported to be positive by students in higher track classes, less positive by students in lower track classes. Students in lower track classes also reported that they "often felt left out," and they were less positive about their own participation. More disruption and student apathy were present in low track classes and more time was spent on student behavior and discipline. The environments of classes at different track levels differed noticeably in terms of social relations. And such differences certainly seemed to indicate an inequality in opportunity to develop an affiliation with the classroom, the other people in it and, perhaps, with schooling itself.

Students in low track classes had less positive general and academic self-concept scores and, as the reader might guess, their educational aspirations were lower than those of high track students. By junior high, students in the different tracks clearly had different expectations for their future roles in society. The schools had done an effective job of sorting even though not one school had any statement about this as one of its functions.

We asked all students to agree or disagree with the following statement: "If you don't want to go to college, this school doesn't think you're very important." The mean response at all schools was mildly disagree. However, as is shown in Table 6.3, large numbers of students did agree. Further, the pattern of response was interesting in that the six schools with minority populations had the greater percentages of agreement. Certainly many students sense the value placed by schools on academic attainment and our data would suggest that minority students sense it the strongest. We do not know how responses to this item varied from track to track in these schools.

Table 6.3

Student Perceptions of School Not Valuing
Non-College Bound Students

School	$\overline{X}$	% Agree	sd	N
Woodlake	1.77	16.6	.83	432
Atwater	1.81	21.3	.90	310
Euclid	1.85	24.0	.97	125
Vista	1.87	21.2	.88	644
Crestview	2.01	28.3	.96	398
Bradford	2.05	30.0	.96	491
Palisades	2.12	33.8	1.00	435
Fairfield	2.14	31.5	.96	432
Manchester	2.14	34.4	1.05	586
Newport	2.16	33.7	.99	665
Rosemont	2.31	44.4	1.10	548
Laurel	2.34	44.2	1.10	235
TOTAL	2.06	30.6	.99	5301

Response $\overline{X}$ categories: 1.00 - 1.49 = Strongly disagree
1.50 - 2.49 = Mildly disagree
2.50 - 3.49 = Mildly agree
3.50 - 4.00 = Strongly agree

Despite lower feelings of self-worth vis-a-vis schooling, lower track students reported the same levels of satisfaction with school as other students. As Oakes said, "We can only speculate, but it may be that low track students see themselves and their own inadequacies, not the hierarchical structure or differential treatment of the school, as responsible for their current positions and future roles in the hierarchical structure."[11] She goes further to state that this cannot be interpreted to mean that the school is, in fact, neutral and one's position in it is dependent upon individual merit. Since there is such a disproportionate distribution of societal groups into track levels, we must suspect that tracking, itself, contributes to societal inequities.

Oakes also examined the degree to which there were different curricular experiences in vocational education courses taken by students of different racial and ethnic groups.[12] She divided the twelve junior highs into three categories. Six schools with an enrollment of 95% or more white students were categorized as "white" schools. Four schools with approximately 50% non-white enrollment were classified as "mixed." The remaining two schools enrolled 95% or more non-white students and were classified as "non-white." The white junior highs enrolled a total of 4,055 students, the non-white schools 2,540 students and the mixed schools 3,515 students (1,664 white and 1,851 non-white).

Each school's vocational program was examined in terms of teacher resources allocated to it, the content and format of courses, and the race/ethnicity of the students taking courses.

While vocational education was the first-ranked subject at the high school level in terms of percentage of allocated staff (referred to as FTE--full-time equivalency), at the junior high it ranked fourth with science. English (22%), math (18%), and social studies (14%) occupied greater percentages of FTEs. Vocational education and science each had 12% of the total and P.E., art, and foreign language ranked lower with 11%, 10%, and 1% respectively.

The percentage of FTEs in vocational education varied across the schools. Laurel had only 4%, with programs at Atwater, Crestview, Palisades, Rosemont, and Woodlake at 7-8%. Manchester stood out at the top with 22%.

Among the sample of mixed junior high schools, disproportionate percentages of non-white students were not found in vocational classes at Palisades or Laurel. At the former, over 70% of the students in sampled classes were white and at Laurel 60% were white. Vocational courses involved all eighth graders at Laurel and all non-music or non-foreign language students at Palisades. At Fairfield five vocational classes were sampled and in these small, work-experi-ence classes, only five students (20%) were white.[13] The lack of individual race/ethnicity data at Newport prevented an analysis.

There were distinct differences in both the content and format of vocational education programs between the white schools and the mixed or non-white schools. Seven types of courses were offered at the secondary schools in the sample (high schools and junior highs): business, skill or trade preparation, military prepara-tion, agricultural, general home economics, general industrial arts, and general career or consumer educa-tion.

In Table 6.4, characteristics of the vocational education courses offered at the twelve junior high schools in the sample are set forth. Information presented includes: (a) the number of distinct courses offered by schools in each vocational education content category, (b) the format of available courses, (c) the racial/ethnic category of schools, and (d) the racial composition of the vocational education courses.

Junior high vocational education courses were more similar than different. Eleven of the 12 schools offered courses in home economics and 10 offered industrial arts. White and non-white students appeared to have fairly equal access to such courses.

Three types of courses were not consistently offered. Business courses (typing) were offered at five schools, consumer or general vocational education at three and trade preparation at only one. Oakes pointed out that "...despite the overall similarity in offerings, the differences in junior high school programs seemed to be associated with the composition of the student body..."[14] While home economics and general industrial arts dominated the vocational curriculum at the white schools, courses preparing students with specific occupational skills dominated the course offerings at non-white and mixed schools.

The program at Fairfield was illustrative of these differences. It was the only junior high to offer courses preparing for specific trades. The courses were two hours in length and took students off campus. The courses included home and community services,

213

duplicating skills, horticulture, general mechanical repair, building maintenance, and general construction trades. Non-white students made up the bulk of the enrollment.

The high school data from A Study of Schooling showed even more marked differences in the vocational education experiences of white and non-white students. Even so, the data were not generalizable on this point. What did emerge was an hypothesis which needs further testing: "non-whites more than whites are being directed in their vocational training toward futures in lower class social and economic positions;" and such differentiation is well begun by junior high.

One of the more positive findings of A Study of Schooling was the outcome of Oakes' comparison of tracked with untracked (heterogeneous, or mixed-ability) classes. Conventional wisdom has generally held that heterogeneous classes operate at the level of the lowest common denominator and that the faster students are held back. That is, teachers aim their instruction just below the average of the students in the class. Oakes' findings, however, clearly showed that heterogeneous classes were much more similar, in both content and process, to upper average and high-track classes. Students in such classes had the advantage of better teaching, more time spent on instruction, and the most positive class climate. They also had the advantage of working with students of different interests and ability levels, home backgrounds, and future plans. They were learning in a pluralistic setting and, we could assume, they were learning to appreciate and respect differences.

In junior high English classes, there were no significant differences between track levels and the heterogeneous groups with regard to student satisfaction. However, significant differences were found in math classes. Heterogeneous classes tended to have more students with higher levels of satisfaction than did tracked classes.

Our data seemed to corroborate the findings of the High School and Beyond Study.[15] That is, students in high-track classes at school A are likely to have more in common with high-track students at school B than with students in low-track classes in their own school.

Table 6.4

Characteristics of Vocational Programs and Race/Ethnicity
of Students Enrolled in Junior High Schools

CONTENT TYPE	Regular School Class		Extended time/Off Campus	
	White Schools	Non-white/ Mixed Schools	White Schools	Non-white/ Mixed Schools
Business	Vista(1)[a]	Rosemont(1)[a]		
		Newport(1)[d]		
		Laurel(1)[b]		
		Manchester(1)[c]		
Trade Preparation				Fairfield(6)[c]
Military				
Agriculture				
Home	Vista(1)	Rosemont(1)[c]		
Economics	Crestview(1)	Newport(2)[d]		
	Woodlake(1)	Palisades(2)[b]		
	Atwater(1)	Laurel(1)[c]		
	Bradford(1)	Manchester(2)[c]		
	Euclid(1)			
General	Vista(1)	Rosemont(1)[c]		
Industrial	Crestview	Newport (3)[d]		
Arts	Woodlake(1)	Palisades(1)[b]		
	Atwater(2)	Manchester(1)[b]		
	Bradford(3)			
	Euclid(1)			
Consumer/ Career/Misc.	Bradford(1)	Palisades(1)[d]	Vista(1)	

---

a. school name (number of distinct courses offered)
b. mixed school, course enrollment predominantly white
c. enrollment predominantly non-white
d. mixed school, race/ethnicity of enrolled students not known

215

It is difficult to conceive of a less democratic, less egalitarian system. Students in high tracks felt superior, and many in lower tracks, we discovered, had feelings of inferiority. There was little common ground. Among students, friendships were formed with others in their own tracks. Many were deprived of getting to know others who had different needs, learning styles, life goals, values, and backgrounds. Carried to its extreme, a system of tracking in a school could alienate students whose schooling was preparing them to work with their hands from those who were preparing to work with their heads. Since track placement has been shown to relate to ethnicity and socioeconomic status, it would appear that tracking is a major factor in solidifying a system of social class in America.

These findings seem inevitably to lead to the hypothesis that heterogeneous grouping is an organizational pattern that would provide more equitable and more desirable educational experiences for junior high students than does a system of tracking. What stands in the way of such a reorganization is tradition and a fear that heterogeneous grouping will make teaching a far more difficult task.

Mixed ability classes need not be a burden for teachers, however. Indeed, many teachers already work primarily with heterogeneous groups of students. The management techniques for mixed-ability teaching already exist and can be mastered relatively easily: diagnostic pre-testing, within-class grouping on the basis of specific learning needs, student tutoring, and the use of learning centers, for example. While such techniques would tend to cut down on direct teacher talk and increase student decision-making and active learning, there would still be many times when the teacher could and should present material to the class as a whole.

It seems to me that a corollary to mixed-ability grouping is a reorganization of our so-called elective programs. We need to think through carefully what common experiences all students need and develop the school accordingly, thus eliminating the "headedness-handedness" dichotomy which is so prevalent in our junior highs. The idea of a unified arts program such as we found at Crestview Middle School and Vista Junior High seems a step in the right direction. As an aside,

216

it is interesting to note that most other western nations do just what is proposed here: they have junior secondary schools which serve early adolescents who are heterogeneously grouped and who have a common set of experiences.

It is a truism that "we teach as we were taught," and most teachers probably experienced some form of tracking as well as much "whole class" teaching. Little pre-service teacher training deliberately prepares teachers to work with mixed-ability classes, so non-tracking policies would call for changes in teacher training as well. The effects of such a policy change would be far-reaching. Our findings suggest that such a reorganization would be beneficial for students, stimulating for teachers, pedagogically sound, and ultimately healthier for our society as a whole.

Perceived Racial Prejudice

I have already discussed a number of variables having to do with the relationship between differentiation and ethnicity. The reader will recall from the previous chapter that there was a relationship between race/ethnicity and class climate scores. Minority students were more positive about their classes than white students but Hispanic students found them more difficult than did the Anglos. Also, earlier in the present chapter, the relationship between race/ethnicity and tracking was discussed. We found disproportionate numbers of minority students in lower tracks.

We also asked students and teachers to agree or disagree on a four-point scale to statements about teacher prejudice. The student item was, "Many teachers at this school don't like some students because of their race or color." Teachers responded to the statement, "Many teachers at this school are prejudiced."

Over 70% of all of the students at the twelve junior highs disagreed with the statement. They did not see the teachers as prejudiced. The student agreement with the statement was closely related to their ethnicity. That is, agreement was lowest at the all white schools. It ran from 13.7% at Woodlake to 22.8% at Crestview. Agreement was higher at the two

217

schools with nearly all minority students. At predominantly black Manchester it was 29.7% and at predominantly Hispanic Rosemont it was 35.2%. Agreement was highest at schools with mixed enrollments. Table 6.5 presents student data about perceived teacher prejudice from three schools with ethnically heterogeneous populations. We did not get data on the race/ethnicity of the fourth heterogeneous school in our sample, Newport.

Table 6.5

Student Agreement That Many Teachers Are Prejudiced --
By Ethnicity at Ethnically Heterogeneous Schools

| | Student Ethnicity | | | |
| | White | | Minority | |
School	% Agree	N	% Agree	N
Fairfield Junior High	29.6	189	42.9	198
Laurel Middle School	40.1	127	52.1	119
Palisades Middle School	30.0	263	50.9	169

At each ethnically heterogeneous school, a greater percentage of minority than white students perceived prejudice in many teachers. We did not probe this area farther with students. Thus, there remained many unanswered questions. Were these perceptions unique to these students and/or these teachers? Were they related to the location of the schools? Which teachers, white or minority, were perceived as being prejudiced? We did know that there were sizeable numbers of minority teachers at both predominantly minority and heterogeneous schools.

In summary, then, students at schools where both the student body and the teaching staff were ethnically mixed tended to perceive teacher prejudice more than did the students at schools where the student body and teaching staff were all or nearly all white. And it was the non-white students who perceived teacher prejudice in greater proportions.

I was quite surprised by the amount of agreement on the part of teachers to the statement, "Many teachers

218

at this school are prejudiced." It ranged from a low
of 9.4% at Manchester to an astounding 61.5% at Palisades (see Table 6.6). We must remember that Palisades
was the only school where there was busing for the
purpose of desegregation and that the faculty was
nearly half white and half black (58% - 42%). The
faculty had been integrated along with the students and
we observed that white and black teachers did not mix
unless assigned to--e.g., they ate separately. Thus,
the prejudice perceived was probably as much teacher to
teacher as teacher to student.

Table 6.6

Comparison of Student and Teacher Agreement
That Many Teachers Are Prejudiced -- By School

School	Students	Teachers
Atwater	19.2	22.7
Woodlake	13.7	22.2
Vista	14.6	41.7
Crestview	22.8	25.0
Bradford	18.9	25.9
Manchester	29.7	9.4
Euclid	14.4	33.3
Newport	34.1	31.1
Fairfield	37.5	17.6
Rosemont	35.2	29.3
Palisades	37.9	61.5
Laurel	45.9	38.1

On the other hand, at the all black school, Manchester, there was also a faculty which was nearly half
white and half black (44% - 56%). The faculty had been
segregated over time with attrition accounting for
fewer white teachers and a gradually larger percentage
of blacks. We observed no animosity between black and
white teachers at Manchester as we did at Palisades.

At the all-white schools, the percentage of teachers who perceived teacher prejudice was always greater
than the percentage of students who perceived it. In
two cases, Euclid and Vista, the difference was quite
large. Except for Palisades, teacher percentages of

agreement were lower than those of students at schools with predominately minority or mixed populations. The meaning of such trends was not readily obvious. However, it does seem safe to say that dealing with the physical aspects of desegregation is not enough to make it successful (e.g., busing). The racial prejudices of students, parents, administrators, community members and particularly teachers must be dealt with, too, if we want schooling not to be differentiated for the wrong reasons: race or ethnicity.

Differentiation and Sex

The reader will recall that in Chapter 5 the perceptions of school experience were different for boys and girls, with girls more positive. Girls saw teachers as better organized, more concerned, more enthusiastic, and as giving them more feedback on their work than did boys. Conversely, boys saw teachers as more punitive, authoritarian, and as showing favoritism. They also found school work more difficult.

There are other issues involved with these data. For instance, it is quite true that by the time they enter junior high, most girls have been socialized into a "proper" sex role. Having learned "how to be girls," they behave as everyone, including teachers, expect them to. They are generally more passive, more accepting of direction, less rowdy, and so forth. Quite possibly, if girls in larger numbers began behaving much more assertively, they might find themselves enjoying far fewer positive relationships with teachers and other school experiences. That is unlikely to happen since the rewards for passivity and being cooperative are just too appealing.

Differentiation by sex in the junior highs in our sample was obvious in some instances. Despite Title IX, for example, boys and girls were generally separated for P.E. and in most cases, boys had industrial arts while girls had homemaking.

In other ways, such differentiation was less obvious, but still there. Extracurricular activities were a good example. Table 6.7 shows that higher percentages of girls participated in all extracurricular activities except sports teams and student government. More boys participated in sports teams and

participation in student government was about equal for
girls and boys. These trends became even stronger at
the high school level as more and more girls did those
things deemed appropriate for them to do.

Table 6.7

Percentage of Students Participating in
Extracurricular Activities--Junior High and
High School by Sex

Activity	Percentages			
	Junior High		Senior High	
	Boys	Girls	Boys	Girls
Sports teams	60.3	45.4	52.4	33.0
Clubs	30.1	39.5	34.1	47.5
Student government	15.2	15.2	11.6	13.1
Music, Drama	36.1	44.1	22.0	33.3
Honor society	20.6	22.4	14.1	19.4
Service activities	29.5	32.6	27.8	37.3

Differentiation of Classroom Instruction

In the previous chapter, I presented data from
teachers which indicated that they only did a moderate
amount of individualizing in their classrooms by
varying instructional methods, grouping arrangements,
activities, objectives, content and/or materials for
different students. Also, the advocates of modern
instructional practice suggest that there should be
constant assessment and grouping and regrouping of
students for instruction.[18] Our data did not suggest
that such assessment and differentiation were practiced
very often in our sample of schools.

We did ask teachers how often they had students
work alone, with a small group, or with the whole
class. Usually, although teachers indicated that they
often had students work in all three modes, it was
clear that working alone was the most frequent.
However, there were differences from subject to subject, as shown in Table 6.8.

221

English and math teachers perceived that students worked alone most in their classes, followed by working with the whole class and then with a small group. Social studies teachers responded similarly except that they perceived that students worked alone and with the whole class about the same amount of time.

Teachers of the arts and foreign language indicated that students worked most with the whole class and somewhat less with a small group and alone. However, there was a good deal of disagreement among teachers of the arts, probably due to the fact that the category included so many kinds of classes--e.g., art, music, drama, creative writing.

Table 6.8

Teachers' Perception of Student Mode of Work
in Their Classes (By Subject)*

Mode of Student Work

Subject	Alone		With a Small Group		With the Whole Class	
	$\overline{X}$	sd	$\overline{X}$	sd	$\overline{X}$	sd
English	3.10	.61	2.69	.66	2.88	.69
Math	3.34	.67	2.62	.76	2.63	.78
Social Studies	3.00	.72	2.68	.64	3.00	.65
Science	2.68	.76	2.93	.80	2.55	1.81
Arts	2.60	.86	2.67	.65	3.07	1.02
Foreign Language	2.90	.74	2.90	.57	3.20	.63
Vocational Educ.	2.95	.75	2.86	.88	2.20	.76
OVERALL	2.99	.75	2.73	.73	2.74	.82

* Response $\overline{X}$ Categories: 1.00 - 1.49 = Never
1.50 - 2.49 = Not very often
2.50 - 3.49 = Often
3.50 - 4.00 = Always or most of the time

The science and vocational education teachers reported quite different patterns. Science teachers

222

most often indicated that students worked with a small group, followed by working alone and then with the whole class. Vocational education teachers said alone, with a small group and then with the whole class. In fact, they indicated that students did not very often work as a whole class.

These data substantiate what has been reported before. There appeared to be a good deal of whole class teaching and student work followed by students working alone: writing, reading, or doing work sheets. The conclusion has to be that, when all data are considered from the classroom level, there seemed to be little differentiation of instruction, at least in most classes and in most subjects.

Conclusions

In this chapter, I have dealt with perhaps the most controversial, if not the most insidious, practice in junior high education: ability grouping or tracking. The practice is based upon a set of assumptions widely held by educators which do not hold up under scrutiny.

Studies of tracking have consistently found correlations between race and socioeconomic status and track level. Minorities and the poor have been found in disproportionate numbers in the lower tracks. Also, there has been shown to be a relationship between class composition and achievement. That is, achievement has been found to be lower in classes composed mostly of minority and/or low SES students. Given this linkage from achievement to race and SES and then to tracking, it is understandable that tracking is considered to be controversial.

Existing research shows no gains in student achievement due to ability grouping. On the other hand, studies have shown that it can have negative effects on students placed in average and lower groups because they often get different content and even poorer teaching. In the final analysis, after all of the unsubstantiated claims for tracking are cleared away, what really emerges is that tracking makes life a bit easier for teachers and administrators.

Unfortunately, ability grouping reinforces the least desirable teaching techniques. When teachers

223

assume that they have a somewhat homogeneous group of students, they also assume that they need not further individualize instruction. Whole class teaching followed by students passively reading, writing, or completing an inevitable worksheet becomes the predominant mode of instruction. I would suggest that grouping students heterogeneously coupled with helping teachers learn to better deal with the obvious individual differences would be the most direct means of altering this mode.

We found ability grouping at all of the junior highs in our sample, particularly in academic areas. We found the linkages with ethnicity reported in other studies, also. We found that the experiences of students in the lower tracks were far less positive than those in the higher tracks on a variety of measures. Students in higher tracks saw their teachers as more enthusiastic, concerned, clear in teaching, and less punitive. Peer relations were reported to be more positive and general and academic self-concepts were higher, too.

Tracking substantially contributes to the "headedness-handedness" dichotomy so prevalent in our society. Students in the higher tracks are expected to work with their brains and go on to higher education and the professions. Students in lower tracks are expected to work with their hands and eventually enter a trade. At the junior high level, largely because of ability grouping, we significantly add to the unfortunate sorting of students which begins in elementary schools.

We found this "headedness-handedness" dichotomy had a relationship to student ethnicity, also. It has already been pointed out that we found disproportionate numbers of minority students in lower tracks. We did not find disproportionate numbers in vocational courses. However, we did find that general industrial arts and home economics dominated the vocational curriculum at the white schools in our sample while courses preparing students with specific occupational skills constituted a substantial proportion of the course offerings at the non-white and mixed schools.

We have become quite aware in the past two decades of the need to equalize educational opportunity for all students, including minority students. Much has been done at a global level. Even if the gains made through

224

desegregation and programs such at Title I and Head-start are not reversed by the political system either by intent or default, we will still need to move forward at an even deeper level. Certainly, the significant modification or elimination of tracking practices at the junior high level should be high on any agenda of action.

Conventional wisdom has generally held that hetero-geneous classes operate at lower levels and hold back the faster students. Our findings, however, showed that heterogeneous classes were much more similar, in both content and process, to upper average and high track classes.

These findings lead me clearly to the belief that junior highs should adopt heterogeneous grouping. Of course, tradition and a fear that it will make teaching more difficult stand in the way of such a change. However, mixed ability grouping need not be a burden for teachers. Appropriate classroom management tech-niques exist and can be mastered through in-service training. Also, pre-service training could equip new teachers with such techniques. I believe that a conscious policy of heterogeneous grouping is educa-tionally justifiable. Further, I believe that it would be more socially equitable, psychologically healthier for students and even professionally more challenging for teachers.

We also found the school experience different for boys and girls in our sample of junior highs. Not only were they generally separated in P.E. and for industri-al arts (boys) and homemaking (girls), but also, their experiences were often different when they were in the same class. Girls were far more positive about their experiences at school than boys. We attributed this to the fact that the girls were socialized to be more passive; and, as such, they were behaved in more "acceptable" ways since schools demand passivity. Teachers responded accordingly.

The elimination of tracking, prejudice, and sex stereotyping and the movement from passive to active schooling, all of which are at the heart of these inequitable and unconscionable practices, will not be easy. Such elimination should be high on our agenda for action, however.

Thus, the function of differentiation, which arose in an earlier time when the junior high school was first charged with taking on the non-college bound, seems outdated today. In its place, we need to consciously design programs which will bring together pre- and early adolescents with varying backgrounds, interests, aptitudes, abilities, personalities, and needs. Most of the rest of the western world has already moved in this direction with their junior secondary programs. The question is one of values. Do we value a healthy, democratic and pluralistic society or do we prefer a class society at least partially based on race, ethnicity, and/or sex? If we do prefer the former, we will have to do far more heterogeneous grouping at least up through the junior high school years, and probably beyond.

Chapter VI, Notes and References

1. William Van Til, et al., Modern Education for Junior High Schools (Second Edition), op. cit., p. 31.

2. Much of the material about tracking in this section is drawn from: Jeannie Oakes, Tracking and Ability Grouping in Schools: Some Constitutional Questions. I/D/E/A Study of Schooling Technical Report 19. Arlington, Va.: ERIC Document Reproduction Service, 1981.

3. See, for example: Glen Heathers, "Grouping," in R.L. Ebel, Encyclopedia of Educational Research (4th Edition). New York: McMillan, 1969. W. Shaefer and C. Oleka, Tracking and Opportunity. Scranton, Pa.: Chandler Publishing Co., 1971. B. Heyns, "Social Selection and Stratification Within Schools," American Journal of Sociology, Vol. 79 (1974), pp. 1434-1451.

4. James S. Coleman, et al., Equality of Educational Opportunity. Washington, D.C.: U.S. Government Printing Office, 1966.

5. W.G. Findley and M.M. Bryan, Ability Grouping: 1970 Status, Impact and Alternatives. Athens, Ga.: University of Georgia Press, 1971.

6. Jeannie Oakes, Tracking and Ability Grouping in Schools, op. cit., p. 7.

7. Most of this section is drawn from Jeannie Oakes, Tracking Policies and Practices: School by School Summaries. I/D/E/A Study of Schooling Technical Report 25. Arlington, Va.: ERIC Document Reproduction Service, 1981.

8. See, also: Benjamin S. Bloom, Stability and Change in Human Characteristics. New York: John Wiley & Sons, 1964.

9. Jeannie Oakes, A Question of Access: Tracking and Curriculum Differentiation in a National Sample of English and Mathematics Classes. I/D/E/A Study of Schooling Technical Report 24. Arlington, Va.: ERIC Document Reproduction Service, 1981.

10. See, for example: Baruk Rosenshine and N. Furst, "Research on Teacher Performance Criteria." in B.O. Smith (Ed.) Research in Teacher Education. Englewood Cliffs, N.J.: Prentice-Hall, 1971.

11. Jeannie Oakes, A Question of Access, op. cit., p. 191.

12. Jeannie Oakes, Limiting Opportunity: Student Race and Curricular Differences in Secondary Vocational Education. I/D/E/A Study of Schooling Technical Report 28. Arlington, Va.: ERIC Document Reproduction Service, 1981.

13. At this school, these students were already identified as "handed." They were essentially being prepared to leave school. The school officials perceived this as a very positive thing since the students would have a "saleable skill."

14. Jeannie Oakes, ibid., p. 15.

15. National Center for Educational Statistics, High School and Beyond. Washington, D.C.: U.S. Government Printing Office, 1981, p. 1.

16. John B. Carroll, "A Model of School Learning," Teachers College Record, 64:723-33,1963 and Benjamin S. Bloom, Human Characteristics and School Learning. New York: McGraw Hill, Inc., 1976.

CHAPTER VII

SOCIALIZATION

Introduction

Van Til and his colleagues state that socialization is an aim of junior high school education. They define that aim as:

"...To provide increasingly for learning experiences designed to prepare pupils for effective and satisfying participation in the present complex social order, and to adjust themselves and contribute to future developments and changes in that social order."[1]

The definition is so broad that it could include about everything done in the junior high. In fact, it is difficult to see how the function can be attributed to the junior high alone. It should be argued that socialization, as defined here, is an aim of all schooling.

Most educators, and lay persons for that matter, would have no difficulty with the concept or the definition. They would probably suggest that students are equipped by schools with basic skills which allow them to participate in and contribute to society. They might even suggest that education for citizenship is a major feature of schooling, particularly in the social studies.

It is my contention that schools, including junior high schools, in fact, do socialize students. However, much of that socialization is not part of the planned curriculum. Rather, it is embedded deeply in what Sarason calls the "regularities" of schooling. These regularities are part of the structural arrangements of schools that are so taken for granted that they seem beyond question.[2]

However, such regularities should not go unquestioned for many of them are harmful to the development of individual students and have effects which are

229

directly contrary to what we say schooling should accomplish.

For example, in Chapter 6, we saw how tracking practices contribute to the maintenance of the existing social class structure in the United States by sorting minority and poor students into low track classes where knowledge and skills gained tend to prepare them for manual occupations and preclude them from the advantages associated with higher education. We also saw how reluctant school people were to discuss this regularity.

Tracking certainly has the effect of socializing individuals into their ultimate roles in society. However, the outcomes of tracking practices seem a long way from the idealized definition of socialization provided by Van Til. In fact, what socialization actually means is that the schools prepare students for their adult role in society by teaching them the norms, attitudes, and values of the adult society and by sorting them into adult roles. For many students, this does not amount to "satisfying participation" as suggested by Van Til and his colleagues. Actually, the opposite is true. Options are limited and participation in the complex social order is minimized for far too many.

I will not return to a discussion of tracking practices in this chapter. It was discussed thoroughly enough in Chapter 6. Neither will I discuss again the fact that the schools socialize boys and girls into their respective sex roles. Suffice it here to remind the reader that in both Chapter 5 and Chapter 6 I discussed how expectations for boys and girls were often quite different, with girls generally more passive, more accepting of direction, less rowdy and, in fact, more positive toward school.

I will return first to a discussion begun in Chapter 5 about the preoccupation of teachers and the school with control. The school socializes students to believe in the need for external authority and, I would hypothesize, this is one reason why there is an apparent lack of self-reliance, self-discipline, and internally generated motivation in many of our youth and throughout much of our society.

Following a discussion of the controlling nature of
schools, I will examine the relationships of students
with their peers, with specific reference to such
things as competition and cliquishness. Also, I will
explore student perceptions of who the most popular
students were. The power and importance of the peer
culture at the junior high level has been recognized
for many years. The examination of these variables
gives some insights into how students in our sample saw
this culture.

I will briefly describe student, teacher, and
parent perceptions of student attitudes toward learning. While the peer culture holds strong attraction
for most students, the same cannot be said for learning.

Next, I will examine responses from students,
teachers, and parents to items about one contemporary
and controversial issue, desegregation of schools.
Several of the items were arranged in order from
general (support for desegregation) to specific (willingness to be bused to accomplish desegregation).
Comparison of responses to these items gives us some
idea of the social press upon young people regarding
such an issue.

Most people acknowledge the fact that the peoples
of the world have become interdependent. The question
remains, though, as to the role of the school in
teaching about this interdependence and in the development of attitudes of students toward other peoples and
nations. In this chapter, I will examine data about
the global attitudes of students, teachers, and parents. Also, I will report on items administered to
students in our schools designed to measure their
global knowledge.

Following all of this, I will return to the issues
of the school's socialization role, what it is, and
perhaps what it might better be. The chapter ends with
recommendations drawn from this discussion.

The School As A Controlling Place[3]

A Study of Schooling yielded a variety of information about the use of time in classrooms. We felt this
was important because of the attention which has been

focused on time as a factor in student learning.[4] We have teachers' perceptions of the approximate percentage of class time spent on instruction, routines, and getting students to behave. Students rank ordered the three categories according to which took the most, the next most, and the least amount of time: daily routines, learning, getting students to behave. Observers noted the percentage of class time spent in instruction, routines, behavior, or socializing.

Junior high students reported that learning took the most time (62.5%), while they said that getting students to behave took the next most (24.2%), and routines the least (12.4%). The mean rankings for time on learning were generally greater in academic classes and a good deal higher for foreign language. P.E. was highest on routines and second highest on behavior, while arts was highest for time spent on behavior.

There were moderate negative correlations between track level and student ratings of time on learning. As might be expected, as track level got higher more students rated instruction as taking more time and behavior as taking less.

In general, the junior highs that ranked highest in terms of the mean for time on learning were predominantly white schools, while the schools that ranked lowest were racially mixed or minority schools. Conversely, the order of school means for behavior showed the opposite trend. The racially mixed or minority schools had higher mean scores and the white schools had lower mean scores. Differences were not very great, however (see Table 7.1).

Teachers reported that around 70% of class time was spent on instruction, about 13% on behavior, and about 14% on routines. Evidently, teachers perceived that there was also activity that did not fall into these three categories. As with students, the perception of teachers was that most time was spent on instruction in the academic areas (see Table 7.2). Also, as with students, foreign language teachers had higher mean ratings for time spent on instruction than did teachers of other subjects. However, math and social studies teachers had the highest ratings for time spent on behavior.

Table 7.1

School Mean Rankings of Junior High Students'
Perceptions of Proportionate Time Spent on Learning,
Behavior, Routines

Learning				Behavior			
School	$\overline{X}$	sd	N	School	$\overline{X}$	sd	N
Vista	2.72	.55	934	Manchester	2.08	.82	1008
Woodlake	2.66	.63	779	Fairfield	1.95	.81	679
Euclid	2.65	.58	366	Newport	1.88	.77	898
Atwater	2.58	.66	519	Laurel	1.84	.80	568
Palisades	2.58	.64	695	Rosemont	1.82	.81	822
Crestview	2.55	.64	660	Palisades	1.81	.77	693
Newport	2.54	.66	899	Crestview	1.81	.80	660
Fairfield	2.46	.71	678	Bradford	1.80	.80	949
Bradford	2.45	.70	947	Woodlake	1.79	.73	781
Laurel	2.45	.72	562	Atwater	1.77	.76	522
Rosemont	2.39	.73	823	Euclid	1.75	.79	366
Manchester	2.32	.74	1003	Vista	1.72	.70	936
Total	2.52	.68	8865	Total	1.84	.79	8882

Routines

School	$\overline{X}$	sd	N
Rosemont	2.73	.76	815
Laurel	1.70	.73	563
Bradford	1.66	.74	946
Atwater	1.62	.67	523
Euclid	1.61	.63	368
Crestview	1.60	.69	661
Palisades	1.60	.69	694
Manchester	1.58	.72	1007
Newport	1.57	.71	899
Vista	1.54	.64	938
Woodlake	1.53	.63	782
Fairfield	1.52	.70	680
Total	1.60	.70	8876

Response categories: 3.0 = Most amount of time
2.0 = Next most amount of time
1.0 = Least amount of time

233

Table 7.2

Teacher Perceptions of Percentage of Class Time
Spent on Instruction -- by Subject

Subject	%	N
Foreign Language	80.0	12
English	75.6	86
Social Studies	69.2	51
Math	68.6	69
Arts	68.0	46
Science	67.8	45
Vocational Education	67.3	49
Physical Education	60.6	34
Overall	69.5	393

There appeared to be no relationship in the teacher report between race or ethnicity of the student body and time spent on instruction. Highest mean scores were reported at Vista and Laurel and the lowest at Rosemont and Euclid. However, the racially mixed or minority schools tended to have higher mean scores from teachers with regard to time spent on behavior.

There were two observation measures of how time was spent in classrooms. The Five Minute Interaction measure (FMI) recorded teacher behavior only, and the Snapshot described what everyone in the classroom was doing. Both measures suggested that about three-quarters of class time was used for instruction. According to the FMI, about 3% was devoted to behavior, about 18% was recorded for routines, and about 2% for socializing.

The subject and school patterns for the observation data were somewhat different from student and teacher reports. Foreign language was still perceived as having most instruction. However, the academic/non-academic dichotomy was not as pronounced for either instruction or behavior. Neither did observers at schools particularly see less time spent on instruction nor more on behavior at schools with minority or mixed populations. Overall, observers saw more time spent on

234

instruction and less on behavior than did students or teachers.

Generally, junior high teachers reported that they had a lot of control over decisions about their teaching and planning. Our data supported the image of the teacher as quite autonomous in the classroom. There was an overall teacher control scale and scores on this scale varied a good deal form school to school. There were also subject differences with arts and math teachers perceiving most control and P.E. teachers the least.

While teachers appeared to support the need for and the desirability of their control of students and classroom events, they were not extreme in this view. Teacher control scale scores, averaged at the school level, varied between mild and moderate agreement.

Our data suggested that classrooms were settings where teachers perceived they were largely, but not completely, in control and where students perceived that they complied with teachers' requests. Our observation data did not suggest that there was much punishment, either. Junior high classrooms were basically well-controlled settings and instruction occupied most of the time.

Actually, this reality was quite in line with conventional wisdom, with standard expectations for schooling. At one point in my career, I was interviewed for a position as a junior high principal. Prior to the interview I prepared myself to answer a host of questions about curriculum and staff relations. However, the first question I received from a superintendent member of the interview committee was, "What are your views on student discipline?" And he wasn't looking for any nonsense answer about having an interesting, active, and challenging program. He wanted to know how I proposed to <u>control</u> the students.

That such expectations are common was shown in our data, too. We had students, teachers, and parents identify what they considered to be problems at their schools. On the average, the mean score for "student misbehavior" was the highest of all problems for all three groups. In addition, the mean for "teacher discipline" was fifth ranked (of 13 possible choices) by parents and sixth ranked (of 16 possible choices) by teachers. The mean score for students placed it a low tenth of twelve possible choices. Interestingly, the problem "too many rules and regulations" was sixth ranked by students.

There were only four schools where the mean score for student misbehavior did not rank first among all groups as a problem. At Euclid, the mean response for drug/alcohol abuse ranked first for parents. At Rosemont, Laurel, and Bradford, teacher mean scores for student misbehavior ranked fourth, third, and fourth respectively. The reader will remember that Bradford was the school where teachers were quite proud of their new "get tough" policy.

This orientation toward control is greater at the junior high level than at either the elementary or high school levels. This is due to the fact that pre- and early adolescents are at such an active developmental stage. However, I would argue that added control is the opposite of what is needed. At this stage, students need to learn self-control and this can best be done through active involvement in learning, experimentation, participation in decision-making, and self-evaluation. Because of tradition and conventional wisdom, this aspect of socialization is a very hard one to change.

Engstrom, in his analysis of class climate variables from the Study, found a number of relationships which tend to suggest that emphasis upon control contributes negatively to a host of important aspects of schooling at the junior high level.[5] For example, he found that teachers who believed in greater teacher control and less student participation were viewed quite negatively and were seen by students as less capable in their instructional practices, and their classes were seen as more difficult.

There were two types of classes in which teachers spent a lot of time on controlling behavior. In one type, the teacher expected relatively less homework and spent less time on instruction. Students in these classes perceived these classes as more apathetic, cliquish, and dissonant. They also saw them as having less warmth from the teacher, as having less peer esteem, and as having poorer instructional practices. In the second type, in addition to spending a lot of time on behavior, the teachers reported being better prepared and expected more homework. Students in these classes perceived their classes negatively, just as the first group, and they also found the classes more difficult. Such data strongly suggest that teacher preoccupation with behavior produces a negative class climate.

Peer Relationships

There were four class climate scales which measured student perceptions of their relationships with their peers: Peer Esteem, Student Competitiveness, Classroom Dissonance, Student Cliquishness.

There were seven items which combined to form a Peer Esteem Scale:
-- I help my classmates with their work.
-- If I am absent, my classmates help me to catch up on what I missed.
-- I like my classmates.
-- I like working with other students in this class.
-- In this class, people care about me.
-- If I had trouble with my work, most of my classmates would help me.
-- My classmates like me.

In general, as might be expected, students had positive feelings about their classmates. They felt that their peers were likable, cared for them, and were helpful. As can be seen from the standard deviations in Table 7.3, there was little variance from class to class.

There were four items which were clustered to form a scale of student competitiveness:
-- There is a lot of competition in this class.
-- In this class, students compete with each other for good grades.
-- When I'm in this class, I feel I have to do better than other students.
-- Students in this class feel they have to do better than each other.

Junior high classes, on the average, had Student Competitiveness scores which fell at about the middle of the response range. As with Peer Esteem, the standard deviation suggests similarity in scores from class to class.

237

Table 7.4

Student Peer Relationships

Scale	X̄	sd	N
Peer Esteem	2.96	0.21	369
Student Competitiveness	2.48	0.25	367
Student Cliquishness	2.79	0.27	368
Classroom Dissonance	2.30	0.44	368

Response categories: 1.00 - 1.49 = Strongly disagree
1.50 - 2.49 = Mildly disagree
2.50 - 3.49 = Mildly agree
3.50 - 4.00 = Strongly agree

Students perceived somewhat more cliquishness than competitiveness in their classrooms. However, these scores were not very high. Scores were similar across classes, too. It would appear that the classroom was not the place to spend time with friends. Most socializing obviously occurred outside of class. In fact, in response to a separate item, "It is easy to make friends at this school," over 70% of the students at each school agreed. Items in the Student Cliquishness Scale were:
-- Some groups of students refuse to mix with the rest of the class.
-- Certain students stick together in small groups.
-- When we work in small groups, many students work only with their close friends.

There were three items which made up the Classroom Dissonance Scale:
-- The students in this class fight with each other.
-- The students in this class argue with each other.
-- Students in this class yell at each other.

Students generally disagreed with the classroom dissonance items. Although the standard deviation was slightly higher than for other scale scores, it was still low enough to indicate common scores across classes.

In summary, then, we can characterize the junior high classes in our Study as ones where the students felt positively about each other, where there was a modest amount of cliquishness, and where competitiveness was only moderate. We have seen from the data presented that the peer relationships _within_ the classrooms tended to be much like the teacher-student relationships. On the average, they were neither strongly positive nor strongly negative. Neutral is the only word that keeps returning to describe aspects of the classroom.

We live in a world badly in need of people who can work together, who can cooperate with each other to solve the many problems that are faced collectively. However, in our junior high classrooms we found teachers and organizational patterns which encouraged independent learning and dependence upon teacher direction. Far more could be done to develop cooperative learning and problem solving.

We did ask students who the most popular students were. Clearly, the norms of the greater society were reflected in their responses. We are bombarded daily from the media about the value of youth and beauty and sure enough, on the average, "good looking students" were chosen by the greatest percentage as the most popular (36.8%).

Not surprisingly, the second greatest percent said "athletes" (23.1%), followed by "gang members" (14.8%), "smart students" (13.5%), "members of student government" (8.4%), and "wealthy students" (3.4%).

Figure 7.1 shows the four basic response patterns at the 12 schools. The most common pattern was found at four schools (Vista, Crestview, Fairfield, Bradford). At those schools, the pattern was the same as the overall pattern: the greatest percent of response was for "good looking students," followed by "athletes" and then "gang members." The second most common pattern was found at three schools (Newport, Woodlake, Atwater). There "good looking students" and "athletes" were followed by "members of student government." At Palisades and Laurel, the greatest percent of students chose "good looking students," and "smart students." At Euclid, "athletes" was chosen by the greatest percent. Interestingly, and not common in much of our data, there seemed to be a regional pattern to these

239

responses. That is, schools in the same region of the country had similar responses (i.e., Vista and Crestview, Woodlake and Atwater, Palisades and Laurel).

Pattern A - Good Looking Students, Athletes, Gang Members

Vista
Crestview
Fairfield
Bradford

Pattern B - Good Looking Students, Athletes, Members of Student Government

Newport
Woodlake
Atwater

Pattern C - Good Looking Students, Smart Students

Palisades
Laurel

Pattern D - Athletes, Good Looking Students, Smart Students

Euclid

Pattern E - Smart Students, Athletes, Good Looking Students

Rosemont

Pattern F - Gang Members, Smart Students, Good Looking Students

Manchester

Figure 7.1 The Most Popular Students

The two outstanding exceptions were Rosemont and Manchester. At Rosemont, the greatest percent of the totally Hispanic, low SES population chose "smart students" (37.6%), expressing the cultural value of

240

education as a way of getting ahead in the greater
society. At all black, middle SES Manchester, by far
the greatest percent chose "gang members (53.3%),
followed by "smart students" (18.1%). "Athletes" was a
distant fourth (6.2%).

Clearly, the majority of junior high students in
our sample were well socialized to the belief that, if
you wanted to be popular, you should be a good looking
athlete and a member of the "gang." Some things
haven't changed much for early adolescents over the
past several decades.

Attitudes Toward Learning

While peer culture was found to be a strong attraction for students, the same could not be said of the
learning atmosphere. We asked students, teachers, and
parents to respond on a four point agree/disagree scale
to the following item, "Many students at this school
don't care about learning."

On the average, all three groups mildly agreed with
the statement. Agreement was the greatest for teachers
and least for parents. The range of response from
school to school was quite a bit for teachers. Teachers at Fairfield strongly agreed with the statement
while teachers at Woodlake actually disagreed. Except
at Euclid where students disagreed with the statement,
the range of responses across schools was not too great
for students. A similar pattern existed for parents
except for those at Woodlake and Euclid where, on the
average, they disagreed.

As can be seen from Table 7.4, there were four
distinct patterns found at the schools for this item.
In the first pattern (Fairfield, Crestview, Atwater),
teacher agreement with the item was greatest followed
by student agreement and then parent agreement. At
Pattern Two schools (Laurel, Bradford, Rosemont),
teacher agreement was the greatest but student and
parent mean scores were about the same. At Pattern
Three schools (Manchester, Vista, and Euclid), teacher
and student means scores were about the same and parent
agreement with the statement was somewhat less.
Finally, at Pattern Four schools (Newport, Palisades,
Woodlake), student agreement with the item was the

241

greatest followed by teacher and parent agreement which were about equal.

Table 7.5

Agreement That Students Don't Care About Learning

	Students			Teachers			Parents		
	$\overline{X}$	sd	N	$\overline{X}$	sd	N	$\overline{X}$	sd	N
Pattern One									
Fairfield	3.05	.91	428	3.59	.61	34	2.87	.95	214
Crestview	3.00	.95	405	3.12	.79	32	2.83	.92	253
Atwater	2.79	.88	310	2.95	.78	22	2.59	.86	153
Pattern Two									
Laurel	3.01	1.05	242	3.47	.75	21	3.05	.94	78
Bradford	2.98	.94	514	3.22	.70	27	2.89	.99	208
Rosemont	2.94	1.07	544	3.26	.88	42	3.00	1.03	144
Pattern Three									
Manchester	2.98	.97	632	3.03	.99	32	2.78	1.00	282
Vista	2.71	.89	648	2.77	.86	48	2.53	.90	407
Euclid	2.48	.93	126	2.50	.90	12	2.20	.94	40
Pattern Four									
Newport	3.01	.92	680	2.91	.81	57	2.92	.91	242
Palisades	2.85	.92	439	2.72	1.01	40	2.69	.97	288
Woodlake	2.71	.88	425	2.37	1.04	27	2.44	.89	279
Total	2.90	.95	5388	3.00	.90	394	2.73	.96	2588

Response categories: 1.00 - 1.49 = Strongly disagree
1.50 - 2.49 = Mildly disagree
2.50 - 3.49 = Mildly agree
3.50 - 4.00 = Strongly agree

Special note has to be made of teacher responses at Pattern One and Pattern Two schools, particularly Fairfield. Not only was teacher agreement that students don't care about learning strongest at these schools; but, also, the smaller standard deviations indicated that the range of agreement within each school was narrow. There were fewer dissenters from this viewpoint. Perhaps what existed at these schools, at least in part, was a kind of self-fulfilling prophecy. Teachers did not feel that students cared about learning, treated students accordingly, and students came to not care about learning. Other data at Fairfield which showed a good deal of student and teacher dissatisfaction seemed to at least partially confirm this.

Attitudes About Desegregation and Racial Prejudice[6]

We asked students, teachers, and parents a series of questions about desegregation and, more specifically, about busing for desegregation. The response patterns were interesting because (1) they changed from item to item as the questions became less general and more specific to the individual's own participation in desegregation/busing, and (2) students were more positive than either teachers or parents. That is, they favored desegregation more.

We asked students to agree/disagree on a four-point scale with the statement, "I think students of different races or colors should go to school together." On the average, over three-quarters of the students agreed and the range of agreement was from 88.7% at Woodlake to 62.8% at Crestview.

Overall, non-white students seemed slightly more receptive to the idea of desegregation than white students. Further, there was a definite and related pattern in the school-by-school responses (see Table 7.5). That is, the greatest agreement was found at the two all-white schools where there was no chance that desegregation would actually take place in the near future (Woodlake, Euclid). The lowest level of agreement was found at the four all-white schools where there were sizable black populations in a neighboring large city and where there was some discussion of metropolitan busing plans (Atwater, Vista, Bradford, Crestview). In between were all the schools with minority or mixed populations.

Teachers and parents were asked to agree or disagree with a comparable statement, "Schools should be desegregated." Teacher responses were only slightly less positive than students, with about 70% agreeing. The range of responses was from 90.6% at Manchester to 47.9% at Vista. The school-by-school pattern was similar to the pattern of student response, too. Also,

243

a smaller percentage of teachers than students at the two schools with large Hispanic populations agreed. At Fairfield, Vista, and Euclid there was a difference of over 20 percentage points between student and teacher responses. Teachers at these schools were far less favorable to desegregation than their students.

Table 7.6

Schools Should Be Desegregated
% of Agreement

School	Students	Teachers	Parents
Palisades	80.2	89.8	74.2
Manchester	78.5	90.6	72.4
Woodlake	88.7	81.5	60.3
Laurel	76.9	75.0	61.4
Newport	77.9	75.4	56.4
Fairfield	79.1	58.8	56.8
Euclid	85.0	50.0	51.4
Rosemont	78.7	65.8	47.5
Atwater	73.6	72.8	35.7
Bradford	68.0	66.7	34.8
Crestview	62.8	64.5	34.1
Vista	70.2	47.9	29.6
Average	76.2	70.3	49.3
N	5505	390	2546

Overall, just fewer than half of the parents agreed with the statement. The range of responses was from 74.2% at Palisades to 29.6% at Vista. Again, more positive responses were from minority or mixed schools. The levels of disagreement were quite high from parents at schools where there was a perceived threat of busing to achieve desegregation with neighboring cities. An interesting response came from Rosemont, an all-Hispanic school. There, over half of the parents disagreed with desegregation.

The next desegregation statement we asked students to agree or disagree with was, "I think students should be bused so that students of different races or colors can go to school together." On the average, just over half of the students agreed with this statement. The range of agreement was from 71.4% at Woodlake to 29.0% at Crestview. At every school, percentages of agreement were smaller for this item than for the previous one and school rankings in terms of agreement were similar with two exceptions. Rosemont ranked much higher on this item than on the more general one and Manchester ranked much lower. In general, there was more agreement with this item at the minority and mixed schools (see Table 7.6).

Table 7.6

Students Should Be Bused to Achieve Desegregation
% of Agreement

School	Students	Teachers	Parents
Palisades	69.7	27.3	38.6
Woodlake	71.4	40.0	12.7
Manchester	50.0	32.3	32.1
Laurel	69.2	28.6	25.6
Rosemont	69.1	17.0	27.5
Newport	49.5	21.9	24.3
Fairfield	65.0	5.8	21.0
Euclid	61.4	16.7	12.9
Atwater	53.3	9.1	5.3
Bradford	38.3	22.2	3.0
Crestview	29.0	18.7	4.0
Vista	30.2	4.2	3.6
Average	52.7	19.5	-
N	5444	138	-

Teachers were far more negative about busing for desegregation than students. The statement they and parents were asked to agree or disagree with was, "Students should be bused to achieve desegregation." Overall, only 20% agreed with the statement. The range was from 40.0% at Woodlake to 4.2% at Vista. Except for Woodlake, the pattern previously established was continued with this item. That is, there was generally greater agreement at minority and mixed schools than at all-white schools.

245

While teachers were more negative than students when it came to busing for desegregation, parents were even more negative. Overall, only 16.8% agreed that there should be busing for desegregation. The range was from 38.6% at Palisades to 30% at Bradford. The pattern of more agreement at minority and mixed schools continued.

The third agree-disagree statement had to do with willingness to be personally involved with busing. The statement for each data source was slightly different, as follows:

Students - I would be willing to take a bus to a different school so that school could have students of more than one race or color.

Teachers - I would publicly support busing to achieve desegregation.

Parents - I would allow my child to be bused to achieve desegregation.

The student response to this item, on the average, was negative with 63% disagreeing. The range of agreement was from 56.4% at Laurel to 18.9% at Vista (see Table 7.7). Over half of the students at eight schools disagreed. Furthermore, with a choice of "mildly disagree" or "strongly disagree," at every school the highest percentage appeared in the "strongly disagree" column.

The familiar pattern of more negative responses from the all-white schools continued. Responses from white students in mixed schools were slightly more positive than those from white students in all-white schools. At Palisades, the one school where busing for desegregation was taking place, 44.2% of the white students and 60.2% of the black students agreed.

Overall, 80% of the teachers sampled disagreed with the statement about publicly supporting busing (57% strongly disagreed and 23% mildly disagreed). The range of agreement was from only 34.6% at Woodlake to 8.3% at Vista.

Only about 20% of the parent respondents said they would agree to allow their children to be bused to accomplish desegregation. The range of agreement was from 42.2% at Palisades to 5.3% at Bradford. Palisades and Manchester were the only schools where over 40% of the parents agreed that they would allow their children to be bused. There was already busing at Palisades, and Manchester was an all-black, urban school. Interestingly, parent agreement at these two schools was higher than teacher agreement to the comparable item. Both of the staffs were fairly well integrated. At the all-Hispanic school, Rosemont, only 25.2% of the parents agreed with the item.

Table 7.8

Personal Commitment to Support Busing For
Desegregation -- % of Agreement

School	Students	Teachers	Parents
Laurel	56.4	33.4	24.7
Palisades	50.3	30.0	42.2
Manchester	38.8	32.3	41.3
Woodlake	43.8	34.6	22.7
Rosemont	51.9	21.9	25.2
Newport	31.8	28.6	25.9
Fairfield	50.3	8.9	26.2
Euclid	43.6	16.7	15.8
Atwater	30.3	9.1	7.9
Crestview	19.8	15.6	5.9
Bradford	25.6	14.8	5.3
Vista	18.9	8.3	7.7
Average	36.9	21.2	-
N	5446	390	-

Three major themes emerged from these data. First, at a general level there was a good deal of agreement that desegregation was a good idea. However, there was disagreement with busing as a means of bringing desegregation about; and very few students, teachers, or parents indicated a willingness to make a personal commitment to busing.

Second, students were clearly the most positive toward the idea of desegregation and were the most willing to make a personal commitment to busing to facilitate desegregation. At all but four schools, over half of the students said that there should be busing. At no school did half or more of the teachers or parents agree that there should be busing to achieve desegregation. Teachers were the next most positive group, and only about half of the parents even agreed that schools should be desegregated.

Finally, there were differences in responses based upon the ethnicity of the respondents and the school situation. Minority respondents were generally more positive toward desegregation and busing than were white respondents. Also, white respondents at already racially or ethnically heterogeneous schools were more positive than white respondents at all-white schools. Whites at schools near cities with large minority populations where there was some talk of metropolitan busing were the most negative to both the idea of desegregation and the idea of busing.

The fact that students were more positive to desegregation could be taken as an indication that they were less prejudiced than the corresponding adults-- their teachers and their parents. Perhaps they were being socialized to newer, more tolerant racial atti- tudes.

Before accepting that hypothesis, we need to examine some additional data. For example, we asked students to agree or disagree on a four point scale with the following statement, "Lots of students at this school don't like other students because of their race or color." Nearly half of the students at the junior high level agreed with the statement. The range of agreement was from a low of 19.7% at Euclid to a high of 68.5% at Laurel.

Three patterns emerged from these data. First, levels of agreement were highest at mixed schools (Fairfield, Palisades, Newport, Laurel), followed by all-white schools, and then all-minority schools (Rosemont, Manchester). Second, they were also higher at the two low-SES all-white schools, both of which were close to large cities with large minority popula- tions (Crestview, Bradford). Third, responses of minority and white students at mixed schools were almost equal.

Another item in this cluster was one which asked students, teachers, and parents whether prejudice/ra- cial conflict was a problem at the school. The now

248

familiar patterns were apparent again. Agreement was higher for all data sources at the racially mixed and low-SES all-white schools.

All of these data pointed to some clear patterns. In schools in our sample that did not have heterogeneous populations, there was a tendency to deny that there was a problem. At all-white schools where there was the possibility of desegregation in the near future, a great deal of prejudice was perceived. And in those schools that did have heterogeneous populations, both white and non-white students perceived that racial prejudice existed. There was some hope for positive attitudes, as at Palisades, where there was busing for desegregation and where there was also a fairly strong commitment to desegregation on the part of students, teachers, and parents.

It is not enough just to bring students together. Physical desegregation has to be accompanied with efforts to change well-entrenched attitudes. We saw in Chapter 6 that there was still the perception of far too much racial prejudice in teachers, many of whom were supposed to be dealing with the prejudices of their students.

Further, we need to attack the regularities of schooling which promote the racial and ethnic separation of students physically and psychologically even while they are in attendance at the same school. Tracking, of course, is the major regularity which causes such separation.

Finally, we need a long-term commitment to the solution of a problem as complex as racial prejudice in our schools. Unfortunately, we seem to be retreating from the problem of desegregation. As a nation we are very much like the data sources at all-white Euclid, Atwater, and Woodlake in our sample. At those schools, there were no minorities and consequently no one perceived any prejudice. But that is only a way of avoiding the truth, isn't it. What we do to prepare young people during the next several years for living in a multi-ethnic, multi-racial world probably will determine the future of this nation for decades to come.

249

Global Knowledge and Ethnocentrism

We collected data about student, teacher, and parent attitudes toward foreign peoples, foreign countries, and toward the school's role in teaching about these things. I have labelled this construct "ethnocentrism." In addition, we collected data on students' knowledge of the world which I have referred to as "global knowledge."

We asked students twelve global knowledge questions. The average number of correct responses across the total sample (N=4656) was 4.68 or 39%. Junior high students in our sample knew very little about the world, at least as their knowledge was measured by our items.

The items were all multiple choice. Two of them had to do with the United Nations. They were:

To work for peace in the world, most countries belong to the:
_____ United Fund
_____ United States
___X___ United Nations (50.9%)
_____ United Kingdom
_____ I do not know

The United Nations:
___X___ Discusses world problems (48.3%)
_____ Controls international trade
_____ Governs all people on our planet
_____ Is part of America's government
_____ I do not know

Only about half of the junior high students responded correctly to these items.

Two other items tested student knowledge of Latin America. Only about one-third of the students responded correctly to these items. The items were:

Other countries depend most on Latin America for:
_____ Televisions and radios
_____ Cars and trucks
_____ Corn and wheat
___X___ Coffee and sugar (32.5%)
_____ I do not know

Latin America is:
```
_____  A large country
  X     A group of countries south of the United
        States (34.1%)
_____  An island
_____  A part of the United States
_____  I do not know
```

There were four questions which were concerned with
relationships among nations. The four concepts tested
for were: balance of power, disarmament, alliance, and
treaty. The items and the overall percentage of
correct responses are reported below.

When two or more nations have the same military
capability, it is called:
```
_____  An alliance
_____  Free trade
_____  Prosperity
  X     Balance of power (43.1%)
_____  I do not know
```

When countries give up their guns and weapons, it
is called:
```
_____  A treaty
  X     Disarmament (45.4%)
_____  Freedom
_____  Balance of power
_____  I do not know
```

A partnership between two or more countries is
called:
```
_____  A passport
  X     An alliance (36.8%)
_____  Literacy
_____  Free trade
_____  I do not know
```

An agreement between two countries might be called:
```
_____  Free trade
_____  Balance of power
  X     A treaty (56.7%)
_____  A passport
_____  I do not know
```

The topic of population was dealt with in three
items, as follows:

In which of the following nations is the population most rapidly outgrowing the supplies of food, clothing, and shelter?

```
_____  Japan
_____  Mexico
_____  Canada
___X__  India (36.7%) [7]
_____  I do not know
```

The movement of people from rural areas to the city is called:

```
_____  Mobilization
_____  Industrialization
___X__  Urbanization (35.6%)
_____  Mechanization
_____  I do not know
```

Over half the world's population is located in:

```
___X__  Asia (28.8%)
_____  Europe
_____  Africa
_____  The United States
_____  I do not know
```

The final question was:

People who live in the United States might speak:

```
_____  English
_____  Spanish
_____  Japanese
___X__  Any of the above (53.0%)
_____  I do not know
```

The average of correct responses varied considerably from school to school. Bear in mind that 12 questions were asked. At Vista, the average number correct was 6.10, highest of the twelve junior highs. The lowest average number correct was 2.66 at Laurel. Average scores at the all-white and higher SES schools tended to be better than at the minority and lower SES schools. Also, scores at middle schools which had sixth graders were lower than at junior highs without sixth graders.

We compared scores by sex, race, and grade level of the respondents. Boys, on the average, got more correct than girls, 5.01 to 4.32. White students had the highest scores, on the average (5.16), followed by

252

Asian (5.11), Mexican (3.72), and black students (3.48).

As might be expected, scores were progressively better as students advanced through the grades. The mean score for 6th graders in our sample was only 3.14 while it was 4.29 for 7th grade, 5.05 for 8th grade, and 6.06 for 9th grade. These data show the potential of the junior high years for the development of global knowledge. While even the 9th grade score was low, there was rapid advancement through the junior high years, and this with very little curricular emphasis upon global knowledge.

There were ten items which made up the ethnocentrism scale. Students were asked to strongly agree, mildly agree, mildly disagree, or strongly disagree with each item.

On the average, students were positive about aid for other peoples and nations of the world. Nearly 70% of them agreed that "Helping other countries is a good way to use our money." About the same percentage disagreed that "A country where people have too many children should not receive food or aid from the United States" and agreed that "The United States should share its food with other countries."

The two questions about American pre-eminence received different responses. Only slightly more than 30% agreed that "America is so great that it can solve all of the world's problems by itself." However, nearly 60% agreed that "The American people are the best in the world."

Similarly, the two questions about foreign influence received different responses. Only slightly more than one-third of the students in our sample agreed that "People from foreign countries should be prevented from living in the United States" while 56% said "The greatest danger to America comes from foreign ideas and countries."

Slightly fewer than one-third agreed that "Schools should not waste time teaching about other countries and people" and slightly more than one-third agreed "Schools should teach that our country is the best in the world."

253

Finally, nearly 90% of the students agreed that "Talking things over with another country is better than fighting."

Responses to the ten items were combined into an ethnocentrism scale score. With this score we were able to determine that ethnocentrism was greater at lower SES schools, that boys were slightly more ethnocentric than girls, that ethnocentrism declined somewhat as students advanced through the grades, and that ethnocentrism was greater in students who did not aspire to education beyond high school.

There were eleven items which measured teacher ethnocentrism. Parents also responded to four of these which had to do with the school's role in teaching about other people and nations of the world. Nearly 95% of both teacher and parent respondents agreed that "It is important that every child have the opportunity to study and learn about the political and economic systems of other countries." About 95% of the teachers and 90% of the parents agreed that "Schools should offer classes that will help students develop positive attitudes toward people from other countries." However, only about 40% of both teacher and parent respondents agreed that "Schools should teach students to place world citizenship ahead of national citizenship." About 63% of the teachers and 71% of the parents agreed that "Schools are not placing enough emphasis on patriotism or the flag." Finally, 55% of the teachers and about 60% of the parents agreed that "This school is doing a good job of teaching students about the political and economic systems of other countries."

The range of responses from school to school for each item was not too wide. On the average, the parents at the all-white schools tended to be slightly more ethnocentric in their responses than those at minority or racially mixed schools. This was not true of teachers, however. Responses to these five items were remarkably similar for teachers across all schools.

Teachers were quite ethnocentric, on the average, as their responses to the remaining six items showed. Nearly two-thirds agreed that "The United States is closer to being ideal than any other country has ever been." About 60% agreed that "The immigration of foreigners to this country should be kept down so that

254

we can provide for Americans first." Thirty-seven percent said that "Our country should not cooperate in any international trade agreements which attempt to better world economic conditions at our expense" and fewer than 30% felt that "If necessary, we ought to be willing to lower our standard of living to cooperate with other countries in getting an equal standard of living for every person in the world." Nearly one-half agreed with the statement, "A populous country should not receive food or aid from the United States until it can prove that it is working toward the control of its birthrate." Finally, only about 30% agreed that "It would be better to be a citizen of the world than of any particular country."

There were differences from school to school in teacher ethnocentrism as measured by our items. By far the most ethnocentric group was at Fairfield. Readers will remember that about half of the students at the school were Mexican-American but that over 90% of the faculty was Anglo. They will also remember that only slightly over half of the teachers at Fairfield Junior High agreed that schools should be desegregated.

Teachers at Rosemont, Palisades, Crestview, Atwater, and Euclid, on the average, were among the more ethnocentric as measured by our items. Least ethnocentric were teachers at Bradford, Newport, and Manchester. The common characteristics of these three schools seemed to be their urban settings and the fact that teachers were unionized and generally politically more liberal than teachers at other schools.

It seems fair to state that the junior highs in our Study were providing little in the way of global education. As we saw in Chapter 4, there were few examples of social studies courses which included much content other than the history or geography of the United States. Occasionally, there was coverage of the Western Hemisphere or Europe but even that was rare. Additionally, we saw that the global knowledge of students was poor.

Given the ethnocentric attitudes we found in teachers and parents, it is no wonder that this state of affairs existed. The global attitude items administered to students were different from those given to teachers and parents. Thus, no direct comparison was possible. However, based on the items we did use, students at every school did seem to be less ethnocentric than the adults there. Also, and despite all of the obstacles cited above, student ethnocentrism did appear to decline as students went through the grades. One wonders what could be accomplished if these obstacles could be overcome. Given the nature of our interdependent world, a good global education curriculum would appear to be desirable. Perhaps if one were developed, the social studies might not be perceived as one of the least interesting, least liked subjects as it was in our Study.

Conclusions

I began this chapter by presenting the idealized definition for socialization by Van Til and his colleagues which suggested that junior high learning experiences should be "...designed to prepare pupils for effective and satisfying participation in the present complex social order.$_9$.[and] contribute to... changes in that social order."

An examination of the data from A Study of Schooling verified that junior high students, indeed, were socialized, albeit not in line with this normative definition. Rather, it was found that there were many "regularities" of schooling, not part of the planned curriculum but taken for granted, which actually mitigated against the definition given above. That is, students were socialized but not for effective and satisfying participation in the social order, present or future. And certainly the emphasis was not upon change in the social order. In fact, the overriding message seemed to be, "Conform."

The evidence was quite varied and quite compelling. We saw, for example, that tracking practices contributed to the maintenance of the existing social class structure by sorting minority and poor students into low track classes where they were precluded from knowledge which would prepare them to move up through the social class structure. We also saw that male and female stereotypes were forced upon boys and girls. Further, the preoccupation with authority and control and the absence of the development of self-reliance, self-discipline, and internally generated motivation were documented in our sample of schools.

256

Much has been made of the fact that students of today are "turned off" to school. Our data tended to agree with this view in that, on the average, students, teachers, and parents all agreed to an item that stated, "Students don't care about learning." However, our data did show that junior high students were quite positive about their peers. When asked what the one best thing about school was, the greatest percentage of students at each school said, "My friends." Thus, the school seemed to have a strong social attraction for students while, at best, necessary learning was only tolerated because school was a place to go to be with friends.

Our data also showed that the junior high students in our sample were more positive about school desegregation than were their parents or teachers, and that they were less ethnocentric as well relative to their teachers and parents. However, we found that students had little knowledge of the world outside of the United States and that there was little being taught which would increase such knowledge. In short, students were also being socialized to be ethnocentric.

Teaching, controlling behavior, sexual stereotyping, racial prejudice, and ethnocentric curricula all play a part in the socialization of our young people. We may not wish to change the ways in which these things happen in our schools; however, I believe that such changes are imperative if we hope to have a vital and meaningful society, one in which all citizens participate effectively and with satisfaction.

Such changes will not be easy to bring about because they frequently require corresponding changes in deeply held beliefs, attitudes, and values. We delude ourselves if we avoid these basic issues in the name of being "value free." The fact is that tracking and the other socialization mechanisms I have discussed exist and are undergirded by definite sets of values.

A beginning strategy, albeit not an easy one to implement, would be to acknowledge the issues noted here and to discuss them openly at each school. It has probably been a long time since most school faculties, with their parent bodies, boards of education, or even state education officials have engaged in serious dialog about the purposes of schooling. Such serious dialog would tend to take away from our politicians the superficial use of schooling as a political issue. If schooling <u>does</u> continue to become politicized, it may well be because school people themselves, by not discussing the issues openly and often, have created a vacuum into which opportunistic politicians can easily move.

Also, we need to take every opportunity to globalize our curricula and to develop cross-cultural understanding. The social studies program is an obvious beginning point. Courses in world history, geography, economics, and politics should become a regular part of the curriculum and the focus should be upon relationships among and the interdependence of peoples. Further, other subjects should also be globalized. Placing emphasis upon the metric system; international sports, games and dances; and literature, music, art, and scientific contributions from other parts of the world can help make this happen. Also, wherever possible, experiences should be provided for students to work and otherwise interact with students of different cultural backgrounds. We live in a multi-cultural society and schools can easily take advantage of this fact. Because of the often sensitive and value-laden nature of intergroup relationships, such activities do need careful planning.

The strategies described here comprise only a minimal list. In Chapter 10, the concluding chapter of this book, there is a great deal more discussion of what our schools can do to help students become effective and satisfied participants in our society and contributors to needed changes in the social order.

It does seem to me that the socialization of our youth to passivity, ethnocentrism, and prejudice in a time of global interdependence truly puts our nation "at risk" far more than the rather superficial things pointed to by the recent National Commission on Excellence in Education.[10] It is time that we stop tinkering with our institutions, including our schools, and really face squarely the question of what this nation stands for. Correspondingly, we need to determine the contribution our schools should make to that vision.

Chapter VII, Notes and References

1. William Van Til, et al., <u>Modern Education for Junior High Schools</u> (Second Edition), op. cit., p. 31.

2. Seymour B. Sarason, <u>The Culture of the School and the Problem of Change</u>. Boston: Allyn and Bacon, 1971.

3. Much of the material in this section comes from Joyce Wright, <u>Teaching and Learning</u>, op. cit.

4. See, for example: Benjamin S. Bloom, "The New Direction in Educational Research: Alterable Variables." <u>Phi Delta Kappan</u>, Vol. 61, No. 6. (1980), pp. 382-385; Baruk Rosenshine, "Content, Time, and Direct Instruction." in P.L. Peterson and H.J. Walberg (Eds.) <u>Research on Teaching</u>. Berkeley, Ca.: McCutcheon, 1979; David E. Wiley, "Another Hour, Another Day: Quantity of Schooling, A Potent Path for Policy." <u>Studies in Educative Processes, No. 3</u>. Chicago: University of Chicago Press, 1973.

5. Gerald A. Engstrom, <u>An Examination of the Viability of Class Climate As a Useful Construct in Secondary Schools</u>, op. cit.

6. Much of the material in this section was drawn from an unpublished I/D/E/A report by Barbara Benham Tye, "Responses of Students, Teachers, and Parents To Five Questions About Desegregation and Busing," February, 1979.

7. This was the correct response at the time of the Study. Currently, the correct response would be Mexico.

8. Bradford was classified as suburban for the Study but it was located adjacent to a large, midwestern city.

9. William Van Til, et al., <u>Modern Education for Junior High Schools</u> (Second Edition), op. cit., p. 31.

10. National Commission on Excellence in Education, <u>A Nation at Risk: the Imperative for Educational Reform</u>, op. cit.

Introduction

At some point, the lucky individual realizes that there is more to life than preparation for the future. With that realization, the individual decides to live in the present tense and to explore the contemporary world with its accumulated knowledge, natural wonders, and intricate human relationships. I say "lucky" individual because many people never reach this point.

There are many reasons for our preoccupation with the future, for the notion that gratification must be postponed. At one level, throughout history, the idea of delayed gratification has made life a little more bearable for the poor, the ill, or the oppressed because they could at least look forward to a better afterlife. At another level delayed gratification has been a way of dealing with the young while they wait to grow to adulthood.

Our educational system strongly reflects this ethic of delayed gratification. Each level of schooling is perceived as preparation for the next--elementary school for junior high, junior high for high school, high school for college, college for graduate school, and graduate school for post graduate studies or on-the-job training. For some students, preparation for on-the-job training comes earlier in the sequence, now as early as high school.

The junior high school was established originally for just these purposes: (1) to prepare some students sooner for college, and (2) to prepare others for the world of work. Those purposes have been modified as a result of the extension downward of the age of compulsory school attendance. Now, the junior high is simply viewed as preparation for high school.

The aim most often suggested specifically for the junior high school is articulation. Van Til and his colleagues state it as "...to provide a gradual transition from pre-adolescent education to an educational program suited to the needs and interests of adolescent boys and girls."[1] In other words, one of the major aims of the junior high is to provide for the transition of students from the elementary school to the high school.

With most of the aims described prior to this one, and with the notable exception of differentiation, I have generally taken the position that they are valid but improperly carried out in some ways. In this case, that of articulation, I believe that the aim itself is not valid for the junior high. In fact, it is my contention that the emphasis upon articulation at the junior high level is dysfunctional to the program of the schools; and, worse, to the students the schools serve.

To begin with, the concept--at least as it is defined by Van Til--gives pre-eminence to the education of adolescents; and, thus, to the high school. The definition itself is not inaccurate. The high school years are considered more important by our society and by most school people, and decisions are made accordingly. For example, in describing the twelve junior highs in our Study, I noted that several of them were housed in old high school buildings. That is, when a school district had to build a new secondary school, it built a high school and used the old building as a junior high. In only two triples, Bradford and Manchester, did we find relatively modern junior highs built much later than the high school. Junior highs are often treated as younger brothers and sisters in families. They get the "hand-me-downs."

Junior highs are supposed to provide a "gradual" transition from elementary school to high school. However, only one of our twelve schools, Crestview, had any block-time or subject integration. All others, including those labelled as middle schools, were totally departmentalized like high schools. Students were tracked, and classroom experiences closely resembled those at the high school level except that classes were larger, options for students were fewer, and resources were generally not as available.

In the remainder of this chapter, I examine how various aspects of the junior high programs in our sample compared to those same aspects in our elementary and/or high schools. To begin with I return to the question of functions explored in Chapter 2. It is these data which most clearly tell us how today's students, teachers, and parents view the transitional role of the junior high in relationship to preparation for college, work, and other aspects of later life. In this regard, I also look at data on the future plans of junior high and high school students to see how they differ. I examine, along with these data, differences in student perceptions of counseling services. Actually, the underlying exploration in this section is the degree to which there is articulation regarding the vocational preparation of students.

The second and most comprehensive section of this chapter focuses upon a comparison of the classroom experiences of elementary, junior high, and high school students in our sample. Teaching practices, classroom affect, how time is spent, and issues of control are all examined and compared. It is here where we see the degree to which junior highs are even more controlling places than schools at other levels.

Third, I compare many of the social aspects of junior and senior highs including: (1) what students perceive as the one best thing about school, and (2) who the most popular students are. Here we see some of the real uniqueness of early adolescence.

Finally, an attempt is made to judge the degree to which junior highs are actually "transition" schools and some suggestions for the improvement of this role are given.

Functions of Schooling[2]

As we saw in Chapter 2, all groups in the junior high sample (teachers, parents, and students) perceived that the intellectual function of schooling received the most emphasis and the personal function the least.[3] Also, they all thought that the intellectual function should receive the most emphasis. They all also thought that there should be more emphasis upon the personal function. Such patterns were true at the elementary and senior high level of schooling, too.

In most ways the junior high and senior high data about functions were very similar. The pattern at the elementary schools differed in many ways from that at the secondary schools, however. Students and parents at several and teachers at <u>all</u> elementary schools expressed a preference for less emphasis on the intellectual function--even while saying it was the most important. All elementary data sources also perceived that the social function of schooling received less emphasis than did data sources at the secondary level.

While intellectual development was seen as the most emphasized apparent and ideal function, there was a shift through the levels to the other aims--mainly personal and vocational. This was particularly true of students.

Such a response is not hard to understand in light of our preoccupation with school as "preparation for life." The reader will recall in Chapter 4 how many junior high students responded to our one open-ended question by stating that the classes they were taking were important because they would help them "get a job." This utilitarian view of school grows from level to level of schooling and the junior high is truly "in the middle." In this sense, it clearly is seen as a transitional school. We asked both junior and senior high school students what they would probably do in the future vis-a-vis schooling. Possible responses ranged from "quit school as soon as possible" to "go to graduate school after college." Table 8.1 shows responses from the 5,222 junior high students and 7,014 high school students. The responses at both levels were almost identical. Clearly, future educational plans were pretty well understood and set as early as junior high.

Just over one-third of the respondents at both levels said that they would probably go to a college or university. Otherwise, there was a shift in less than 10% of the responses. Fewer students at the high school than at junior high level said that they didn't know or that they only expected to finish high school while more said that they expected to go to technical school or junior college.

We also asked students at all secondary schools to respond to three statements about the counseling services available to them. Responses were different at the junior and senior high levels. At the high school level, the most positive response was about help

264

for planning a career, followed by help for planning
the school program. Fewer high school students perceived that it would be easy to get help for a personal
problem. At the junior high level, it was help with
the school program, a personal problem, and planning a
career, in that order (see Table 8.2).

Table 8.1

Junior and Senior High Student Perceptions
of Their Probable Future Educational Plans

Response	Junior High %	Senior High %
Quit School As Soon As Possible	3.2	1.7
Finish High School	28.4	25.6
Go to Trade or Technical School	6.4	11.8
Go to Junior College	7.8	11.5
Go to a Four Year College or University	34.6	34.4
Go to Graduate School After College	8.0	7.0
Don't Know	11.6	8.0

Table 8.2

Perceived Ease of Getting Help From a Counselor

	% Agree	
	Junior High	High School
It is easy for me to get help from a counselor when planning my school program	68	66
If I have a personal problem, it would be easy for me to get help from a counselor	66	56
If I needed help planning for a career, it would be easy for me to get help from a counselor	64	69

265

Given the tremendous pressure on both junior and senior high students to plan for the future, it is appalling to think that from 30-40% of them did not perceive that it would be easy to get help from a counselor for this. We need not dwell here on the misuse of counselors as sub-administrators as glorified clerks. That was discussed at length in Chapter 5. The point is that while we insist that school is a "preparation" for adulthood, we provide inadequate counseling and guidance support for students. Clearly, some structure such as the teacher advisor program described in Chapter 5 is needed at both the junior and senior high levels.

The actual provision of vocational education programs varied greatly from school to school and from the junior high level to the senior high level. Table 8.3 shows the percentage of full-time equivalent staff members (FTEs) assigned to teach vocational classes at each secondary school. Nearly one-quarter of the teachers at the senior highs in our sample were vocational teachers, while only slightly more than 10% of junior high teachers were. The range at the high schools was from a low of 13% at Newport and Palisades to a high of 42% at Fairfield. At the junior high level the range was from only 4% at Laurel to 22% at Manchester.

There appeared to be no relationship between the amount of vocational education offered at junior and senior highs and the race/ethnicity of the students. However, there did appear to be a difference in kind. Vocational programs at all-white schools tended to focus on industrial arts and home economics which seemed appropriate for all students. Business courses at all-white schools stressed such topics as management, taxation, and the stock market. There were even such elite courses as aviation or marine technology available at one school. At another all-white school there was a course entitled "bachelor cooking."

In contrast, vocational programs at mixed or minority schools tended to focus on training for specific and often fairly low-level occupations: building maintenance, commercial sewing, cosmetology, TV repair, and the like. Business courses at these schools stressed clerical skills and retail sales. At the high schools many of these courses took place off-campus and outside of the regular schedule.

266

Vocational programs such as these are often labelled as "work experience." As Oakes concludes, the result:

> ...may be that large numbers of predominantly non-white students are channeled early into training for specific low-level occupations, rather than encouraged to continue in more academic programs. These students may be eased out of the school setting through on-the-job training during the school day. They may be likely to leave school early believing they have been trained in a marketable skill, only to find that they cannot translate these skills into occupational advantage.[4]

Table 8.3

Rank Order of Schools in Vocational Emphasis:
Percentage of FTEs in Vocational Subjects

High Schools		Junior High/Middle Schools	
School	% of FTEs	School	% of FTEs
Fairfield	42	Manchester	22
Euclid	41	Fairfield	15
Dennison	35	Newport	13
Woodlake	27	Vista	13
Crestview	24	Bradford	12
Vista	22	Euclid	12
Atwater	21	Atwater	8
Rosemont	21	Crestview	7
Manchester	19	Palisades	7
Laurel	15	Rosemont	7
Bradford	14	Woodlake	7
Newport	13	Laurel	4
Palisades	13		

Range = 29 points	Range = 18 points
Mean = 23.61	Mean = 10.58
sd = 10.04	sd = 4.92

As was pointed out in Chapter 6 and again here, we begin to sort and label children as "headed" or "handed," as material for the professions or manual labor. We begin this sorting and labeling almost as soon as children enter school and, in great measure, we do it on the basis of race, ethnicity, and socioeconomic status. There seems no school practice quite so unfair, undemocratic, or wasteful of human potential.

In Chapter 6, I argued for the elimination of tracking and for the deliberate grouping of students heterogeneously through junior high years. Actually, I would suggest that such heterogeneous grouping be practiced through grade 10. By about grade 11, today's youth are generally capable of choosing interesting paths to explore. A junior college type program for grades 11 and 12 with an open campus, courses offered throughout the day and evening, no age ceiling upon the time of completion or floor upon entering a program, and adequate counseling services would serve our youth well. Such schools would be centralized and thus large enought to provide a host of offerings. Barbara Benham Tye describes in detail such high schools in her companion volume from A Study of Schooling entitled Multiple Realities, A Study of 13 American High Schools.[5]

I would not want to define the age or grade limits of the junior secondary school which would inevitably find itself between the elementary school and the high school. That would depend on local needs, enrollment patterns, and the like. What I would hope to see would be a commitment to heterogeneous grouping, quality teaching, and a common set of experiences for all pre- and early adolescent boys and girls.

The Classroom Experience[6]

In Chapter 7, I reported on teacher, student, and observer perceptions of how class time was spent at the junior high level. Here I report on how those data compare to similar data from other levels of schooling.

Instructional activities comprised the main part of life in our sampled classrooms at all levels of schooling. On the average, observers recorded more occurrences of instructional activities than of any other type, teachers reported that instructional activities accounted for the largest percentage of class time, and students responded that learning took the most time. On the average, teachers at each level reported that around 70% of class time was devoted to instruction. Observers estimated slightly more. We shall examine student data in a moment.

268

These data say nothing of the qualitative dimensions of instruction. However, they do partially respond to the critics of classroom life and school who suggest that not enough time is spent on instruction. At all levels of schooling, it would seem that the question of time is a qualitative and not a quantitative one.

The second pattern which emerged from the data had to do with time spent on behavior. Findings from all three sources--teachers, students, observers--indicated that time devoted to student behavior decreased at each higher level of schooling. This was most dramatically noted in the student data (see Table 8.7). Sampled students were asked to choose the one type of activity which took the most time. The response for behavior ranged from 38% at the early elementary level to only 15% at the senior high.

Table 8.4

Percentage of Students Who Selected Each
Category as Taking the Most Class Time

	Early Elementary (N = 1775)	Upper Elementary (N = 1611)	Junior High (N = 8876)	Senior High (N = 10,872)
Instruction	44.6%	52.8%	62.5%	72.8%
Behavior	37.4	31.9	24.2	14.7
Routines	18.0	14.4	12.4	11.0

These findings point out the preoccupation at the elementary school level with socializing students into acceptable behavior patterns. As children progress through the grades, they either learn to conform to those patterns or they drop out.

An examination of the data on teachers' activities revealed some interesting patterns, also. Lecturing/ explaining/instructing/demonstrating -- frontal teaching -- was the most prevalent type of activity at all levels of schooling as it was shown to be for the junior highs in our sample in Chapter 3. And, as with the time spent on instruction, the pattern was for there to be more frontal teaching as the level of schooling increased (see Table 8.5).

Table 8.5

Proportion of Total Observed Teacher Activity
Spent on Explaining, Lecturing,
or Demonstrating to Students

Level of Schooling	%
Early Elementary	23.3
Upper Elementary	24.7
Junior High	27.9
Senior High	30.8

Classroom space and furnishings both partially supported and partially explained the predominance of frontal teaching. By and large, a single teacher was assigned to a single 30' x 30' classroom which had 25-35 desks organized into 4-6 rows. A very few elementary classrooms had learning centers and tables for several students instead of single desks. Almost no secondary classrooms had such arrangements.

Obviously, such arrangements supported the type of instruction which called for teachers to lecture and to monitor students while they did written work. Further, it probably inhibited many teachers who would have liked to have had students involved in more active forms of learning.

We found other differences in teacher activity as well. Elementary teachers interacted more with individuals and small groups than did secondary teachers. We found that a little less than two-thirds of observed teacher lecturing/instructing activity at the early elementary level included the total class. The proportion increased to more than two-thirds for upper elementary teachers and about three-fourths for secondary teachers. Junior high teachers were like senior high teachers in this regard.

In addition, teacher questioning and responding or giving feedback declined as the level of schooling got higher. Thus, we found in our sample that elementary teachers interacted more with their students; and again, junior high teachers were more like the high school teachers.

Several different types of data contributed to the impression that the prevailing classroom atmosphere was a neutral one. Teachers were seldom observed to either praise or reprimand students. In those cases in our sample where affect was even observable, neutrality characterized the classroom environment over 95% of the time, regardless of the level of schooling. Despite the lack of much teacher behavior which could be seen as overtly positive, students at all levels perceived their teachers to be concerned about them and not overtly punitive.

Teachers may have been concerned for their students; they certainly were in control of events in the classrooms. Our data supported the image of the classroom teacher as being quite autonomous. By their own report, at all levels of school, they perceived that they had "complete" control over selecting teaching techniques and learning activities. Secondary teachers reported "complete" control over evaluating students while elementary teachers, on the average, said "a lot." Teachers at all levels reported "a lot" of control over all other aspects of curriculum and instruction in the classroom.

Observation data substantiated these teacher reports. However, there were level differences. Senior high students were observed making decisions more often than were junior high students, and they made a greater percentage than did elementary students. In fact, elementary teachers made 95% of the observed classroom decisions while junior high teachers made 89% and senior high teachers 79%. At all levels, when students were observed making decisions, it was usually about seating, space, or materials.

At all levels of schooling, the majority of students perceived that they were not much involved in classroom decision-making. However, a greater percentage of elementary students than secondary students reported that they helped to make classroom decisions. They also indicated more of a desire to have choices about what they did in classes. We do not really know whether or not the elementary students did make more decisions or whether they just thought they did. Since we have just seen that observation data showed elementary students making fewer decisions than secondary students, I tend to believe it was the latter. Perhaps, too, students become more compliant, more accepting, more socialized as they progress through the grades. By junior high they are "ready to play the game."

Table 8.6

Student Perceptions of Their Involvement
In Classroom Decision-Making

Item	Level	% Agree	% Disagree	N
Students help decide what we do in this class	High School	32.9	67.1	10,693
	Junior High	34.8		
			65.1	8,174
	Upper Elem.	44.6	55.4	1,616
I would like to be able to make more decisions about what goes on in this class	High School	52.9	47.1	10,758
	Junior High	61.2	38.9	8,301
I would like more chances to help choose what we do in this class	Upper Elem.	69.6	30.4	1,621

		Yes	Sometimes	No	N
I choose what I want to do in this class	Early Elem.	18.1	26.0	55.8	1,789

We also had data from teachers on their educational beliefs and one set of items measured their beliefs about classroom control (Teacher Control scale).[7] Teachers at all levels mildly agreed with the items in the scale. In other words, they supported the need and desirability of teacher control of students and classroom activities. Mean scores for elementary and high school teachers were almost identical while the junior high teachers indicated a slightly stronger belief in teacher control. They also endorsed traditional beliefs more strongly than elementary or high school teachers. It would appear that they were reacting to the volatile nature of early adolescence.

In summary, then, it appeared that instruction took up the most time in classrooms at all levels. Time spent on behavior decreased at each higher level of schooling. Frontal teaching was the most common teacher activity at all levels and it increased at each higher level. Also, elementary teachers did more small group and individual teaching than secondary teachers. At all levels of schooling, the prevailing classroom atmosphere was one of neutrality, neither warm nor harsh. Even so, students at all levels perceived their teachers as being concerned about them. At all levels, teachers were very much in control of their classes. Students were little involved in decision-making. The one unique pattern in the data was one which showed junior high teachers believing more strongly in teacher control in the classroom than teachers at other levels.

While it is true that early adolescents are very, very active, it seems to me that more external control is not what is needed. They need to practice and learn self-control and this can best be done through active involvement in learning, through participation in decision-making and problem solving, and through continual formative evaluation on their part of their own actions.

The School as a Social Place

We asked students a number of questions which gave us a picture of what it was like to attend school. We asked them about their relationships with other students in their classes and about competitiveness and cliquishness in their classes. At the secondary level, we asked what the one best thing about school was, what extracurricular activities they participated in, and who the most popular students at school were.

Early elementary, upper elementary, and secondary students were asked different questions about what we labelled Peer Esteem. Response modes were different from level to level. While it was not possible to make precise level comparisons, it appeared that students at all levels felt, on the average, that their peers were likeable, cared for them, and were helpful.

273

It also appeared that the mean score at the junior high level was slightly less positive than mean scores for the early elementary, upper elementary, or high school levels.

At the upper elementary level, about one-half of the students agreed with the statement that they felt a competitive spirit in their classes. Schools with minority and mixed populations had the highest percentages of students who responded affirmatively to this item. This seems to support earlier findings which suggest that minority students place a high value upon educational attainment.

At the secondary level, scores on the Student Competitiveness scale fell at about the middle range, and junior high scores were slightly higher, indicating slightly more competitiveness at that level than at the high school level.

About three-quarters of the upper elementary students perceived student cliquishness in their class while there was only mild agreement at the secondary levels. Junior high students did perceive more cliquishness in classes than did senior high students.

Thus, we found that junior high students, on the average, saw their peers as likeable, caring, and helpful in class. They saw the classes as only moderately competitive and they perceived some cliquishness. At the pre- and early-adolescent stage of development, they perceived slightly less positive peer relations and slightly more competitiveness than either younger or older students, suggesting a need for a strong emphasis upon personal guidance.

We asked secondary students to select the "one best thing" about their school. At every school, junior and senior highs, by far the greatest percentage of students selected "my friends." Running a distant second was usually "sports activities" and sometimes "good student attitudes," two other peer-related choices. Things that had to do with the school program (e.g., the variety of class offerings, the classes I'm taking, teachers) were chosen by very few students.

In all triples except two, the percentage of students who chose "my friends" was slightly lower at the high school than at the junior high. The two instances where a greater percentage of students at the high school chose "my friends" were Bradford and Crestview, the two schools with low SES, white student populations. I would hypothesize that secondary school programs of today are not generally perceived by low SES, white students as offering much other than an opportunity to socialize. On the other hand, many white middle and upper SES students see secondary schools as preparing them for higher education, and minority students of all SES groups often see education as a means of getting ahead socially and economically.

Junior and senior high students were asked who the most popular students in the school were. They chose between athletes, gang members, smart students, members of student government, good looking students, and wealthy students. Results are reported in Table 8.7.

Table 8.7

Student Perceptions of Which
Students Are the Most Popular

Type of Student	% of Response	
	High School	Junior High
Athletes	55.0	23.1
Good looking students	23.6	36.8
Gang members	7.0	14.8
Smart students	7.0	13.5
Members of student gov't	4.6	8.4
Wealthy students	2.8	3.4

At the senior high level, the common pattern of response at most schools was for 50-60% of the students to respond "athletes," followed by 25-35% responding "good looking students." Other responses tended to be 10% or less with the usual pattern being "smart students" or "gang members" next, followed by "members of student government" and finally "wealthy students."

Patterns at the junior high were quite different and more varied from school to school. Generally, "good looking students" received the largest percentage of responses and "athletes" received the second greatest response. Notable exceptions were Rosemont,

275

Laurel, and Manchester. At Rosemont and Laurel, "smart students" received a larger than usual response—37.6% and 26.7%, respectively. Again, this finding suggests the value placed upon education by minority students as a means of "making it" in the greater society. At Manchester, "gang members" received a very large response: 53.3%. This reflects the extremely strong attraction of the peer culture during early adolescence, perhaps especially in urban areas such as Manchester.

Conclusions

This chapter examined a number of variables as a means of testing the notion that the junior high serves an articulation function. The question, simply put, was "Did the junior highs in our sample provide for a gradual transition for early adolescents from the self-contained, more child-centered elementary program to the departmentalized, subject-centered high school program?"

The summary answer is, "No, not really." What it seemed that they did do, in the name of articulation, was to reinforce many of the practices of schooling which growth and development literature tell us are not good for early adolescents.

To begin with, the name of the school, junior high school, gives us a clue to one of its main problems. It is thought of and dealt with as if it is "junior." Its role is to prepare students for high school. High school is believed to be more important and junior high is a poor copy of high school: it is departmentalized and students are tracked.

In the schools in our Study there was no evidence of block time or core classes as a transition step from elementary schooling to the high school. Classroom experiences at the junior high resembled those at the high school except that classes were larger and less well-equipped.

Neither does it matter if schools are called "middle" schools. That still translates as being between elementary school and what is perceived to really matter, adolescence and high school. In our sample, student experiences were about the same at middle schools and junior highs except that they were begun earlier (grade 6) in the middle schools.

In our sample, we found that intellectual development was seen as the most-emphasized apparent and ideal function of schooling at all levels by all data sources. However, there was a shift toward the personal and vocational aims, particularly for students, at the higher levels. In this instance, junior high responses were in the middle, between those from elementary data sources and those at the high schools.

When it came to plans for the future, junior high data were not in the "middle." By junior high, student perceptions of what they wanted to do and what they were going to do were pretty well set. At both the junior and senior high levels, about one-third said they would probably go on to college, and about a quarter said they would finish high school. The remainder were divided among several options including attendance at trade or technical school and attendance at junior college.

Neither were the junior high data from students about the school as a social place in the "middle." These students, on the average, saw their peers as likeable, caring, and helpful in class. They saw the classes as somewhat competitive and they perceived some cliquishness. Also, about a third of them reported that it was not easy to get help with a personal problem from a counselor.

Pre- and early adolescents are at a particularly sensitive developmental stage. Given these perceptions, it would seem necessary to have adequate counseling services at each junior high. This could be in the form of more guidance counselors, relieving counselors of a paperwork load which takes away from their time spent with students, or some form of teacher advisor program wherein each teacher has responsibility for a very small number of advisees.

Many aspects of classroom life were similar at all levels of schooling. Instruction, for example, took up the most time at all levels. Time spent on behavior decreased at each higher level. Frontal teaching was the most common teacher activity at all levels and it increased at each higher level. At all levels, the prevailing classroom atmosphere was one of neutrality

277

although students did perceive, on the average, that their teachers were concerned for them.

What did stand out at the junior high level was the strong belief of teachers in their need to be in control in the classroom. This may well be a reaction to the active nature of pre- and early adolescents. This is just the opposite of what probably ought to occur. Rather than external controls being applied, junior high students should practice and learn self-discipline through active participation in decision-making, problem solving activities, and evaluation of their own actions.

Student perceptions of which students are most popular were different at junior and senior high levels, too. They were more varied at the junior high with "good looking students" usually perceived as most popular but "smart students" and even "gang members" chosen at some schools. At the high schools it was always "athletes." This difference is mostly explained by the heavy emphasis upon inter-school athletic programs at the high school level. However, some of it also is probably attributable to the great importance placed by pre- and early adolescents upon peer and adult recognition and acceptance.

Earlier in this chapter, I called for the elimination of tracking and for the deliberate heterogeneous grouping of students through about grade 10. What I was suggesting was the adoption of the pattern of junior secondary education common in many European countries. While I would not want to precisely define the age or grade limits of the junior secondary school, I would want that school to be committed to heterogeneous grouping, a common set of experiences for all students, and active participation by students in the learning process.

It is my belief that the idea of articulation creates its own self-fulfilling prophecy which has many serious consequences for the junior high program. Preoccupation with preparation for high school, a job, and the future in general is just one set which tells early adolescents that they will be worthy individuals if they can just get through until adolescence. Designing programs which are poor copies of those at the senior high is another which does not take into account the uniqueness of early adolescents.

It would be interesting if somewhere a junior high program was planned which did not have to carry the burden of articulation. Such a program would be concerned with the characteristics of pre- and early adolescents and would take into account their active nature, their penchant for exploration, their sensitivities and insecurities. With those characteristics addressed, I believe, pre- and early adolescents would, in fact, be better prepared for the future.

Chapter VIII, Notes and References

1. William Van Til, et al., Modern Education for Junior High Schools (Second Education), op. cit., p. 31.

2. The four functions defined by this item were:
   a. SOCIAL DEVELOPMENT: Instruction which helps students learn to get along with other students and adults, prepares students for social and civic responsibility, develops students' awareness and appreciation of our own and other cultures.

   b. INTELLECTUAL DEVELOPMENT: Instruction in basic skills in mathematics, reading, and written and verbal communication; and in critical thinking and problem-solving abilities.

   c. PERSONAL DEVELOPMENT: Instruction which builds self-confidence, creativity, ability to think independently, and self-discipline.

   d. VOCATIONAL DEVELOPMENT: Instruction which prepares students for employment, development of skills necessary for getting a job, development of awareness about career choices and alternatives.

3. Bette C. Overman, Functions of Schooling, op. cit.

4. Jeannie Oakes, Limiting Opportunity, op. cit., p. 25.

5. Barbara Benham Tye, Multiple Realities, A Study of 13 American High Schools. Lanham, Md.: University Press of America, 1984.

6. In this section, I have drawn heavily from two I/D/E/A technical reports: Joyce Wright, Teaching and Learning, op. cit., Kenneth Sirotnik, What You See Is What You Get, op. cit.

7. See: David P. Wright, Teachers' Educational Beliefs, op. cit.

CHAPTER IX

THE REALITIES OF BRINGING ABOUT CHANGE

Introduction

From the previous chapters, it is obvious that much is in need of change in our junior highs. Recognition of this fact, of course, is an important first step. Identification of what is to be changed is also an early task in the change process.

Getting the initial recognition of the need for change is not an easy task. There is a good deal of comfort in doing things "...in the way they've always been done." To suggest the need for change is often to suggest that people are doing things wrongly and humans are reluctant to admit that.

Knowing what to change to is also not so easy. In fact, one of the problems American education has faced for the past several decades has been the advocacy of countless "innovations," each to be tacked on to the school program, each promising to solve one educational problem or another. Unfortunately, most innovations of the past several decades have seemed to make little difference in the actual lives of school children. We have been "tinkering" with our schools.

Much of the research on change and a substantial amount of opinion based upon experience seem to suggest that the total school—its curriculum, structures, people and their relationships, as well as linkages to the greater community—must be the focus of improvement efforts. In short, the school has to be viewed as a complex social system.[1]

In the remainder of this chapter, I examine a number of variables which, I believe, are critical to the change process. These particular variables were chosen because, in a preliminary examination of data from A Study of Schooling, I found that teachers did not interact with each other very much, nor did they come in contact with a great deal of professional knowledge from outside the school. The change literature assumes that the school is an "open" social system.[2] The reality may be that it is hardly open. The need may be to make it more so.

The data that follow are from and about junior high teachers and are divided into three sets. First, data about the relationship between teachers and selected external forces are examined (e.g., consultants, in-service training). Second, professional relationships within the school are discussed. Third, selected professional characteristics of the teachers themselves are explored. The chapter concludes with a statement about the implications of these findings for future change efforts.[3]

External Forces

We asked teachers to respond to an item which named potential sources of influence on what they taught within a given subject area. A substantial number of teachers (over 75%), regardless of subject area taught, indicated that they were greatly influenced by two sources: (1) their own backgrounds, interests, and experiences and (2) student interests and abilities. On the average, they also responded that four sources had very limited or no influence: (1) district consultants, (2) parent advisory councils, (3) state equivalency exams and (4) teacher unions. Four sources were perceived as having moderate influence: (1) textbooks, (2) commercially prepared materials, (3) state and district curriculum guides and (4) other teachers (see Table 9.1).[4]

There were some interesting variations across subject areas. For example, foreign language and English teachers reported that they were highly influenced by more external sources than did teachers of other subjects while teachers of the arts and vocational education reported the least number of external sources as being influential.

We also asked teachers about the availability, use and value to them of resource persons. Over 80% of the responding teachers said that district resource people were available to them. When asked whether or not they actually consulted district resource people, only approximately one-half said "yes." Also, approximately one-half of the teachers indicated that they found

282

district consultants of little or no value. That
figure was approximately 75% and 80% for help from
intermediate agency consultants and from state or

Table 9.1

Sources and Amounts of Influence on Teachers and Subjects

Amount of Influence by Subject

Sources	Arts	English Reading	For. Lang.	Math	Phys. Ed.	Science	Social Studies	Voc./ Car. Ed.
District Consultants	Low	Low	Mod.	Low	Low	Low	Low	Low
State/District Texts	Low	Mod.	High	High	Low	Mod.	High	Mod.
State Guides	Low	Low	Low	Mod.	Mod.	Mod.	Mod.	Mod.
District Guides	Mod.	Mod.	Mod.	Mod.	Mod.	Mod.	Mod.	Mod.
Commercial Materials	Mod.	High	High	Mod.	Low	High	Mod.	Mod.
Teacher Background	High	High	High	High	High	High	High	High
Other Teachers	Mod.	High	Mod.	Mod.	High	Mod.	Mod.	Mod.
Student Interests and Abilities	High	High	High	High	High	High	High	High
Parent Advisory Councils	Low	Low	Low	Low	Low	Low	Low	Low
State Equivalency Exams	Low	Low	Low	Low	Low	Low	Low	Low
Teacher Unions	Low	Low	Low	Low	Low	Low	Low	Low

283

federal projects/agencies, respectively. Thus, we found that while outside resource people were generally available, teachers neither used them much nor felt that they were of any great value. Whether they were or not was not the issue. The issue was teacher perceptions, and behavior based upon those perceptions.

We asked teachers about their professional contacts with other teachers outside of their own schools. They most often came in contact professionally with other teachers through college courses, in-service classes or workshops, meetings of educational organizations, and informally arranged consultations to share problems, ideas, etc. They less often came in contact through visiting other schools or receiving visitors from other schools, or at formal conferences on specific topics (see Table 9.2). Teachers reported that they seldom had professional contacts with teachers from other schools as a result of written correspondence; serving on district committees; or serving on local, state, or national committees.

In order to obtain information about the content of in-service programs and workshops, we gave teachers a list of seven general topics and eight subject areas and we asked them to indicate whether or not they had attended programs at which these topics were discussed (see Table 9.3).

One-half of the programs attended by 20% or more of the teachers at any school were initiated by the school staffs, almost 40% were initiated by the district or county and only about 10% by other agencies. The most widely attended topics were teaching methods or strategies, curriculum development and behavioral objectives/evaluation. The least attended were cross-cultural/cross national education and adult group dynamics.

Table 9.4 lists the schools by topic where 20% or more of the teachers attended in-service programs. In addition to the general topics reported already, the only subject-specific topic to which 20% or more of any staff responded was English, reading, language arts.

We had no way of knowing how many teachers attended more than one program or how many attended none. Neither did we have any way to know how effective in-service programs were. Our data only told us how many teachers were exposed to various topics according to their own report.

Table 9.2

Frequency of Teachers' Professional Contacts
With Other Teachers

Type of Contact	Never	Occasionally	Fairly Often
In-service classes or workshops	21%	65%	14%
College courses	24	52	24
Meetings of educational organizations	28	58	14
Visiting other schools or receiving visitors from other schools	40	54	6
Formal conferences on specific topics	42	54	4
District committees	61	33	6
Local, State or National government committees	81	17	2
Informally arranged consultations to share problems, ideas, etc.	35	52	13
Written correspondence	61	37	2

A first reaction to the data in Table 9.4 is that few teachers attended in-service programs. That is true if you consider single topics at any given school. However, when cumulative totals at some schools are considered, a different picture emerges. For example, at Manchester 25% or more of the teachers indicated that they had attended programs on six different topics during the previous year and one-half.

Large numbers of teachers at two other schools, Palisades and Rosemont, also indicated attendance at a

285

variety of programs. These three schools had several things in common: they were urban, they served large minority populations, and they had federal funding. One might hypothesize that the Elementary and Secondary Education Act (ESEA) has worked, at least insofar as the provision of in-service for teachers in urban, minority schools was concerned. Federal aid made a difference.

Table 9.3

Percentage of Teachers Attending
General Interest Programs

	School Staff	District or County	Other Agency
Adult group dynamics (i.e., human relations, interpersonal relationships)	16(2)	10	9
Teaching methods or strategies	18(3)	16(3)	14(3)
Child growth and development	7	6	8
Classroom Management	12(1)	10(1)	8
Behavioral objectives/ evaluation	16(2)	10(2)	7
Curriculum development	12(3)	12(2)	8
Cross-cultural/cross-national education	5	6	2

Note: Numbers in parentheses denote the number of schools in which 20% or more of the teachers reported they had attended programs at which the topic was discussed.

Table 9.4

Schools in Which Twenty Percent or More of the Teachers Attended
Programs at Which Topics of General Interest Were Discussed

Topics	School Staff		Sponsored by District or County		Other Agency	
Adult group dynamics	Manchester Atwater	38% 26	Atwater	30%		
Teaching methods or strategies	Manchester Palisades Crestview Vista	38 25 22 21	Rosemont Fairfield Palisades	35 20 20	Atwater Vista Woodlake	39% 29 22
Classroom management	Manchester	32	Rosemont	23		
Behavioral objectives/ evaluation	Manchester Palisades	50 22	Rosemont Palisades	23 22		
Curriculum development	Palisades Crestview Manchester Newport	30 28 25 21	Crestview Rosemont	25 23		
English, reading, language arts	Manchester Palisades	31 20	Rosemont	21		

Unfortunately, we had no measure of the perceived effectiveness of in-service training programs for teachers. The greater attendance at school-based programs may have been an indicator of their being perceived by teachers as more worthwhile. The low percentage of attendance overall suggests that a great deal more needs to be done to provide better programs of teacher in-service and/or to find ways to have more participation in what is offered.

We asked teachers about their membership in educational organizations: how many were belonged to, how they affected working conditions, and how much they affected professional growth. About 40% of the

teachers said they belonged to three or four educational organizations and about one-third said they belonged
to only one or two organizations. Seventeen percent
said they belonged to no organizations and about 10%
said five or more. Forty-two percent of the teachers
felt that their memberships in professional organizations had little or no effect on the working conditions
at their schools and exactly 50% felt it had little or
no effect on their own professional growth.

We also asked teachers how many articles, books and
reports in education they read, and how helpful they
thought professional literature was to them. Over half
of the teachers reported reading nine or more books,
reports and articles in education in the year preceding
the Study. They perceived that this literature had
"some" value for their professional development.

The set of data just reported gives us a view of
the interactions of teachers with the professional
environment outside of the school. While these findings are not generalizable to all teachers in the
United States, we can say that teachers in this sample
were most influenced by their own background, interest
and experiences as well as their own perceptions of the
interests and abilities of their students, rather than
other sources including parents, consultants, curriculum guides and textbooks.

Teachers reported that outside resource people were
available to them, but that they found them to be of
little value and used them very seldom. Contacts with
other teachers were, more often than not, at the choice
of the individual (e.g., at college courses, in-service
classes attended on an individual basis, or meetings of
educational organizations). Educational organizations
and professional literature were viewed by teachers as
having only "some" influence on their professional
development.

There was some evidence to suggest that teachers
attended a variety of in-service programs. However,
there appeared to be very few school-wide planned
in-service efforts which were either offered or, if
offered, attended by teachers. The situation, it
seems, is still much as Rogers described it in 1962:
change occurs slowly, as a result of the involvement of
individuals haphazardly in a variety of programs.
Occasionally, topics arise and seem to become more

important (e.g., behavioral objectives). But even so, only a fraction of the teachers at the schools in our sample attended even these kinds of programs. Knowledge flows unevenly and without focus or plan in our schools. There is still a need for new strategies or for better application of existing strategies in response to the problem of linking schools to new knowledge.

Organizational Forces

While the linking of teachers to professional knowledge from outside of the school appeared to be haphazard and weak, it might be assumed that there were cohesive linkages within the schools. That was not found to be the case, either.

Three quarters of the junior high teachers in our sample taught alone in a self-contained classroom. Eleven percent considered themselves members of a "teaching team." Eight percent taught with aides, 6% taught in self-contained classrooms with informal help from other teachers, and only 1% taught with student teachers.

Approximately one-half of the teachers indicated that they could arrange to have another person take over their classes so that they could engage in some professional activity.

When asked if they observed instruction in classrooms other than their own in the school, 60% said "never." Of the remainder, the majority indicated that they observed once or twice a year. Interestingly, approximately three-fourths of them stated that they would like more opportunity to observe other teachers at work in the school.

Teachers were asked about their knowledge of other teachers in the school. The question was, "For about what percentage of the teaching staff do you feel you know each of the following things: the way they behave with students, their job competence, their educational beliefs." On the average, teachers said that they knew how about one-third of their colleagues behaved with students. They acknowledged knowing slightly less about job competence of their colleagues and even less about their educational beliefs.

There were variations across schools. The junior high with the highest score on the three variables was Euclid. Bradford had relatively high mean scores on "the way they behaved with students" and "job competence" (i.e., teachers said they knew these things of about one-half of their colleagues). Atwater had similar scores for "job competence" and "educational beliefs." Palisades and Laurel were the schools with the lowest mean scores (i.e., teachers said they knew of the three things for just over 10% of the teachers).

It seemed that mean scores were higher in smaller schools and/or schools where teachers had been together for longer periods of time (i.e., Euclid, Bradford, Atwater, Vista). They were lowest at schools where staffs were of "split" race or ethnicity. That is, at smaller schools and/or at schools with staffs which have been together longer, teachers perceived that they knew more about their colleagues than at other schools, particularly large ones. Also, teachers at schools where there were nearly an equal number of teachers from two racial or ethnic groups perceived that they knew less about their colleagues. This latter finding could have been because such "balancing" was a recent thing in those schools. It also suggests that racial or ethnic "balancing" of staffs needs to be accompanied by special efforts or in-service work to acquaint teachers on a staff with each other. The fact is, however, that at all of our schools, teachers expressed only a moderate knowledge of their colleagues.

We asked teachers about the importance of matters dealt with at staff and department meetings. In general, teachers considered staff meetings to be only "moderately important." However, department meetings were seen to be "very important" by nearly one-half of the junior high teachers in our sample. Over three-fourths of the respondents indicated that they attended all staff and department meetings.

In addition to asking teachers about the importance of matters dealt with at staff and department meetings, we also asked them how many staff members they thought were spending a lot of time and effort on major school problems. Only about 25% said either "a considerable number" or "almost all." All the rest responded "very few," "some," or "a moderate number." Clearly, teachers in our sample did not feel that school-wide problems were being dealt with by their colleagues.

We asked the degree to which teachers thought information was shared between <u>different</u> departments, teams, or grade levels. The responses tended to suggest that there was less school-wide sharing than would be desirable. School size appeared to make a difference: the smaller the school the more cross-grade, cross-team, between department communication.

The teacher survey included an organizational climate measure designed to assess various aspects of the working relationship among teachers and between teachers and the principals. One of the scales of this climate measure was labelled "Quality of Problem-Solving/Decision-Making Processes." Items in this scale were:
- When decisions are made, it is usually clear what needs to be done to carry them out.
- The administrator(s) and teachers collaborate in making the school run effectively.
- When a problem comes up, this school has viable procedures for working on it.
- In faculty meetings, there is a feeling of "let's get things done."
- If I have a school-related problem, I feel there are channels open to try to get the problem resolved.
- It is often unclear as to who can make decisions. (-)*
- After decisions are made, nothing is usually done about them. (-)
- Decisions are made by people who have the most adequate and accurate information.
- Problems are recognized and worked on; they are not allowed to slide.

The overall mean for this scale was 4.23, which indicated mild agreement on the part of teachers that problem-solving/decision-making processes were satisfactory at the junior highs in our sample.

The response mode for the organizational climate measure was: 6 = Strongly Agree
5 = Moderately Agree
4 = Mildly Agree
3 = Mildly Disagree
2 = Moderately Disagree
1 = Strongly Disagree

---

* items with minuses are reversed for scoring.

Teachers at one school, Fairfield, mildly disagreed that such processes were satisfactory (3.37). Scores were highest at Atwater (4.95), Vista (4.94), Manchester (4.56), Bradford (4.56), and Woodlake (4.50).

There was also a scale which measured a construct labelled "Staff Self-Renewal." Items in the scale were:
- The staff is continually evaluating its programs and activities and attempting to change them for the better.
- People do a good job of examining a lot of alternative solutions to problems before deciding to try one.
- Teachers prefer the "tried and true;" they see no reason to seek new ways of teaching and learning. (-)
- Teachers are continually learning and seeking new ideas.
- Teachers would be willing to take a chance on a new idea.

At all twelve of the schools in the Study, scores on this scale were slightly positive, indicating that teachers considered themselves and their colleagues as somewhat open to new ideas. Scores were highest at Vista (4.67), Atwater (4.54), and Woodlake (4.52). They were lowest at Fairfield (3.51).

Items in a scale called "Staff Openness" were:

- Information is shared between teachers from different departments, teams or grade levels.
- Staff members don't listen to each other. (-)
- Teachers from one department, team, or grade level have personal respect for those from other departments, teams, or grade levels.
- Information is shared between teachers within the same department, team, or grade level.
- Staff members are tolerant of each others' opinions even if those opinions are different from their own.
- When conflicts occur between the staff members, they handle them constructively rather than destructively.
- Staff members are flexible; they can reconsider their positions on issues and are willing to change their minds.

Scores on this scale also were slightly positive, indicating that teachers believed that they communicated fairly openly with each other. Scores were highest at Atwater (4.88), Vista (4.78), Euclid (4.70), and Woodlake (4.67). Again, the lowest score was at Fairfield (4.04).

On an individual item, "It is possible for teachers to deviate from prescribed curricula for the school," scores were somewhat higher ($\bar{X}$=4.37), indicating that, in general, teachers did not feel held back from trying new things by the principal, the district, or other superordinate authority. This was true even in districts with rather precise negotiated contracts.

From responses to the "Staff Job Satisfaction" scale, we found that teachers were generally satisfied with matters at the school level. Items were:
- Most people who are teaching in this school find their job rewarding in other than monetary ways.
- Staff members are proud to be working in this school.
- The morale of staff members is rather low. (-)
- I usually look forward to each working day at this school.
- Conditions in this school motivate staff members to work hard.
- In general, it is a waste of time for me to try to do my very best.

The mean score across all junior highs in the Study was 4.36, indicating an overall mild level of satisfaction. Again, teachers at Fairfield indicated dissatisfaction (3.41) and the level of satisfaction at Laurel also was low (3.71).

We looked at teachers', parents', and students' ratings of "problems" in all schools. A couple of observations are worth noting. First, the three schools with the lowest "Staff Job Satisfaction" mean scores also were the highest-ranking schools in terms of a composite "problems" score from all three data sources: teachers, parents, students.[5] Second, there was an apparent discrepancy between teachers' perceptions and the perceptions of parents and students in regard to the severity of certain problems. In general, in these schools, students and parents perceived many problems to be more severe than did teachers.

293

"Poor curriculum" was often identified by parents and/or students as a problem, but not by teachers.

Much literature on change in schools suggests that the principal plays a key role. We asked teachers a number of questions about their principals. To begin with, at Fairfield and Newport, the administration was seen as a "minor" problem on the teachers' "problems" inventory discussed above.

We asked teachers some specific questions about their contacts with principals. Table 9.5 summarizes teacher perceptions of how often they talked with their principals about pupil discipline, curriculum and instruction, parents, staff relations and their own job performance.

Table 9.5

Frequency of Teachers' Talks with Principals
About Various Topics
(Percentage of Teachers)

Topic	Never	Once a Month or Less	Once a Week or More
Pupil Discipline	21	66	13
Curriculum and Instruction	19	70	11
Parent	25	68	7
Staff Relations	42	44	14
Job Performance	18	78	4

Over 20% of the teachers said they "never" talked with their principal about discipline, nearly 20% said "never" regarding curriculum and instruction, one-fourth said "never" about parents, over 40% said "never" about staff relations and nearly 20% said "never" about job performance. On the other hand, fewer than 15% said they talked with the principal once a week or more about any of the five topics and,

294

specifically, only 4% said they talked to the principal once a week or more about their own job performance. Teachers did not perceive a great deal of talk with principals about these matters and there were great differences from school to school. It would seem logical to hypothesize that differences were related to the size of the school; that is, it might have been that teachers talked to principals more at smaller schools simply because there were fewer subadministrators (i.e., vice principals, deans, counselors). But that was not true. In fact, the amount of such talk and the topics seemed totally idiosyncratic to the schools and their principals.

We asked teachers who usually initiated these discussions between themselves and the principal. For all topics except their own job performance, more teachers perceived that they initiated such discussions. They almost always initiated discussions about discipline. About two-thirds of the teachers indicated that discussions of their own job performance were initiated by the principal, however.

Approximately 30% of the teachers perceived the discussions with principals about discipline to be very helpful, about half said "somewhat helpful," and around 20% said "not helpful." For discussions of curriculum and instruction, the responses were approximately one-quarter very helpful, half somewhat helpful, and one-quarter not helpful. About 25% thought that discussions about parents were very helpful while fewer than 30% thought that discussions about their own job performance were very helpful. More teachers found discussions with the principal about staff relations to be not helpful than found them to be very helpful. The greater number of teachers perceived discussions of all topics as only somewhat helpful.

A slightly greater percentage of teachers felt that there should be more discussions of all topics than felt there should be fewer. For all topics, the greatest percentage felt that the amount of discussion should remain "about the same."

Teachers at all schools except Fairfield agreed with the statement, "The principal encourages teachers to experiment with their teaching." Since principals did not initiate discussions and yet teachers felt moderately encouraged to experiment, it could be hypothesized that what existed was a laissez-faire "do your own thing" attitude in these schools. Certainly, there was little evidence of curricular and/or instructional leadership behavior on the part of the principals. They, in general, appeared to reinforce the isolation and autonomy of teachers.

Such an hypothesis is not meant to be critical of principals. Most school systems do not encourage curriculum leadership on the part of principals. Usually, they are encouraged and rewarded for "keeping the lid on," for completing administrative tasks for the superordinate system, and for creating the impression that learning takes place in the school.

Teachers were asked to rank five reasons for doing things the principal suggested. The item read:
I do the things my principal suggests or wants me to do because:

(Personal)   a. I admire the principal for personal qualities, and I want to act in a way that merits the principal's respect and admiration.

(Competence)   b. I respect the principal's competence and good judgment about things with which he/she is more experienced than I.

(Reward)   c. The principal can give special help and benefits to those who cooperate.

(Punishment)   d. The principal can apply pressure or penalize those who do not cooperate.

(Legitimate   e. The principal has a legitimate
Right)   right, in that position, to expect that the suggestions he/she gives will be carried out.

In analyzing these data, Overman found that the configuration which appeared with greatest frequency was (1) Legitimate right, (2) Competence, (3) Personal, (4) Reward, and (5) Punishment. Five schools showed this pattern (Crestview, Newport, Woodlake, Atwater, Palisades). There were five other distinct configurations.[6]

Overman looked at the six different configurations in relation to the composite Principal Leadership Scale of the School Climate Inventory, teachers' grading of the school, and teachers' perceptions of the amount of influence they had in decision-making. Two distinct types of configurations of the Principal Power rankings were identified, one positive and one negative. The positive type was characterized by high ranking of the Competence and Personal dimensions and lowest ranking of Punishment. Vista was the only junior high with this configuration. One junior high, Fairfield, was a negative type, characterized by low ranking of the Competence and Personal dimensions, with Legitimate Right having the highest rank. Overman found that this "power" typology seemed to be a good predictor of several other perceptions teachers had of their principals and a moderately good predictor of other school climate factors. Because of the small N (12), this is strictly hypothetical. However, it certainly deserves further study.

The School Climate Inventory included four scales relative to principal behavior: Principal Receptivity and Staff Influence, Principal Openness, Principal-Staff Affection, and Principal Leadership. Items in the first scale were:
- People are involved in making decisions which affect them.
- I feel that I can have input regarding important decisions that affect me.
- The principal usually consults with other staff members before he/she makes decisions that affect them.
- The principal uses group meetings to solve important school problems.
- The principal frequently seeks out the ideas of staff members.

The mean score for all junior highs was 4.16, (the highest possible score was 6.00) indicating that principals were seen as moderately receptive to teachers' ideas. Teachers at Vista (4.93) and Atwater (4.90) were quite positive, on the average, and those at Fairfield (3.14) and Laurel (3.34) were negative about their principals on this dimension. On the single item, "The principal frequently seeks out the ideas of staff members," the range of agreement was from 79% at Vista to only 5% at Laurel.

297

Items in the Principal Openness scale were:
- The principal encourages "team work."
- The principal encourages teachers to experiment with their teaching.
- The principal is reluctant to allow staff members any freedom of action. (-)
- The principal would be willing to take a chance on a new idea.
- The principal is continually learning; seeking new ideas.
- The principal could accept staff decisions even if he/she were not to agree with them.

The mean score for this scale across all schools was 4.46, the highest of the four principal scale means. Only the Fairfield teachers were negative about their principal on this scale (3.45) and most faculties were fairly positive. Those at Laurel (3.88), Bradford (3.89) and Crestview (4.12) were only "mildly" positive.

Items in the third scale, Principal-Staff Affection, were:
- Conflicts between the principal and one or more staff members are not easily resolved. (-)
- Staff members support and encourage the principal.
- The principal's behavior toward the staff is supportive and encouraging.
- The principal looks out for the personal welfare of staff members.
- The staff members trust the principal.
- The principal trusts the staff members.
- When the principal acts as as spokesperson for this school, he/she can be trusted to fairly represent the needs and interests of the staff.
- Staff members feel free to communicate with the principal.

The mean score across all schools was 4.31. Teachers at Vista (5.18), Atwater, (4.92) and Euclid (4.85) were quite positive, on the average, and those at Fairfield (3.35) were negative about their principals.

The final principal scale was labelled Principal Leadership. Items were:
- The principal knows the problem faced by the staff.

- The principal tries to deal with conflict constructively; not just "keep the lid on."
- The principal inspires staff members to work hard.
- The principal helps staff members to improve their performance.
- The principal sees to it that staff members perform their tasks well.
- The principal lets staff members know what is expected of them.
- The principal helps staff members settle their differences.
- The role of the principal is clearly understood by staff members.

The mean score in this case for the 12 schools was 4.31. Teachers at Vista (4.99), Manchester (4.88), Euclid (4.78), Atwater (4.77) and Rosemont (4.63) were positive, on the average, and those at Fairfield (3.68) were negative.

Thus, we found teachers at Vista rating their principal positively on all four climate scales as well as on the Power scale. On the same measures, teachers at Fairfield were consistently negative. Atwater and Euclid teachers were generally quite positive and those at Laurel and Crestview tended to be slightly negative about their principals. Similar patterns showed up for other adult climate scales at these schools indicating that principals, indeed, made a difference in the work lives of teachers.

This section looked at several factors within the schools in our sample in order to see what potential for change resided there. There were many variations from school to school. However, in general, we found that:

1. Most teachers taught alone in self-contained classrooms.

2. Only about one-half of the teachers indicated that they could arrange to have another person take over their class so that they could engage in some professional activity.

3. A majority of teachers reported that they did not observe in other classrooms although they said they would like to.

4. Teachers did not seem to have much knowledge of other teachers in their schools with respect to the way they behaved with students, their job competence, or their educational beliefs. This seemed particularly true at larger schools, and at schools where there was a racial or ethnic split in the staff.

5. Staff meetings were seen as only "moderately" important by teachers, but department meetings were considered more important. Also, teachers did not believe that the majority of their colleagues were spending a lot of time on major school problems.

6. Teachers reported that there was not much sharing among teachers in different departments, teams, or grade levels. This was more noticeable in larger schools.

7. Overall, on our organizational climate measure, teachers indicated mild satisfaction with problem-solving/decision-making processes, thought that they and their colleagues were somewhat open to new ideas and believed that they communicated fairly openly with each other. They also felt that it was possible to deviate from the prescribed curriculum.

8. On the "Staff Job Satisfaction" Scale, teachers indicated a mild level of satisfaction. Where there was some teacher dissatisfaction, we found that teachers' perceptions of problems often differed from the perceptions of parents and students, and that "poor curriculum" was often identified as a problem by parents and/or students, but not by teachers.

9. Principal leadership varied a good deal from school to school, but some interesting patterns were found:

   a. Teachers reported that they did not have frequent discussions with their principals about discipline, curriculum and instruction, parents, staff relations, or their own job performance. They indicated that they initiated most discussions that did take place, except for the ones about their job performance. They also perceived that discussions of all kinds with the principal were only moderately helpful, on the average.

b. Teachers felt moderately encouraged to experiment. It seemed that principal leadership most often was characterized as laissez-faire with a backdrop of "keep the lid on."

c. Two distinct configurations of perceived principal "power" emerged from our data. The positive type found teachers placing competence and personal respect high and punishment low as reasons for doing what principals ask. They ranked competence and personal respect low, and legitimate right high for the negative type. This typology seemed to be a good predictor of other principal leadership and school climate factors and is in need of further study.

d. Overall, on the scales of our organizational climate measure of principal leadership, teachers were mildly positive. At those schools where teachers were negative about their principals, they tended also to be negative about other climate dimensions. Where they were positive about principals, they tended to be positive about other climate dimensions. It appeared that the principal did make a difference to the work life of teachers.

In general, we found teachers to be quite isolated from one another within the school. Also, we found that although there was the possibility that principals could have been a force for opening up that environment, they generally had not been.

Despite the mildly positive response of teachers on the various organizational climate scales, it seems obvious that communication within the schools was quite limited. There was little school-based in-service, teachers knew little about each others' educational beliefs or classroom behaviors, there were few collective problem solving efforts, teachers felt left out of school-wide decision-making, and principals tended to be laissez-faire in their leadership.

301

Herein lie the critial points of intervention for those who wish to bring about meaningful change in our junior high schools. First, structures need to be built which cause school staffs to engage in in-depth problem solving, curriculum development, and in-service training activities. Such activities require release time from classroom responsibilities so that people can meet and work together. Second, principals need the training to be able to facilitate such activities. They need to be able to open the system up to new ideas rather than trying to "keep the lid on." Finally, the school district and other superordinate levels of schooling need to allow and to support such school-based efforts rather than attempting to direct and standardize school practices. The need is for us to develop "self-renewing" schools.[7]

Personal Factors

Change in schools is problematic because of the way in which teachers are or are not linked to knowledge from the outside, and because of the ways in which schools are structured and operated internally. Additionally, it may be that the personal characteristics of teachers themselves stand, at least partly, in the way of change.

We asked teachers how much control they had over decisions about various aspects of their planning and teaching. They reported "complete" control over evaluating students and "a lot" of control over setting goals and objectives; use of classroom space; scheduling time use; scheduling instructional materials; selecting content, topics and skills to be taught; and grouping students for instruction. There was little variation from school to school. When asked about their satisfaction with these various aspects of their planning and teaching, teachers indicated that they felt satisfied with all of them. Overall, they were most satisfied with their selection of content, topics and skills to be taught; with their selection of teaching techniques; and with selection of learning activities.

In a related question, teachers were asked how much influence they thought they had in decisions made at the school about instructional methods used in the classroom. Over 70% of the respondents said "a lot" rather than "some" or "no" influence.[8]

There was great variation in the teachers' responses to 33 items about influence over school policies and decisions. Overall, they felt they had "some influence" over a large number of individual policy issues, "no influence" over fewer issues, and "a lot of influence" over still fewer decisions.

Using the nine subscales of intercorrelated items, it was clear that teachers felt most influential regarding issues of curriculum, instruction, pupil behavior, and communication with parents. They felt least influential concerning fiscal management and the selection and evaluation of personnel. Their perceived powerlessness regarding fiscal management and personnel decisions was stronger than their sense of potency concerning curriculum, instruction, pupil behavior and parent communication.

It seemed that teachers felt most influential concerning classroom policies and then decreasingly so concerning school-wide policies related to pupil life, school-wide policies related to teacher life, other school-wide policies, and the selection and evaluation of school personnel.

The teachers' sense of influence over the entire set of 33 issues varied relatively little from school to school.

David Wright analyzed teachers' educational beliefs.[9] Table 9.6 shows the items, grouped by mean responses. Each item is labelled "P" for Progressive or "T" for Traditional.

Teachers expressed a wide range of beliefs about many educational issues. There was infrequent consensus. When such consensus did occur, it took the form of strong affirmation of belief statements.

Overall, teachers expressed moderate and mild agreement with most belief statements. They mildly and moderately disagreed with few statements and in no case was there strong agreement or disagreement.

Table 9.6

Teachers' Educational Beliefs: Items Grouped by
Mean Responses

Set 1: Moderately Agree (tends toward Strongly Agree)	Means
T. Good teacher-student relations are enhanced when it is clear that the teacher, not the student, is in charge of classroom activities.	5.44
P. Learning is enhanced when teachers praise generously the accomplishments of individual students.	5.31
P. The best learning atmosphere is created when the teacher takes an active interest in the problems and affairs of the students.	5.15

Set 2: Moderately Agree (tends toward Mildly Agree)	
T. In the interest of good discipline, students who repeatedly disrupt the class must be firmly punished.	4.85
T. An orderly classroom is the major prerequisite to effective learning.	4.71
T. Students must be kept busy or they soon get into trouble.	4.66
T. Effective learning depends primarily upon the use of adequate instructional techniques and resources.	4.61

Set 3: Mildly Agree (tends toward Moderately Agree)	
T. The teaching of basic skills and subject matter is the most important function of the school.	4.26
T. Learning is essentially a process of increasing one's store of information about the various basic fields of knowledge.	4.20
P. Student initiation and participation in planning classroom activities are essential to the maintenance of an effective classroom atmosphere.	4.18
T. Proper control of a class is amply demonstrated when the students work quietly while the teacher is out of the room.	4.15

304

Table 9.6 (Cont.)

Means

P. When students are allowed to participate in the 4.12
choice of activities, discipline problems are
generally averted.

P. Student motivation is greatest when students can 4.12
gauge their own progress rather than depending on
regular evaluation by the teacher.

T. Students need and should have more supervision than 4.03
they usually get.

Set 4: Mildly Agree (tends toward neutrality)
T. Before students are encouraged to exercise inde- 3.97
pendent thought they should be thoroughly grounded
in facts and knowledge about basic subjects.

P. The learning of basic facts is less important in 3.94
schooling than acquiring the ability to synthesize
facts and ideas into a broad perspective.

P. In planning their work, teachers should rely 3.77
heavily on the knowledge and skills students have
acquired outside the classroom.

Set 5: Mildly Disagree (tends toward neutrality)
P. Students are motivated to do better work when they 3.19
feel free to move around the room while class is in
session.

P. When given a choice of activities, most students 3.12
select what is best for them.

Set 6: Mildly Disagree (tends toward Moderately Disagree)
P. There is too great an emphasis on keeping order in 2.70
most classrooms.

Set 7: Moderately Disagree (tends toward Mildly Disagree)
T. As long as they have control over teaching in their 2.34
own classrooms, it is not necessary for teachers
to have a voice in school administrative affairs.

Response categories: 6.0 = Strongly agree
5.0 = Moderately agree
4.0 = Mildly agree
3.0 = Mildly disagree
2.0 = Moderately disagree
1.0 = Strongly disagree

305

Overall, teachers tended to endorse traditional beliefs a little stronger than progressive beliefs. They tended to agree with traditional beliefs about teacher control and basic skills and with progressive beliefs about student participation and welfare.

We asked teachers a number of questions about themselves as persons and as professionals. For example, we found that nearly two-thirds of them were under 40 years of age, about 55% were female, nearly 70% were married and approximately 30% had spouses who also worked in education. Rural schools tended to have more teachers under 40 (as well as lower salaries), but not necessarily fewer male teachers or married teachers.

Just under 80% of the teachers in our sample were white, about 15% were black, 3% were Mexican-American and about 2% were Asian. The racial/ethnic makeup of the school staffs varied considerably from school to school and the variance was somewhat related to the racial/ethnic makeup of the student population. At Vista and Euclid, where the student bodies were totally white, the staffs also were 100% white. At Palisades, where there was an approximate 50-50 black-white student body, about 42% of the staff was black. At Laurel, there was also an approximately 50-50 black-white student body, but only about one-third of the staff was black. At Rosemont, only 20% of the teachers were Mexican-American while almost all the students were and at Fairfield only about 6% of the teachers were Mexican-American while half the students were. Clearly, Mexican-American students had the fewest teacher role-models.

More than half of the teachers (53.8%) considered themselves politically "moderate," while 22.4% responded "conservative" and 23.9% said "liberal". Teachers in urban areas tended to perceive themselves as slightly more "liberal" than did those in rural or suburban areas.

The average number of years of teaching experience in our junior high sample was 10.3 years and ranged from 4.4 years at rural Laurel to 15.6 years at nearby, urban Palisades. Rural Euclid (6.7 years) and Fairfield (8.8) were the other schools with large numbers of less experienced teachers. Manchester (12.5 years) and Atwater (12.0 years) had the more experienced teachers. Clearly, experienced teachers tended to move toward the urban, better paying school districts while rural, lower paying districts tended to hire younger, less experienced teachers.

When asked to indicate the highest educational degree attained, the greatest percentage of teachers reported that they had bachelors' degrees (65.5%). About 32% had masters' degrees and just under 2% had degrees beyond the masters'. Just over 1% had less than a bachelor's degree. There appeared to be a moderate relationship between levels of teachers' educational attainment and reported teacher median salaries. That is, where salaries were higher levels of education were also higher. There did <u>not</u> appear to be any relationship between teacher salary or level of education on the one hand and satisfaction or programmatic variables on the other.

The majority of teachers did post-credential work in subject matter (47.1%), followed by teaching methods (29.8%), other subjects (12.5%), and administration (10.6%). When asked what the main purpose of the post-credential work was, slightly more than half of the teachers said "for personal growth" and about 30% said "to advance on the salary schedule." Ten percent said "to change subjects," and 7% said "to become an administrator."

Only 3.5% of the teachers reported that they did not feel adequately prepared to teach the subjects they were currently teaching. The area in which the greatest percentage of teachers reported inadequate preparation was science (7.3%).

Teachers were asked to indicate their primary reason for entering the education profession. Overall, about 70% of the teachers selected from the following four reasons: Subject interest (20%), inherent professional values (18%), to help others (17%), and influenced by others (15%). While there was some variation from school to school, there seemed to be no noteworthy patterns or relationships with any school or community characteristics.

All teachers were asked if their pre-career expectations had been fulfilled, and if they would select the same career again. Two-thirds of the teachers reported that their career expectations had been fulfilled. The range was from over 90% at Atwater to

under 60% at Fairfield. A lower percentage of junior
high teachers than elementary or high school teachers
reported career fulfillment (elementary - 78%; high
school - 75%). Such data tend to support the conventional wisdom that teaching early adolescents is the
most difficult teaching, and also that many junior high
teachers would prefer to teach at the high school
level.

Teachers were asked to indicate what would hypothetically cause them to leave their present position.
Two reasons, "personal frustration or lack of satisfaction with job performance" (33.6%) and "more money"
(25.1%) were selected by the largest percentage of
teachers overall. Interestingly, large numbers of
junior high teachers also chose the reason "difficult
student population (or the characteristics of the
student population)" (14.2%). Only 10.8% of the
elementary teachers and 11.5% of the high school
teachers in our Study chose this reason, testifying to
the active nature of early adolescents.

This section discussed a number of professional
characteristics of teachers, with an eye toward seeing
how such characteristics might relate to the change
process in schools. There were many variations from
school to school. However, in general, we found that:

1. Teachers, on the average, perceived that they
   had "a lot" of control and influence over all
   aspects of teaching and planning for their
   classrooms and, for the most part, they were
   satisfied with that teaching and planning as it
   was.

2. Beyond classroom policies, teachers felt decreasingly influential regarding (a) school-wide
   policies related to student life, (b) school-
   wide policies related to teacher life, (c) other
   school-wide policies, and (d) the selection and
   evaluation of school personnel.

3. Overall, teachers endorsed traditional and
   progressive education belief statements at the
   same time, although they endorsed traditional
   beliefs more strongly. Teachers also considered
   themselves generally to be politically moderate.

4. Almost all teachers felt adequately prepared to teach their subjects and most teachers had taken post-credential work in education.

5. Generally, teachers felt that their pre-career expectations for teaching had been fulfilled. Most said that they would select education again as a profession. However, there were significant differences from school to school, suggesting that the individual school environment had much to do with teacher morale. Teachers who selected "economics" or "working conditions" as reasons for entering the profession felt less fulfilled than did those who entered education for more inherently professional reasons.

6. There appeared to be a general "frustration" among teachers regarding their work.

It is difficult to know just why there was so much teacher dissatisfaction. There were probably many reasons and probably there were different reasons for different teachers. Certainly, those teachers I described in Chapter 1 as feeling that they were "at war" with disinterested students will remain dissatisfied until students are "forced" to listen attentively, follow all classroom rules, do their homework, and the like (or drop out of school). Some teachers may have felt unappreciated because of the general societal negativism which has been associated with schooling for the past several years. A few teachers, I am sure, were frustrated because they were not involved in any significant way in school-level discussions. I believe, also, that there were a number of truly conscientious and hard-working people who knew that their traditional teaching techniques weren't really adequate for today's pre- and early adolescents, and yet they didn't know how to change. The confusion demonstrated by teachers selecting both traditional and progressive beliefs was evidence of this, as was the selection of dissatisfaction with their own job performance as a reason for leaving education.

The fact that many teachers want to improve their teaching but don't know how, adds strength to the argument put forth earlier in this chapter suggesting the development of structures for problem solving by staff members at each local school and the linkage of these efforts to knowledge from outside. Through such local problem solving, teachers will be able to examine, experiment with, and develop more appropriate teaching strategies.

Implications for Change

It would appear from the data which has been presented above that change does occur in our schools. However, it is basically not planned and depends upon what has been labelled as "social interaction."[10] That is, new ideas in education travel rather randomly through the system, from school to school and person to person.

Teachers tend to be isolated in their own classrooms and in control of what goes on there. They feel impotent to effect school-wide decisions, they do not wish to call upon resource people, they individually select their own in-service or post-credential college course work, and they are basically traditional in their educational beliefs. Many teachers like this isolated, controlling existence. However, many would like to change it but don't know how.

According to the "social interaction" pattern, teachers follow a certain sequence whereby new ideas are pursued individually. Initially, a teacher becomes aware of a new idea at a class, in a workshop, from a book, from a fellow teacher or the principal. Secondly, if the teacher is sufficiently interested, he or she searches for further information. After evaluation of the new idea for its relevance to his or her situation, the teacher often tries out the idea. Such evaluation and trial is usually a very informal process, more or less at the level of "how the idea feels." Certainly, evaluation and trial in this context does not imply controlled conditions and/or measurement of any kind. However, if such a trial seems successful to a teacher, the new idea may be adopted and integrated into the ongoing program.

This paradigm of awareness, interest, evaluation, trial and adoption was derived from studies of change in agriculture and medicine and seems, logically, to describe how change occurs in education as well. Certainly, our data suggest that this is generally the case.

This is a slow process, rather random, and certainly unplanned. The "system" has responded to the "social interaction" pattern in a number of ways, either knowingly or unknowingly. The presentation of courses through education extension is a conscious effort to increase the awareness and interest of teachers in new ideas. One could argue that local or regional in-service programs serve the same purpose, although I suppose that most planners of such programs could not articulate the fact that they were attempting to intervene in, and/or speed up a "social interaction" change strategy. Neither would the advocates of in-service by television, nor the advocates of action research which improves the evaluation and trial processes.

The advocates of teaching as a profession would probably suggest that a social interaction pattern is the way it should be. The argument would probably be that the teacher should be in control of his or her own professional growth. Further, the argument would probably state that no one, particularly an administrator, should interfere in this pattern. Our data suggest that, indeed, this is the case at least for principals. Principals in our sample intervened little and no one particularly wanted it otherwise, least of all teachers.

Certainly, there are professional teachers, highly skilled, keen in perceiving their own needs for growth, and vigorous in the pursuit of that growth. But, I think, our data do not suggest that this is the dominant description of teachers. Data presented in this chapter suggest that teachers often reject outside knowledge, that they pursue a narrow range of new knowledge, that they remain relatively isolated within the school, and that they don't want to or don't know how to change. As we have seen in previous chapters, many teachers, in fact, lack a number of the very basic skills of good teaching.

What we have, then, is the appearance of professionalism without the reality. It is no wonder that the "social interaction" pattern, the dominant mode of educational change in our schools, is not adequate to narrow the gap between the idealized version of schooling and what actually goes on in schools. And it is no wonder that many teachers express personal frustration and dissatisfaction with their own job performance.

311

The myth of "teacher as professional" is begun in institutions of pre-service training. Potential teachers are trained in subject matter, teaching methods, and related areas such as the foundation subjects--psychology, sociology, history and philosophy of education. Unfortunately, these disciplines are taught to the potential teachers as compartmentalized, discrete entities. There is very little interdisciplinary teaching in institutions of teacher training. The experience for the potential teacher culminates when he or she is sent out to student teach or "practice" teach in a self-contained classroom, usually with a teacher who may be a good technician but who most certainly is already socialized to the so-called "professional" norms. It is these norms, even more than the technical skills, which are most surely passed on to the potential new teachers.

The pre-service training of principals is not much different. To begin with, the potential candidates have been "successful" teachers (translation: behave well according to the accepted norms). They are trained in relative isolation including, perhaps, an isolated internship. Above all, they are trained (subtly, for sure) to <u>first</u> satisfy the needs of the superordinate system--the state, the board of education, the district administration. Then, and only then, are they expected to assist or intervene with program or teachers. Part of the subtlety is that they are not ever trained as change agents anyway (despite the rhetoric of "instructional leadership").

There is no shortage of teachers or of principals today. Perhaps our training institutions can take advantage of this situation and consider the qualitative aspects of their preparation programs. This would be better than keeping up the quantity by madly scurrying into the in-service business.

Perhaps the training institutions could begin by recruiting more people with progressive beliefs rather than traditional beliefs. At least this could be one criterion for recruitment.

What our data do suggest is that the relative isolation of teachers needs to be overcome. Thus, emphasis in pre-service training might better be upon relationships (i.e., interdisciplinary courses) and collegiality (i.e., forms of team planning, teaching,

312

and evaluation). At a minimum, the student teaching experience should occur in schools where teachers work in teams or at least plan together in grade level or departmental groups. Very few internships, certainly not medical internships, are carried out in isolation.

Certainly, pre-service training for principals has to include a healthy portion of change agentry. This includes an ability to assess the school and an understanding of how the change process works. Just knowing how to cause people to become aware of new ideas or to be able to help them pursue their interest in such ideas, or to assist with the evaluation and trial of new ideas, would go a long way toward enabling principals to begin behaving as change agents.

The improvement of schooling is a systemic problem, which must be approached at a variety of points and with many strategies. While redesigned pre-service training programs can be important, there are also a number of strategies which can be employed at the school level. Recognizing and intervening in the "social interaction" pattern is an obvious strategy. For example, we can identify and enlist opinion leaders, or we can increase the number of in-service offerings, or the rewards for taking in-service classes.

There are other more direct and comprehensive strategies which can be used. Four of these will be briefly discussed here, since they are ones which come to mind from the data presented in this report. These four are (1) networking, (2) organization development, (3) linkage, and (4) situational leadership development.

During the late 1960's, we at I/D/E/A conducted an experiment called the Study of Education Change and School Improvement (SECSI). A major component of this experiment was the formation of the League of Cooperating Schools, 18 school staffs joined together for the purpose of helping each other improve the various programs of instruction. This work was facilitated by a small staff whose members sometimes gave advice but who, most often, organized opportunities for people from one school to share ideas with people from other schools in the League. Thus, the network of schools became the resource base of knowledge and teachers and administrators learned to use each other. They turned

313

outward for ideas, and knowledge flowed more quickly. Also, in-service activities were more collective and focused rather than individual and random.

The SECSI Project also worked at creating a more open problem solving environment among the staffs of the League schools. This was done by measuring and giving feedback to staffs about their collective problem solving efforts, using constructs labelled dialogue, decision-making, action, and evaluation. In a way, this was a form of organization development in that it attempted to improve the problem solving, decision-making, planning, and evaluation processes within the school.

The principles involved in organization development are those of an outside consultant first making an assessment of processes such as those listed above, and then collaboratively with a staff designing a training program to improve those processes. The ultimate goal is for the consultant to withdraw and have the staff know enough to monitor its own processes.

The processes are those measured by the school climate instrument of A Study of Schooling and discuss-ed in this chapter. The assumption behind this strate-gy is that these processes must be operating smoothly before a school staff can focus upon improvement efforts. A consultant can act to bring new knowledge to the setting, but that is not necessarily part of the organization development strategy.[11]

On the other hand, linkage strategies have as their focus the bringing together of a staff (or staffs) with knowledge from outside, as well as the amelioration of the internal processes of the school. The linkage agent is the kind of person who must know both the theory and practice of schooling, must have a broad knowledge (or know where to get knowledge), must understand the processes discussed above, and must be able to help people in schools to improve these proc-esses. There are few, if any, schools of education preparing such people for the field.[12]

Finally, the field of administrative (or leader-ship) training has advanced beyond its earlier traits, styles, and behavioral straight-jackets to realize that neither scientific management nor human relations approaches are adequate in themselves. Administrators, including principals, are trained to emphasize task accomplishment or staff relationships in varying degrees as the <u>situation</u> requires.[13]

It should be noted that A Study of Schooling itself grew out of the belief that we need more data about schools before we attempt to change them. A Study of Schooling demonstrates that the most profitable research yet to be done, at least for the improvement of schooling, is that which illuminates practice.

In the next and final chapter, I attempt to translate the data gathered by A Study of Schooling into proposals for improved junior high schools. I certainly believe that such proposals should be tested and adapted to local needs. Most importantly, I believe that conditions must be created within schools so that such proposals have a chance of succeeding.

Chapter IX, Notes and References

1. See for example: John I. Goodlad, The Dynamics of Educational Change Toward Responsive Schools. New York: McGraw-Hill Book Company, 1975.

2. See: Paul Weick, "Educational Organizations as Loosely Coupled Systems," Administrative Science Quarterly, 21, March, 1976.

3. Much of this chapter is drawn from Kenneth A. Tye, Changing Our Schools: The Realities. Technical Report 30, Arlington, Va: ERIC Document Reproduction Service, 1981.

4. M. Francis Klein, Teacher Perceived Sources of Influence on What is Taught in Subject Areas. Technical Report 15, Arlington, Va.: ERIC Document Reproduction Service, 1980.

5. All respondents were given a list of things that might be a problem at any school and were asked to indicate whether each was a "major problem," "a minor problem," or "not a problem" at their schools. See: Bette Overman, Variety and Intensity of School-Related Problems as Perceived by Teachers, Parents and Students. Technical Report 17, Arlington, Va.: ERIC Document Reproduction Service, 1980.

6. Bette Overman, Bases of Principal Power. Unpublished report. Study of Schooling, Research Division, I/D/E/A, Los Angeles, 1979.

7. See, for example: The I/D/E/A Reports on Schooling, including Mary M. Bentzen Changing Schools: The Magic Feather Principle. New York: McGraw-Hill Book Company, 1974; and Kenneth A. Tye and Jerrold M. Novotney, Schools in Transition: The Practitioner as Change Agent. New York: The McGraw-Hill Book Company, 1975.

8. Much of the following discussion is taken from David P. Wright, Teachers' Perceptions of their own Influence Over School Policies and Decisions. Technical Report 16, Arlington, Va.: ERIC Document Reproduction Service, 1980.

9. David P. Wright, Teachers' Educational Beliefs. Technical Report 14, Arlington, Va.: ERIC Document Reproduction Service, 1980.

10. Everett Rogers, <u>Diffusion of Innovations</u>. New York: Free Press of Glencoe, 1962.

11. Richard A. Schmuck, et al. <u>The Second Handbook of Organization Development in Schools</u>. Palo Alto: The Mayfield Publishing Company, 1977.

12. Nicholas Nash and Jack Culbertson (eds.), <u>Linkage Processes in Educational Improvement: Concepts and Applications</u>. Columbus: UCEA, 1977.

13. Paul Hersey and Kenneth Blanchard, <u>Management of Organizational Behavior: Utilizing Human Resources</u>, 3rd edition. Englewood Cliffs: Prentice-Hall, 1977.

CHAPTER X

TOWARD IMPROVED JUNIOR HIGH SCHOOLS

Introduction

In this book I have taken the position that the concept articulation--supposedly providing a gradual transition from the child-centered elementary school to the more subject-centered high school--does a disservice to the education of junior high students by giving pre-eminence to the education of older, adolescent high school students. Since junior high is seen as preparation for high school, it follows that high school is considered more important. And since high schools are considered more important, decisions are frequently made in school districts which short-change junior highs. We saw, for example, that in many of the districts in A Study of Schooling new high schools were built and junior highs were housed in the old high schools. Worse, we saw that junior highs were little more than poor copies of high schools. They were departmentalized, there were no block-time or core classes, students were tracked and classroom experiences resembled those at the high school except that classes were larger, student options were fewer and resources were less available.

The middle school movement suffers just as the earlier junior high movement did from having to serve the articulation function. A frequently cited early definition of the middle school makes this clear:

> ...a school providing a program planned for a range of older children, preadolescents, and early adolescents that builds upon the elementary school program for earlier childhood and in turn is built upon by the high school's program for adolescence.[1]

The limitation of this 1968 definition was recognized by one of its creators and revised to focus more sharply upon the immediate needs of middle school students. In 1981, Alexander and George defined the middle school as:

319

> ...a school of some three to five years between
> the elementary and high school focused on the
> educational needs of students in these in-
> between years and designed to promote continu-
> ous educational progress for all concerned.[2]

This definition of middle school seems to be
appropriate on a number of counts. First, it does not
require specific age or grade levels which must be
included. Second, it does not argue for this or that
label to be assigned to students (i.e., pre-adoles-
cents, early adolescents, prepubescents, transescents).
Most important, it directs attention to the planning of
school experience based upon the characteristics of the
students to be served and, after all, that is what is
truly critical.

In Chapter 2, I described the physical, emotional,
social and intellectual characteristics of middle or
junior high students. I pointed out that their predominant characteristic is their difference, one from
another. Also, they are quite sensitive and changeable. The point is that the schools which serve these
young people should be organized and operated with a
focus upon the needs and characteristics of the students they serve rather than upon preparation for high
school.

In the remainder of this chapter, I will utilize
data from A Study of Schooling and other sources to
describe an idealized junior high school, one which
does focus upon serving the current needs of its
students. The aspects discussed are: school organization, curriculum, teaching/learning, guidance, and
strategies of change. The chapter concludes with a
statement about what I see as the revised aims of the
junior high school.

School Organization

We found almost no examples of interdisciplinary
integration at the schools we studied. There was a
course labelled "Unified Arts" at two schools. This
was a label for home economics and industrial arts in
one school and these two courses plus music and art at
the other school. At both schools, each subject was
taught separately within "Unified Arts." There was one
integrated domestic arts course at one school with shop

320

and home economics for boys and girls together. Health was taught as part of P.E. at one school. One teacher taught both English and history to three classes. There was a two-period language arts block at one school for all three grades which was planned by teams of teachers at each grade level but which was taught individually. The overwhelming organizational plan at all Study schools was for students to have six or seven separate subject classes each day (See Chapter 3).

We also found that college bound and non-college bound students had quite different experiences in our sample of schools. Foreign language, exclusive of English As A Second Language (ESL), was offered almost solely for the college bound. Poor readers were often automatically scheduled into remedial reading classes and thus excluded from other elective choices. College bound and non-college bound students had different electives and, for the most part, there were more elective choices for the academically oriented students (See Chapter 4).

Finally, we found ability grouping at all of the junior highs in our sample. We found that the experiences of students in lower tracks were far less positive than those in the higher tracks on a variety of measures. We found disproportionate numbers of minority students in lower tracks. Defenders of ability grouping at the junior high generally claim that heterogeneous classes operate at lower levels and hold back the faster students. We found heterogeneous classes to be much more similar, in both content and process, to upper average and high track classes (See Chapter 6).

On the basis of what we know about junior high students (e.g., the importance of the peer culture, the need to learn to accept differences, the need to learn problem-solving behavior), because of the need to develop tolerance in our pluralistic society, because it is wasteful to sort and label youngsters as early as junior high, and because our young people should have an equal opportunity for a quality education, I feel that our junior high schools should be reorganized so that all students have a common core of experiences.

I would not presume to define one single program for all the junior high students in the nation. However, our data do suggest some important guidelines.

First, each school should provide <u>all</u> students with a set of experiences in common organized into a balanced program of academic and non-academic courses which included English/language arts, math, social studies, science, the arts, industrial arts and home economics, and P.E. Our data suggest the following additional half dozen considerations:

1. There is a wide discrepancy in the amount of science offered to junior high students. We found students in one school having three times the amount of science as students in another school which included comparable grade levels. Actually, it is my feeling that science offerings should be considerably expanded for all junior high students.

2. The co-educational "home arts" course offered at one school in our sample seems a good model for all junior highs. Such an exploratory course serves junior high students better than the specific low-level skill trade preparatory courses (e.g., office machines, mechanical repair, building maintenance) we sometimes found offered in predominantly minority schools.

3. Rather than single out performing music students (e.g., band, orchestra, chorus) by scheduling them separately, I suggest that <u>all</u> students have (a) a common set of experiences in the arts and (b) a performance option of some kind--music, art, drama, dance, creative writing, film, etc.

4. I question the need for as much mathematics education as we have in our junior highs. Much of it is review of basic operations learned previously. Perhaps alternate days for math as we see in some Western European junior secondary schools would suffice.

5. We live in an interdependent world. Therefore, I believe that <u>all</u> students should learn a foreign language. In our sample of schools, foreign language classes were taught as academic classes. Because of this, only college bound students were enrolled. How foreign language should be taught will be dealt with in the next section of this chapter.

322

6. With a balanced, common curriculum there is no need for an elective program. Exploration as a function of the junior high should occur <u>within</u> all classes. The elimination of elective programs will stop both the proliferation of the curriculum and discrimination against the non-college bound. If there is a felt need for optional, additional offerings, the extracurricular program can be expanded.

Data from A Study of Schooling overwhelmingly point to the fact that tracking is a harmful practice for students in the lower tracks and that it does not particularly do any good for the students in higher tracks. More insidiously, tracking gives the appearance of dealing with the problem of individualization of instruction. Supposedly, a tracked class in any subject contains students with a narrow range of abilities. Therefore, the argument goes, the teacher can "teach" to the average of that class. This is just not true and, as a result of tracking, individual differences are frequently overlooked. I propose a conscious effort to create heterogeneous classes.

The creation of heterogeneous classes would need to be accompanied by the in-service training of teachers in diagnostic and evaluation procedures, classroom management techniques and instructional strategies including small group instruction. Practically, I would see classes being made up which are representative of the entire school or grade level population insofar as such factors as age, sex, achievement, social-emotional development, and race and ethnicity are concerned. Additionally, I would see consideration given to individual needs and interests. For example, there might be a given group of students who would be best separated from each other or, conversely, a certain pair of students might do best when they are together. The basic consideration is that heterogeneous grouping is critical to the social-emotional and intellectual growth of junior high students (See Chapter 6).

Another organizational pattern I favor because it offers stability to junior high-aged children is the core program. This is not a new idea at all. Core classes were quite common in junior highs as long ago as the 1930's. However, as Alexander and George explain:

323

...the reemphasis on subject organization of the post-Sputnik era of the late 1950's and 1960's caused many junior highs to abandon any design other than a strict subject one. With the advent of the middle school as in part a reaction against extreme subject departmentalization in the junior high school, the opportunity again existed to use some type of core, block or interdisciplinary design...[3]

Some early advocates of core classes recommended the combining of three, four or even more subject areas. I, like Alexander and George, believe that knowledge has become too complex for such a total combination of subjects and that there are intermediate arrangements which can provide for the maximum personal, social and intellectual growth of students. For example, I have taught problem-centered social studies/language arts blocks which have allowed for a good deal of integration of content with skill development.

Throughout this book it has been noted that advantages tend to accrue to the smaller schools wherein people know each other better and wherein they tend to work more closely together. It would be unrealistic for me to recommend that all large junior highs be replaced by smaller schools. However, it is not unrealistic to suggest that schools be organized into sub-units which function much as a set of smaller schools. Such plans, referred to as a school-within-a-school (SWAS), house plan, learning community, or multi-unit have had a good deal of recent success.

The basic organizational feature of the Individually Guided Education (IGE) secondary school initiated and supported by I/D/E/A is the Learning Community. Each Learning Community contains a cross-section of a dozen or so teachers and 200-300 students. Students generally have core and other "basic" courses within the Learning Community, but on occasion they take a course outside if it requires special teachers or equipment. Thus, they might have homemaking and/or industrial arts outside of their Learning Community. IGE provides a structure whereby the several Learning Communities in a school relate together to deal with school-wide problems and set school-wide policy.[4]

The reader will recall that, in general, teachers in our sample did not know a great deal about their fellow teachers: the way they behaved with students, their job competence, their educational beliefs. However, such knowledge was greater in the smaller schools. Likewise, the reader will remember that the facilitation of staff dialog and problem solving is a key element in the school improvement process. Thus, it seems logical that large junior highs should be organized into administrative sub-units. It also seems logical, in light of what we know about the change process, to suggest that sub-unit staffs meet frequently to plan together and to collectively solve problems.

I have not advocated vertical organizational patterns such as non-grading, continuous progress or multi-aging. Neither have I suggested horizontal reorganization plans such as team or cooperative teaching. I have had a lot of experience with such alternative organization patterns and, basically, I am in favor of them. However, I feel that the critical aspect of schooling upon which improvement efforts should focus is teaching/learning in the classroom and while a change in school organization can facilitate improvement of teaching/learning, it can also be distracting.[5]

Curriculum

As suggested in the previous section, each school should provide all students with a balanced program of academic and non-academic courses which include English/language arts, math, social studies, science, the arts, industrial arts and home economics, and P.E.

English/language arts. In our sample of schools, grammar, mechanics, composition and literature were emphasized. Less attention was given to creative writing, study skills, critical thinking including questioning, speaking or listening. Separate reading instruction was often given to 5th and 6th grade middle school students and poor readers at all grade levels were often enrolled in remedial reading classes.

The major weakness in most English/language arts classes at the junior high level is that they focus on the teaching of skills as an end in itself rather than upon using skills of language in communication and/or problem solving activities. The so-called "back-to-basics" movement has caused much of this, as has the move to teach English/language arts separately from the social studies and other subjects.

As I have already stated, I feel strongly that English/language arts should be taught as part of a core or integrated block-time class. I prefer it combined with the social studies because I have successfully experienced that combination. I suspect that other combinations can also be effective given that there are teachers with appropriate expertise.

Second, I believe that learning best occurs when it is experiential. That is, when students are actively involved in interviewing, visiting, acting out or simulating, and/or constructing or otherwise creating something they are learning basic skills as a matter of application and not in isolation. Such active learning is particularly appropriate for junior high students who themselves are so active.

Third, I favor in-class grouping of students for specific skill instruction based upon needs identified from their writing, reading, speaking and listening behaviors. Thus, if a number of students seem to have difficulty writing a clear paragraph, they are brought together for appropriate instruction having to do with needed skills.

Finally, given the strong need for our schools to overcome ethnocentrism, I recommend globalization of the curriculum wherever possible. The use of literature from other countries and reading and discussing the daily newspaper can help.

Social Studies. The social studies, along with English/language arts should comprise a minimum core or block-time class for junior high students. There are those who would argue for the integration of the arts, science, math and other subjects as well into a core. I believe that such total integration is possible, but I also think it takes a very good teacher and that some units of study lend themselves more readily than others to such integration. For example, a unit on world travel could include science material on aerodynamics; money planning, calculation of distances using decimals, scales and metrics for math; construction of models for industrial arts; the preparation of food and clothing for home economics; and various arts, crafts and music of other lands. I think I would prefer to see a limited core with teachers of other subjects correlating their instruction as much as possible upon the request of the core teacher.

Our data showed the social studies curricula in our sample of schools to be very ethnocentric. At every school there was one year of U.S. history and many schools also had only one year of either state or regional history and/or geography. In those schools where there was a third year, that year, too, often contained a nationalistic theme such as U.S. government. Some schools did have a world history/geography course and those courses usually focused upon European history and geography.

Another finding of the Study was that social studies courses were generally preoccupied with coverage of content. For example, U.S. history courses "covered" from the period of exploration through the Civil War and Reconstruction. There was little focus on concept learning.

Classroom activities in social studies were quite traditional. Teachers lectured, students read and answered questions, and there were discussions but teacher questioning almost always required simple recall answers as did tests and quizzes. There was some report writing. However, the investigative methods of social scientists which could help students become critical thinkers were little in evidence.

We live in an interdependent world wherein every aspect of our daily existence has connection to other peoples of the planet. Not only do we import and export goods and services which are basic to our lives; but, more importantly, our mores and values are shaped by these connections. We are rapidly becoming an information society rather than an industrial one. This alters our world role.[6]

We need to globalize our social studies curriculum. Children and youth need to learn about the basic needs common to all humans and they need to recognize the interdependence of all people. Projects such as "Columbus[7] and the World" can be replicated almost anywhere. The project demonstrates the many ways Columbus, Ohio is connected to the rest of the world. Students need to recognize that nations, including their own, and corporations often operate out of selfish interests and that such interests are sometimes but not always the best for the majority of the people in the world or even for the majority of the people in this nation.

Rather than coverage of given bodies of content, teachers would do better to select a set of themes, problems or generalizations around which to organize the social studies program for the entire school. For example, in Chapter 4 I described how teachers at Palisades Middle School organized their U.S. history around six themes: (1) the scientific revolution, (2) disciplines of social and natural sciences, (3) nationalism, (4) business cycles, (5) family patterns, and (6) wars.

Social studies classes should break out of the lecture/answer the questions/take the test cycle. If they do, perhaps the subject will not be one of the least liked by junior high students. Later in this chapter I shall discuss a variety of ways to make learning more active. Suffice it to say here, much learning should take place outside of the classroom through active involvement in the school and community.

Science. While activity in all other academic classes was very predictable, it was less so in our sample of science classes. The curriculum varied greatly from class to class. There was some inquiry-oriented activity, teacher demonstration, and even evidence of students being involved in pre-planned experiments. Few students were involved in experiments or projects which they themselves had planned, and most classes were dominated by listening, watching, reading and writing rather than by "doing."

Curricula were usually organized around life science topics (e.g., cells and organisms, nature cycles, plant and animal diversity) and earth science topics (e.g., geology, astronomy, atoms and molecules). There was generally a subtle pressure to "cover" as many topics as possible and the teaching of facts seemed more prevalent than teaching for the understanding of concepts.

There was a great discrepancy from school to school in the amount of science taught. We found that students in some schools had three times as much science as students in other schools. There was also a discrepancy in facilities for science instruction. Very few schools had actual laboratories. Most science classrooms were standard rooms with desks in rows facing some kind of table at which the teacher would perform demonstrations.

I believe that every junior high student should be enrolled in a science class throughout his or her years at junior high school. Science has the potential of truly meeting the needs of the curious, active students of this age range. However, I would hope to see well-equipped laboratory facilities at all schools and students actively involved in experimentation, much of it planned by themselves. In this way scientific method, inquiry skills, and concept attainment would dominate the curriculum instead of the usually passive, fact-oriented science curriculum we see currently. I would also hope to see a comprehensive unit on the human body, its growth and care. Sex education, drug abuse education, and other health topics would be part of the curriculum also since these are issues of such critical importance to youngsters of this age. Finally, I would like to see emphasis upon the scientific contributions of people from all over the world and examination of global scientific problems (e.g., world-wide damage done by acid rain from industrial waste).

Math. Variability from class to class and inequity in exposure were not characteristic of the math classes in our sample of schools. In fact, this was by far the most predictable subject of any at our junior highs. Every student had one period of math per day. Almost without fail, students listened to the teacher explain an operation, then they practiced a number of problems from a text, a workbook or a worksheet. Finally, they were tested. Frequently, large numbers of students failed such tests. Infrequently, teachers saw such failure rates for what they truly were, evidence of inadequate or inappropriate instruction--teacher failure. Usually, however, teachers simply moved on to the next topic, leaving their students with another unlearned operation. Given that math learning is most often cumulative, this is a very serious matter and probably is at least a partial explanation of why American children and youth do so poorly in math when compared to those of other nations.

I suspect, too, that the recent turn away from the concept-oriented New Math is due, at least in part, to the fact that this "listen/practice/test" pattern has failed to help students understand clearly the relationship between concept and operation. The failure of the New Math is a perfect example, I believe, of our inability to properly diagnose what is wrong with our schools and then to develop the processes necessary to bring about the needed improvements.

In most subject areas, and particularly in math, basic pedagogy is poor because teachers have had poor training. Instead of changing the content, we need to involve teachers in the close examination of what it is they do and then they need to be directed to new knowledge from outside the school concerning what and how to teach. I fear that the current move to increase emphasis upon the academics is another example of misdiagnosis. Increasingly, this emphasis will help little in our schools and runs the risk of doing great damage (e.g., increasing discrimination, causing more drop-outs, encouraging poor teaching).

Another recent innovation which has reinforced poor pedagogy in junior high math, albeit we saw no evidence of this innovation in our sample, is the application of the so-called "management system," often referred to by other names such as individual progress plan. The idea is that math is an exact discipline and thus can be broken down into anywhere from 250-300 skills and/or operations which in turn can be categorized and sequenced. Students are pre-tested (diagnosed), taught (talked to) and/or assigned seat work, and post-tested (evaluated) on one or more skills at a time. A record is kept of each student's progress through the skills and operations. Skills are most often stated in behavioral terms and such "systems" abound in reading and other skills areas, also. These diagnostic-prescriptive approaches have a number of faults which I shall address later. Suffice to it say here, they encourage poor teaching and dependence upon text and worksheet materials.

I have indicated previously that I believe that the amount of time spent on math can be shortened. Typically, math taught beyond sixth grade in the junior high, and except for algebra, is a review of what was previously taught. If math were taught as a set of problem solving skills, it could probably be learned easier and much more quickly. For example, a group of students planning a trip or designing a building would learn everything from addition of whole numbers to division of fractions to subtraction of decimals, not to mention metrics. Likewise, they would learn to work together and would be active rather than passive learners.

Vocational Education. Much of what we saw in industrial arts and homemaking classes in our sample of junior highs came the closest to what seems appropriate for students of this age. That was because they were active courses, ones where students were doing rather than sitting passively. Even so, about half of the students' time was taken up with passive activities-- listening and writing. While I recognize the need for instruction in safety procedures and in how to do and make things, I wonder if this isn't too much time taken away from actual work on projects.

Originally, industrial arts and home economics were among those courses called exploratory courses. They were seen as short courses which preceded longer, often more specific vocational courses. As the junior high has lost its vocational function, they no longer are seen as beginning preparation for work. Rather, they now provide young people with valuable skills of everyday living. They, along with all courses, do provide students an opportunity to explore their interests and aptitudes.

Based upon the data we collected in A Study of Schooling, I would make the following recommendations regarding vocational education. First, I think every student should be enrolled for one full year in a co-educational, heterogeneously grouped industrial arts course. Such a course should cut across presently conceived industrial arts, shop disciplines. Basic home, yard and auto maintenance ought to serve as the basis for the content and actual projects at home as well as at school should be involved. All students should have another year-long, co-educational, hetero- geneously grouped class in family living (as opposed to home economics). The content would include the common subjects of cooking (including, of course, internation- al menus), grooming and sewing. More importantly, perhaps, it would include such topics as budgeting, consumer education, dating, personal hygiene and family relationships. The social aspects of sex education should be dealt with in this class while the physical

331

aspects are dealt with in science classes. Of course, science and family living teachers need to plan and otherwise collaborate with each other in this regard. Later in this chapter I shall refer to these industrial arts and family living classes as the practical arts.

Second, the specific job training courses we found at Fairfield have absolutely no place at any junior high. As we say, they had the effect of selecting some students (predominantly Mexican-American students) for low-paying occupations.

Finally, I take exception to a term we found in use at two schools in our sample. That term was "unified arts." As I explained earlier, it was really an euphemism for all the courses which used to be labelled exploratory: industrial arts, homemaking, art, music, typing, drama, etc. A number of middle schools which promote the unified arts approach suggest that it encourages teaming and interdisciplinary designs. I disagree strongly. All teachers and departments should be encouraged to plan together and integrate curricula whenever possible. However, forcing the music teacher to team with the industrial arts teacher makes no more curriculum sense (although it might help the principal schedule classes) than does putting the P.E. and language arts teachers together. Formal teaming--or better, informal cooperative arrangements--should arise out of the mutual interests of teachers and, more importantly, out of visions of what will help students develop integrative behavior (See Chapter 3).

P.E. Students in physical education classes in our sample of schools, by and large, were very active. Even so, they spent approximately 40% of their time listening to their teachers. Most emphasis was upon competitive team sports rather than upon the development of skills in individual sports in which students could be engaged throughout life (e.g., aerobic conditioning, raquetball, badminton, folk dance).

Other critical findings regarding P.E. were that there was little co-educational activity and teachers, on the average, spent about one-third of their time monitoring or just watching student activity. The most striking feature of our P.E. data was the variability from school to school. Programs ranged from almost nothing but a few team sports to a broad and interesting set of offerings (See Chapter 4). Also, there was only one school which reported a separate program for students with special physical problems.

Most recommendations for an adequate P.E. program generally arise right out of the data presented above. There should be a balanced program of movement and exercise, lifelong individual sports, and team sports. Teachers should be actively involved in skill teaching rather than spending a lot of time monitoring. P.E. should be co-educational as much as possible and special "correctional" experiences should be available for students with unique needs. Finally, emphasis should be placed upon games played in all parts of the world (soccer instead of American football, for example).

An important area not dealt with by our data has to do with interscholastic competition. The data from other studies against such competition is overwhelming. A viable alternative is a healthy intramural program which is co-educational, comprehensive in activities included (not just football, basketball and softball), which involves all students who wish to participate, and which de-emphasizes the competitive aspects of athletics. Such a program can go a long way toward building a strong school spirit and toward meeting the need for frequent physical movement characteristic of junior high students.

Foreign Language. We found foreign language classes in only half of the junior highs in our sample. In addition, we found academically-oriented, college bound students enrolled in those courses. Finally, we found the foreign language classes dominated by the same traditional pedagogical style as all other academic classes. That is, the teacher talked, students did written practice and took written tests. The written practice included a good bit of translation and teachers occasionally did ask students to converse in the language. In short, the purpose of those classes which did exist was to prepare college bound students for the foreign language classes they were to have in high school.

Americans are ethnocentric. That needs to be changed. Many Americans are prejudiced toward ethnic minorities. That needs to be changed. Our interdependent world requires people who can understand and appreciate each other. Good foreign language training can help toward this end.

I believe that all junior high students should take foreign language. Probably, it should be the language of the dominant minority of the region (e.g., French on the border of French speaking Canada, Spanish in Florida and the Southwestern United States). Most important, courses should be conversational and should use drama, role play, games, stories and music extensively. Further, these courses should deal with attitudes,working to overcome prejudices and misinformation and building an understanding of the similarities among all peoples.

A final issue has to do with what happens to students who already speak a language other than English. Some would argue that it is better for such students to be segregated into English As A Second Language (ESL) classes until they are proficient enough in English to be enrolled in a regular program. I tend not to agree. The burden of teaching English to all students, native speakers and foreign born, should be borne by all subjects including foreign language and particularly English/language arts. Wherever there is a large enough minority to warrant instruction in its language, a class should be formed. Spanish and French are obvious cases. Less obvious are the various Asian languages, Iranian, Armenian, and the like. I have two reasons for this proposal. First, very often young people who speak a foreign language do so badly. Instruction in their first tongue can be quite beneficial. Second, many of these students can add a great deal to a class and, in fact, a chance for them to "excel" may be beneficial to them, too. At any rate, I envision all junior high students enrolled in a nongraded, conversational course in one language for approximately one and one-half years.

Arts. When you walk through an apartment complex and hear the loud and strident music coming from several directions, when you see the countless junk items sold in discount stores as home decorations, or when you look at any typical evening's television offerings, you easily come to the conclusion that we are a nation of illiterates where the arts are concerned. On the other hand, when you realize that there are well over 100 live stage productions each week in Los Angeles, or that over 12,000 people in that same city crowd into the Hollywood Bowl to hear a Brahms concert, or that community theatre prospers in small cities such as Little Rock, Arkansas or Dayton, Ohio or Pocatello, Idaho, you get the impression that the arts are alive and well in the nation.

Of course, the truth is somewhere in between. And, unfortunately, if the data from A Study of Schooling are at all representative, arts education at our junior highs has a long way to go before it can claim to contribute significantly to national literacy in the arts. Throughout this book I have shown and argued that we do not need more academics, we need some basic revisions in the curriculum and in teaching of academics. The arts, however, are a different story. We need both revisions and more.

Across all the schools in our sample, offerings in the arts were quite varied. However, at any one school, offerings in the arts were quite limited. The question is largely one of attitudes. The greatest percentage of students, for example, judged the arts to be a subject they liked. At the same time, a smaller percentage judged it important. We know that the arts are often considered a "frill" and among the first things to be cut when there is budget-trimming. Over two-thirds of the parents in our sample responded no to one item which asked if the teaching of things like art, music and drama should be increased. Our data suggest that arts teachers have been influenced by these attitudes. In our sample, they tended to opt for the more formal aspects of their disciplines. In other words, I hypothesize, they were trying to make their courses more legitimate by making them appear more academic.

On the other hand, we also found a problem of a different kind, particularly in music. Every junior high had at least one performing group: band, orchestra, chorus. Many teachers had lost sight of what the goals of such programs should be. We had an interview comment from a chorus teacher, for example, complaining that students were being allowed into chorus who didn't have superior voices. He/she obviously cared more for the performance than for what students learned. Performance had become an end in itself rather than a means of learning. Also, we found that performing music students were often scheduled together throughout the day and thus segregated from other students.

335

I would hope to see at least two years of arts for all junior high school students. To begin they should be heterogeneously grouped in a semester long survey course where they have experiences with art, music, film, dance, drama and various forms of writing (e.g., expository, creative, poetic). Such a course would involve both going out into the community to exhibits and performances and inviting various artists to the school to talk about and demonstrate their arts. During the remaining semesters, students could choose from among a variety of non-graded performing arts classes, perhaps staying with one or perhaps taking many.

The implementation of such a program requires leadership from school people and from committed people in the community. The belief that the arts are a "frill" is deeply held by a majority of Americans. Somehow people have to examine the question as one of the quality of life we wish for ourselves and our children. If I were a superintendent of schools making a presentation to the board of education about an increased commitment to the arts, I might begin the presentation by reading the T.V. listings for the evening.

Computer Science. We gathered no data on the availability or use of computers. I can say that their use was not extensive. If the study were conducted today, they would be more available and, I would guess, their use would vary greatly from school to school.

My own view, based upon recent personal experience in schools and upon my observations of the growth of the use and the importance of computers is that they should become an integral part of all junior high programs. At this writing, in the infancy of computer use in schools, I suggest a developmental program with elementary students becoming familiar and comfortable through the use of a language such as LOGO which teaches rudimentary programming and mathematical logic.[9]

At the junior high level, I would see all students enrolled in an introductory course for one semester where they would become familiar with an instructional language such as BASIC. From there, I would see students using computers as appropriate in a variety of subjects. The potentials of Computer Assisted

336

Instruction (CAI)--not to mention many other forms of technology, including video recording--have never been realized in our schools. The use of technology with inquisitive, active junior high students seems a natural.

Conclusions. The exact configuration of such a curriculum would depend on local needs and resources, availability of teachers, etc. I have provided an hypothetical schedule for a three year school in Figure 10.1. My most fervent hope would be that each junior high school faculty would engage in a discussion involving parents about the various points raised in this book and particularly in this chapter. If such discussion were preceded by the gathering of local data it perhaps would be more meaningful since, as we found in A Study of Schooling, the perceptions of the various actors in the school drama are often at variance and reality most often is some combination of all such perceptions.

Period	Year One	Year Two	Year Three
1	Language Arts -	Language Arts -	Language Arts -
	Social Studies	Social Studies	Social Studies
2	Block	Block	Block
3	Science	Science	Science
4	Math/P.E.*	Math/P.E.	Math/P.E.
	Lunch	Lunch	Lunch
5	Computer/Arts	Performing Arts/	Performing Arts
	Survey	Foreign Language	
6	Practical Arts	Practical Arts	Foreign Language

Figure 10.1 An Hypothetical Idealized Three Year Junior High Curriculum

* Math and P.E. could alternate every other day; other alternating courses could alternate daily or by semester.

Teaching/Learning

While organization and curriculum are important aspects of schooling, what is most critical is what actually occurs in the classroom--teaching and learning. Pedagogy in the majority of classrooms in the junior highs sampled by A Study of Schooling can be characterized in three ways: (1) the teacher was usually in total control of the situation; (2) the sequence of events almost always involved teacher talk followed by student written practice followed by student test taking; and (3) students were almost always to recall specific facts, not demonstrate higher cognitive behaviors.

This description of the teaching/learning act, unfortunately, is consistent with the recommendations which have come out of the current wave of research on time-on-task and effective teaching practices. Take, for example, the description by Brophy of the effective process of basic skills instruction:

> The instruction that seems most efficient involves the teacher working with the whole class (or small groups in the early grades), presenting information in lectures/demonstrations and then following up with recitations or practice exercises in which the students get opportunities to make responses and get corrective feedback. The teacher maintains an academic focus, keeping the students involved in a lesson or engaged in seatwork, monitoring their performance, and providing individualized feedback...[10]

Alexander and George have pointed out that this body of research has focused on the elementary school level, on the teaching of basic skills, and on the less academically successful students. In short, as research it has been rather narrowly targeted. These authors suggest that when objectives go beyond the basic skills, or when teachers deal with students who are more successful in school, or when we consider the inquisitive junior high students, there are other instructional strategies which may be preferable.[11]

I am even more skeptical of the school effectiveness movement. It seems to me that it risks the justification of much poor instruction in the minds of

338

many; and, worse, diverts our attention from a number of truly critical variables of teaching and learning. As my colleague, Ken Sirotnik, has noted, it is the quality--not the quantity--of schooling which best serves as the focus for school improvement efforts. He raises questions about such qualitative aspects of teaching/learning as small group discussion, questioning at higher cognitive levels, various principles of learning, individualization, and student decision-making.

Our data shed light on a number of these qualitative aspects of teaching/learning. In the remainder of this section, I shall examine five: (1) classroom activities, (2) the use of principles of learning, (3) individualization and grouping for instruction, (4) diagnosis and evaluation, and (5) classroom affect.

Classroom activities. As has been noted time and again in this book, teacher, student, and observation data all suggested that classroom activity, particularly in the academic classes, was dominated by teacher talk, working on written assignments, and taking tests or quizzes. Also, a relatively large amount of time was spent on activities preparatory to or following instruction (e.g., passing out worksheets, collecting word done). Overall, more than 65% of our observations were of these four activities (Chapter 3). The non-academic classes and, to a lesser degree, science classes were more active with students involved in activities other than listening and writing. Also, in foreign language classes there was a good deal of observed oral practice although it was more recitational than conversational. Finally, our data suggested that while teachers thought they were providing experiences directed at the development of higher cognitive abilities, they were not. Questioning, for example, was directed at the recall of specific facts--names, dates, places, formulae, sums, rules, and so forth.

Junior highs, intermediate schools, or middle schools serve children who are moving from a developmental stage of concrete operations to a developmental stage of more abstract operations (Chapter 2). Regardless of the ages of the students in any given school, the fact is that there will be a range of intellectual development and abilities. Even though individual differences must be recognized, a major focus of teaching/learning activities at this level of schooling

339

<u>should be the movement of students from concrete to</u>
<u>abstract intellectual operations</u>.

Simulation, role play and other forms of drama are perhaps the best activities for young people to begin with concrete, defined situations and then work through higher cognitive processes to arrive at conclusions, solutions and/or alternative scenarios. King, for example, describes a simulation in a social studies class focused on the French Revolution which causes students to question such realistic conditions as the unfairness of regressive taxes and the special privileges attributed to people in positions of power. He says of the value of simulations:

> ...Among other advantages, simulations or "games" are successful because they involve activity rather than rote learning and they make good use of an almost universal enjoyment of games...[13]

Role play can be used more spontaneously and also can help students understand feelings. For example, reversing roles in disputes or role playing parental views can help students see issues from alternative perspectives. Creating and performing original dramas can make current and historical events far more realistic and understandable, too.

There are a whole host of communication activities that can cause children to practice and develop higher cognitive abilities. Designing interview and observation schedules, constructing questionnaires and then actually collecting, analyzing and preparing and presenting reports of data about contemporary topics is one set of such activities. In short, students learn to conduct research. In such a process they learn about hypothesis generation and testing and such issues as generalizability. Imagine how students with such experiences might react to the simplistic claims of television advertisers.

As a matter of fact, causing students to be more interactive with the media--television, radio, newspapers, magazines, tapes, records--is an important aspect of creating a thoughtful and active populace. There is the danger that the media, particularly T.V., is helping to create a passive, accepting and somewhat mindless populace. If students are passive at school and they go home to be passive T.V. watchers or tape listeners, we probably will have a very different society 20 or 30 years from now. The American media provide us with an unprecedented amount of information. Schools should help students to integrate that information, analyze and evaluate and use it in constructive ways.

Teaching junior high students to establish and apply artistic and other criteria (e.g., use of propaganda) to media presentations is one set of activities which eventually could help create a generation of discriminating listeners, viewers and readers. Less complex activities such as comparing written and visual presentations could help, too. At the simplest level having students summarize presentations can cause them to be more interactive with the media.

The community, too, is a real laboratory for learning which is too seldom used by schools. Environmental studies in science, architecture and transportation studies in math, and culture studies in social studies are examples of studies which could involve students in observing, discussing, and problem solving activities.

The essence of what I have been saying about teaching/learning at the junior high level is that students should be actively engaged in real problem solving activities instead of sitting passively. Partly, this means the development of higher cognitive abilities as they interpret, analyze, evaluate, plan and apply knowledge and skills to real problem situations. Partly, too, it means that the teacher arranges and then uses real student experiences as the basis of teaching/learning. This, of course, is not a new idea. Progressive educators have been calling for the use of truly "educative" experience for many years. For example, in calling for the development of reflective thinking, John Dewey identified the following essentials:

> They are first that the pupil have a genuine situation or experience--that there be a continuous activity in which he is interested for its own sake; secondly, that a genuine problem develop within this situation as a stimulus to thought; third, that he possess the information and make the observations needed to

341

deal with it; fourth, that suggested solutions occur to him which he shall be responsible for developing in an orderly way; fifth, that he may have the opportunity and occasion to test ideas by application, to make their meaning clear and to discover for himself their validity.[14]

Unfortunately, our acceptance of narrow measures of the attainment of skills developed in isolation (e.g., achievement test scores) puts us in the position of rejecting the engagement of junior high students in real problem solving. More time spent on teacher lecture, written practice and taking tests will probably raise test scores.[15]

The question is, however, what are the truly important aims of our junior high schools? I would guess that if people really understood that the engagement of students in real problem solving activities would more likely lead to the development of integrative behavior and an increased sense of personal power and growth, they would opt for such activity and correspondingly call for the application of different criteria to the measurement of school effectiveness.

Principles of learning. One aspect of instruction which has received a good deal of attention in recent years has been the set of teacher behaviors derived from learning theory. These behaviors have been a major focus of the so-called school effectiveness movement. One reason for the interest in such behavior is that they are relatively easy to identify and to train people in. Also, there seems to be a relationship between such behaviors and achievement test scores.[16]

As a matter of fact, students in our sample of junior highs were moderately positive about their teachers' use of principles of learning. They perceived that teachers told them what was expected of them, had them practice what they were to learn, let know how well they were doing, and were organized in their instruction. There was some feeling on the students' part that they often had to do work they already understood (Chapter 5).

Our observation data, while not parallel to our student data, gave a somewhat different picture of the use of principles of learning by our teachers. For

342

example, our observers saw teachers very infrequently involved in giving either positive or negative feedback.

There is no doubt in my mind that teachers should know how and when to utilize such principles. The problem is that some advocates of teaching teachers how to master principles of learning tend to overstate their case substantially, giving the impression that this alone makes good teaching. They tend to overlook more basic issues such as helping students to gain the sense of power and growth suggested by Dewey, or helping them to examine moral conflict situations as a means of moral growth as described by Kohlberg.[19]

Along with attention to principles of learning, the recent effectiveness research and literature attends to issues of classroom management; that is, how teachers can better control student behavior so that more time can be spent on direct teaching and the like, and so that achievement test scores can be improved. Again, I have to ask the question of purpose. Our data showed that teacher control and dominance was one of the major characteristics of our classrooms. Students were not involved in decisions about their learning. Do we want an even more controlled learning environment so that test scores can go up, or are there other criteria we wish to utilize in measuring the success of our classrooms? For example, do we want self-reliant students, ones who would in fact question having to constantly submit to teacher authority?

I think most parents and other adults would opt for teacher control and dominance in our schools. There has been so much discussion of rebellious youth and of students' being "turned off" to school that most people probably support the notion of more authority. However, I suggest that the answer does not lie with more control. The opposite may be true. A large proportion of each data source in our study--parents, teachers and students--suggested that lack of student interest was a problem at their school. Even though students seemed satisfied with how much decision-making they had and even though they did not see their teachers as authoritarian, I would suggest that a more active role for students in problem solving, decision-making and in critical thinking activities would cause them to be more motivated and more interested in school. The reader will recall that the more active, non-academic

343

subjects were the ones students generally liked more and found more interesting.

Appropriate practice is one principle of learning which seemed in question in our data. I have already referred to the fact that many students said they had to do things they already knew. Teachers also reported that many materials of instruction were inappropriate for their students because of interest, ability or ethnicity. I suggest that learning based upon active involvement in real problem solving will lead students to search out materials which are appropriate for them. Rather than giving all students the same assignment, the teacher becomes a facilitator, helping each student find appropriate materials and raising questions which do not require a recall answer but which lead students on interesting journeys of discovery.

Individualizing and grouping. Much has been said and a little done about the need to individualize instruction for the junior high students of our nation. However, much more needs to be done particularly if my recommendation for heterogeneous grouping is taken at all seriously. I believe that I have well established that ability grouping does not help to individualize. In fact, it caused teachers to do more whole-group teaching. The reader will recall that teachers in our junior high sample said that they did only a moderate amount of individualizing by varying instructional methods, grouping arrangements, activities, objectives, content, materials, and/or time spent on tasks. Large percentages of teachers said they never varied instruction in any of these ways for different students (Chapter 5).

Teachers did have students work alone a good deal of the time (Chapter 6). That, of course, was basically when they were doing seatwork as a follow-up to a teacher presentation and almost always all students were doing the same thing. Such a practice was not surprising since teachers also said that they used almost no diagnostic tools to determine individual students' needs. What they did rely upon for gathering information about students was their own observations, homework and tests they prepared.

There is a need for a good deal of in-service training for school staffs in how to diagnose and evaluate learner needs and progress. In addition to

344

learning how to diagnose and evaluate skill and content attainment, teachers need help with assessing student learning styles. Some students learn better verbally, some visually, some through touch. With such knowledge, teachers could vary instruction appropriately using a variety of materials, audio visual resources, computers, and the like.

I would propose that teachers hold frequent cross-departmental meetings wherein they discuss individual students, including their skill and ability growth, content attainment, social-emotional development, and whatever other aspects of student growth and development they might consider important. A counselor and/or outside growth and development specialist might participate, at least in the early stages of such conferences and until teachers gain skill with these diagnostic meetings. Of course, release time should be arranged for much of this conferencing.

Teachers need in-service training, too, in the practical techniques of organizing and carrying out small group instruction. Alexander and George discuss a series of such techniques including peer teaching and group inquiry and team learning. They also discuss a variety of techniques for individualizing instruction and they place in perspective the fact that whole-class teaching, small group instruction and individualization all are appropriate forms of teaching, depending upon purpose.[18]

It is my belief that in our desire to deal with individual needs of students, particularly their academic needs, we have overlooked some of the intrinsic values gained by students from group inquiry and interaction. Many of the individualized learning systems developed and marketed in recent years have isolated students and, in fact, seem sterile to many teachers and students.

Joyce and Weil identify a number of small group teaching models, all of which feature interaction-oriented learning. Of particular import to me has always been <u>Thelen's Group Investigation Model</u>, which is a process model emphasizing not only the importance of rational inquiry but also of democratic participation.[19] Joyce and Weil list the six phases of the proposed model:

1. Encounter with a puzzling situation (planned or unplanned).
2. Exploration of reactions to the situation.
3. Formulate study task. Organize for study (problem definition, role, assignments, etc.).
4. Independent and group study.
5. Analysis of progress and process.
6. Recycling of activity.[20]

Of the model, Joyce and Weil say:

> Provided that one accepts Thelen's view of knowledge and its reconstruction, the Group Investigation Model can be considered a very direct and probably efficient way of teaching academic knowledge as well as social process. It also appears likely to nurture interpersonal warmth and trust, respect for negotiated rules and policies, independence in learning, and a respect for the dignity of others.[21]

It seems unrealistic to me to continue to think that one teacher can plan and carry out a good program with 25-40 students in a classroom, particularly when she/he has to repeat that performance for five or six periods a day. There are many ways to remedy this situation. I have already discussed core classes, at least as far as English and social studies are concerned. Where teachers feel competent and comfortable in other areas, they can also create core classes, for example in science and math. This can cut down on the overall number of students faced by a teacher. The most direct way to reduce teacher-pupil ratios is to limit class sizes. This is expensive, but a worthy goal for a school district or a state legislature. Also, many schools have creatively used part-time teachers, with those part-time people having to get to know fewer students.

A plan I strongly advocate, because it works at the school where I recently was a principal, is that of having two teachers work together in each class. In addition to reducing pupil-teacher ratios, it also helps overcome the teacher isolation I spoke of in Chapter 9.

At Westland, the Group Teacher (lead teacher) is ultimately in charge of planning and carrying out the curriculum and instruction, assessment of student needs and interests, communication with parents, and school-wide responsibilities. He or she is experienced and skilled as a teacher. More importantly, he/she is committed to and articulate about the unique progressive philosophy of the school.

The Co-Teacher participates in all aspects of the program: planning, teaching, communication with parents, and so forth. There are generally two types of people who work as Co-Teachers. First, there are beginners who are learning from the more experienced Group Teachers and the school, in general. Second, there are a number of older people who were teachers some time ago, who left teaching for awhile (e.g., to raise a family, to try some other kind of work), and who have returned to teaching. While there are different salary schedules for Group Teachers and Co-Teachers, this plan is not as complex as many of the commonly proposed differentiated staffing plans. It requires only that two people cooperate (there are larger cooperating groups at the school, but they tend to be informal and organized by the teachers themselves) and it remains fairly informal and non-bureaucratic.

In addition to the lower pupil-teacher ratio, the plan gives us several other advantages. In the case of teacher absence, there is someone available who knows the program and the students. We are able to free people for observing and other in-service activities. There is real sharing between the co-operating teachers. Most importantly, two people, working together, know the students a lot better than the single teacher, no matter how experienced he/she is.

Classroom affect. I have pointed out a number of times that the predominant affective tone of the classrooms in our sample of junior highs was one of neutrality and student passivity. Teachers were very much in control, but they were not treating students harshly. Students perceived their teachers as moderately concerned and enthusiastic, did not see them as too punitive or authoritarian, and did not see them as showing too much favoritism. There was little difference from school to school or from subject to subject (Chapter 5).

There has been a lot written about students being "turned off" to school. In fact, in our study, students, teachers and parents all reported that lack of student interest was a problem at most schools. However, we did have a measure of student satisfaction at the classroom level which showed some promise. When that measure was correlated with other affective classroom measures we found the strongest positive relationship with teacher concern and teacher enthusiasm along with a fairly strong negative relationship with teacher authoritarianism. In short, where teacher affect was more positive, student satisfaction was highest.

We determined two additional relationships among variables having to do with classroom climate. First, we found that teachers who tended to utilize the principles of learning (e.g., teacher clarity, knowledge of results, appropriate practice) were also the ones who were viewed more positively by the students in terms of classroom affect (e.g., concerned, enthusiastic, not punitive). Second, we determined that teachers who were more satisfied with aspects of their own careers and school had classes which were perceived more positively by students.

Other researchers have shown that classroom climate is a dimension of schooling which is related to student achievement.[22]

All of these findings, taken together, seem to indicate that much of school improvement hinges upon dimensions of teachers' attitudes and the resulting climates created in classrooms. A goal would seem to be to create a school climate wherein teacher satisfaction, enthusiasm, and motivation are high. This does not suggest that making teachers "happy" is all that is necessary. What it does mean is that the improvement of technical skills alone is not enough. I shall return to a discussion of the adult climate of the school and school improvement toward the end of this chapter, but first I would like to briefly discuss a program directed at the improvement of student guidance.

Guidance

At the junior highs in our sample, we found that students viewed the counseling programs as satisfactory, but just barely so. Teachers were less positive. Counselors, themselves, felt that they had too much responsibility for record keeping, testing and general coordination and too little time for actual student advisement. We also found counselor-pupil ratios which precluded any hope for regular and sustained counselor-pupil interaction. Very few students really get to spend any time with a counselor.

At the classroom level, we found little if any opportunity for teacher-pupil interaction which went beyond the concerns of the subject matter of the particular subject or class. Obviously, there is need for some intermediate structure which can allow for students to interact with a sympathetic adult about their school concerns, future plans and personal concerns and which also allows for referral of students to highly trained counselors and/or other growth and development specialists (e.g., psychometrists, psychologists) for special needs.

The I/D/E/A teacher-advisor system seems to represent the kind of program which meets the needs described above.[23] When students enter the school, they select an advisor and remain with that advisor throughout their years there. Every teacher, administrator, counselor, librarian, and professional staff member has an advisee group of 15-20 students. Each group is purposely heterogeneous in terms of age, sex, ethnicity, and academic ability.

Teacher-advisors are responsible for all the program planning and scheduling, paperwork, record-keeping and parent reporting for their advisees. They are also the ones to whom students are most likely to take personal problems or future vocational concerns. To keep the advisory periods from becoming just another version of homeroom, they should not be interrupted by PA announcements or filled with administrative routines. Rather, it is better when advisors use the time with their advisees for program planning, group discussion of student problems and concerns, self-awareness building activities, career-awareness experiences (e.g., guest speakers from careers which interest students in the group), and helping individual students with particular problems and needs.

Junior highs which use a teacher-advisor system find it works best when advisee groups can meet at least three times a week for 30-45 minutes each time, since not much can be done in less time. I have found some initial resistance to the idea from both teachers and counselors because both have felt that when you get beyond homeroom type issues, teachers may not have the expertise to sustain advisor programs. Such a criticism is more accurate than not. However, rather than shortening advisor time and making it more like a homeroom, teachers need to be helped to develop their counseling skills and counselors, freed from much of their paperwork responsibilities, can serve as teachers of the teacher-advisors.

Alexander and George, in describing the advisor program as a critical element in the middle school movement, suggest a variety of activities which can be utilized to make these programs successful. Included are such things as using one day a week to focus on the interests, likes, dislikes and aspirations of individual students; silent reading time; keeping individual journals; academic counseling and assistance; indoor and outdoor games; reading to students with discussion of what is read; current events; and the like.[24] My experience is that advisors and advisees become quite creative in designing the constructive use of their time together once the intent of the program has been adequately internalized.

Changing the Junior High School

Based upon my own analysis of data from the junior high school sample of A Study of Schooling, the research and writings of others, and my own experiences, I have proposed a number of substantive changes in school organization, curriculum, teaching/learning practices in classrooms, and guidance procedures for junior high schools. The major changes proposed were:

1. The development of a common curriculum for all students in the school including an increased attention to science and foreign language, a reduction in time devoted to mathematics accompanied by improved instruction, opportunity for all students to participate in at least one performing art, co-educational practical arts experiences, and a course for all students in computer science.

2. The elimination of ability grouping and the conscious formation of heterogeneous classes at the school.

3. The organization of large junior highs into smaller sub-units known as learning communities.

4. The utilization of core or block-time scheduling wherever possible, particularly with English and social studies.

5. The utilization of more active teaching strategies in all classrooms with emphasis upon group problem solving.

6. The globalization of all curricula to help overcome the extensive ethnocentrism which permeates our schools and our society.

7. Improve student guidance through the establishment of a teacher-advisor program.

The question becomes, of course, how do you bring about these or other needed changes in the junior high school? In Chapter 9 we saw that teachers in our sample relied heavily upon their own backgrounds and perceptions, they seldom used available resource people, and there were very few school-wide planned change efforts. Individuals were involved in in-service training and new knowledge tended to "trickle in" to the schools. Within the schools, we saw that teachers were more or less isolated in their class-rooms, that they knew little about their colleagues, and that there was little evidence of collective staff inquiry or problem solving. Principal leadership was characterized as laissez-faire and these individuals were little involved with matters of curriculum and instruction. Finally, we saw that teachers themselves tended to more strongly endorse traditional beliefs, beliefs which stress teacher control of most aspects of classroom operation. Clearly, such beliefs seem incompatible with many of the changes proposed above.

The one strategy which will not work is the mandating of change. Time and again we have seen legislatures, state departments of education, school boards, superintendents and/or others in positions of authority try to force changes upon schools and we have invariably seen those attempts fail. The curriculum reform

351

movement of the 60's and the efforts to introduce individualized instruction systems of various kinds during the 60's and 70's are good examples of comprehensive reforms with substantial political and financial backing which were mandated at various levels but which frequently failed because attention was not paid to overcoming the conditions in schools just described: teacher isolation, lack of opportunity for group inquiry, laissez-faire principal leadership, an emphasis upon teacher control in the classroom, and the like.

Many of the proposals for change which I have made in this book have been proposed before. Some have been suggested by advocates of middle school organization. I would hypothesize that the fact that there are a growing number of schools called middle schools which are really not much different than the junior highs they replaced is also due to a lack of attention to such conditions. The amazing aspect of what I am saying here is that we do know how change occurs and what it takes to bring it about in schools. We do know know to address these conditions. There is a substantial body of research and literature on change in education. Unfortunately, it lies largely ignored by those in authority and by practitioners alike.[25]

It seems to me that there are five major tasks we must undertake if our junior highs are to be able to change to meet the challenge of educating today's pre- and early-adolescents. These are: (1) create an environment in each school that causes it to become a self-renewing organization, (2) develop the capabilities and possibilities for individuals to truly exert leadership in our junior highs, (3) create linkages between each school and knowledge from outside necessary to its improvement process, (4) select and adequately train the individuals who will staff the junior highs of the future, and (5) engage parents and staff members at each school in dialog about the functions which should be performed by their junior high for their students.

Self-renewing schools. In Chapter 9, I briefly described the Study of Educational Change and School Improvement Project (SECSI) conducted by the Research Division of I/D/E/A during the late 60's. I told of how the project measured and gave feedback to school staffs about their collective problem-solving efforts, using constructs labelled dialog, decision-making, action, and evaluation (DDAE). This was done for the total staff and for sub-groups in each school (e.g., teams, departments). The measures were both quantitative and qualitative, and involved the judgment of the staff members as well as of trained observers.[26]

The DDAE paradigm gave those staffs a way of looking at their group interaction, particularly their problem-solving. Data from A Study of Schooling showed that staffs in that sample did not communicate much with each other and did little about collective school-wide problems. Even so, they were fairly satisfied with their problem-solving processes. The question becomes: How can we get schools to utilize a process such as DDAE as an improvement tool?

Staffs in the SECSI Project did not just adopt DDAE outright. They were very tentative at first. They needed to see that problems dealt with were _their_ problems and not ones imposed on them by their superordinates. And they needed to see that _their_ problems could get resolved as a result of the process. Initially, too, there was a great need for trust to be built between staff members and the SECSI facilitators/researchers. Basically, such trust resulted from the SECSI personnel being good listeners, by their following through on commitments they made, and by their being able to diagnose the disposition of the various staff members to the stages of changes noted by Rogers and described in Chapter 9 (i.e., awareness, interest, evaluation, trial, adoption).[27]

The DDAE paradigm represented an intervention strategy not dissimilar to many of the organization development efforts in schools during the 60's and 70's and to the even earlier school change efforts known as action research. The organization development strategy (OD) involves the initial use of an outside consultant or consultants who diagnose the health of various processes within a school: communication, goal setting, conflict resolution, group operation, problem solving and decision-making. Following diagnosis, the consultants design and carry out appropriate in-service training of staff members with the aim of the improvement of such processes. OD operates with three assumptions:

(1) healthy organizations have shared leader-
ship--everyone participates and assumes responsibility, (2) members of the organization are
involved in continual and formative evaluation
of the health of organization processes, and
(3) eventually members of the organization take
over from the consultant(s) and the organization becomes self-renewing.[28]

The main reason such strategies have not been
utilized more frequently is that the superordinate
system too often has been afraid to give up its authority. The classic comment of the SECSI Project was made
by a district superintendent who said to the project
principals, "Change anything you want in your schools,
just don't rock the boat." Data from A Study of
Schooling made it clear that teachers were not involved
in school-wide decisions. Their area of concern was
pretty much limited to the classroom.

If we are truly interested in improvement in our
junior highs, we have got to first see that they become
self-renewing organizations. That means that our ways
of thinking about decision-making, control, authority
and power need to be revamped. While policy making
should remain a legislative function carried out by
boards of education and legislatures, programmatic
decisions should be made at the school level. Quality
assurance and the provision of support become the major
functions of district administration. Until such
re-thinking is done, change will probably not take
place in our schools--at least not on any major scale.

The one prerequisite to DDAE or OD processes is
that schools staffs have time to meet, plan, and
problem-solve together. Expecting that all staff,
department and/or team meetings will take place before
or after school is unrealistic. To date, many school
districts have been unwilling to grant the necessary
release time for such meetings. While cost, transportation problems, and disruption of instructional time
are often cited as reasons for not having release days,
the real reason is often that authorities are reluctant
to fight the norm of schools performing a custodial
function for children while parents are otherwise
occupied. A realistic goal would be to have one-half
day per week set aside for staff meetings and for the
class schedule to somehow rotate so that the same
subjects would not be missed by students each week.

354

Leadership. It has almost become a platitude to suggest that the principal is a key person in the process of change. Of course, I believe this. I have been writing about principal leadership and teaching university and in-service courses for principals for years.[29] However, I suggest that it will take a great deal of effort to develop effective school principals. It will take an almost entire re-thinking of the role.

To begin with, expectations for principals will have to change drastically. Data from A Study of Schooling showed that teachers did not have frequent discussions with principals about substantive matters, and that discussions which did occur were generally felt by teachers to be of little value. These principals were seen as laissez-faire in their leadership, preoccupied with "keeping the lid on." Even so, teachers were mildly positive about their principals. They had come to expect such behavior and had no vision that it could be different.

School districts, loosely coupled or not, are bureaucracies. Aside from some individual and idiosyncratic characteristics which are more or less viewed as beneficial (e.g., the ability to speak or write well, physical attractiveness), bureaucratic organizations tend to promote people who follow the "rules" or norms, who maintain the status quo, who "don't rock the boat" as our superintendent so clearly put it. The behavior of the junior high principals in our sample was predictable. And neither should they be criticized for that behavior. More than likely, they would not have been principals had they been more assertive and/or creative or had they been leading a call for major changes.

Teachers identified competence and personal respect as the major reasons why they responded to their principals. It seems clear to me that we need to mount significant in-service efforts as well as change markedly the pre-service preparation directed at preparing principals. Such training, coupled with selection based upon criteria of competence rather than system loyalty, could go a long way toward improving our junior highs.

Data from A Study of Schooling suggest three sets of competencies needed by those in leadership positions in our schools, including principals. The first set arises out of the organization development needs described previously. Principals need to be able to create and facilitate staff communication, goal setting, problem solving and the like and they need to know when and how to involve parents appropriately in such processes. The second set has to do with curriculum and instruction. Being able to facilitate the improvement of teaching through direct work with teachers or through the organization of needed inservice is critical. Third, it seems obvious that principals need to be able to make assessments themselves of the adult work environment, the condition of teaching/learning in the classroom, and the relationship between the school and its community needs and wants.

Finally, I believe that those in leadership positions in our schools should be introspective. They should attempt to know their own values and, further, attempt to understand how these values cause them to behave toward others. Important to the process of self-understanding is a willingness to "hear" from others about how they behave. Such openness, coupled with competence, is what our schools badly need from those in leadership positions.

Linkage. A major finding of A Study of Schooling was that teachers were poorly linked to knowledge from outside their schools. Basically, they were isolated in their classrooms and what new knowledge did come to them came rather randomly through reading, class attendance and the like. Creating a self-renewing organizational environment will both facilitate internal communication and cause people to seek more knowledge from outside.

There are structures which can be built which can increase the flow of knowledge to schools. For example, an important component of the SECSI Project described earlier was the League of Cooperating Schools (LCS). The SECSI staff office served as a facilitating "hub" for the 18 schools in the LCS. The SECSI staff worked in the individual schools, consulting on the DDAE process or other topics. They arranged for cross-school visitations, group meetings around topics of interest to several people from different schools, and all-league meetings which featured speakers and discussions on a variety of topics identified by League members.

356

County departments of education, regional education centers and even district offices could serve schools in much the same way if they were organized to do so. Unfortunately, most are not. Currently, consultants to schools are either subject area specialists or they represent programs and projects decided on in their own offices or by federal or state authorities who provide categorical monies. Readers will recall that teachers in our sample used consultants very little and thought them of little value.

There is a need for people who are knowledgeable in the various subject areas. However, a prior need is for a cadre of people trained in school assessment procedures, in organization development processes described previously, and knowledgeable about where to get other resource people and information when school staffs identify a particular need, problem or interest. Such people are not being trained in our schools of education and few intermediate agencies seem to see the need to retrain their staff members in change agentry. In order for schools to become self-renewing, they need to be linked to outside knowledge and they need help which can facilitate this linkage.

If I were the director of an intermediate educational agency, I would set as one of my goals the enlistment of every school within my service area in some kind of improvement project or another, decided upon by each school staff and linked to my office through one of my agency staff members. Of course, staff members in my agency would be retrained for the task.

Pre-service training. Our institutions of higher education have a major responsibility to assist with the improvement of our junior highs. To the degree that staff members in schools of education are capable, they should be working in the field to help people there solve their problems. That, too, probably requires much re-training, for few people in schools of education know a great deal about how change occurs in organizations.

I have already described the kinds of competencies needed by school principals. It is my belief that schools of education should re-design their administrative training programs so as to assure that their graduates attain such competencies. Similarly, I

357

believe that some pre-service institutions should initiate advanced programs in change agentry. Such programs might well be interdisciplinary, drawing upon social-psychology, political science, sociology and perhaps the field of management.

Pre-service teacher education, too, could learn from A Study of Schooling. Some years ago, many teacher education programs moved away from methods courses and emphasized instead subject content. Yet our data suggest that teachers are not equipped to plan active learning experiences. They basically lecture, assign worksheets and give tests. There needs to be a better balance in pre-service teacher education between methods courses and subject content. Teachers need to be able to plan and implement discussions, good questioning, simulations, role plays, small group inquiry and a variety of other teaching strategies which require active participation by students.

Our data suggest that teachers need more training and practice in utilizing principles of learning and techniques of individualizing instruction, including techniques of student assessment. Additionally, our data point to the need for teachers to know more about affective guidance.

An important part of teacher training is student teaching. Currently, the common practice is to assign a single student to a single "master" teacher. While many students probably have good experiences and learn a lot in this way, there are a whole host of "hidden" learnings which occur, also. For example, if a student teacher is in a school where teachers are isolated from each other, he or she learns that this is the norm. Perhaps a better strategy would be to find or develop self-renewing schools and saturate them with student teachers, interns and other learners. The object would be to infuse students with a sense of inquiry rather than a need to be in "control."

A serious problem faced by our junior highs is that very few teacher training institutions prepare teachers specifically to teach at this level. Most are prepared as secondary teachers which means the focus is on high school students and teaching them. We need people thoroughly trained in dealing with active, changeable and challenging junior high aged students.

Finally, I would like to see teacher training institutions do a better job of recruitment and screening of the people who apply to enter teaching. People with a high need for control should be screened out before they enter teaching. Conversely, people committed to lifelong inquiry need to be recruited into teaching. Perhaps the recent attention accorded our schools will cause teaching salaries to become competitive with other occupations. If that happens, teacher training institutions might better be able to recruit people with such a commitment and with a strong interest in working at the junior high level.

Purposefulness. The major need of junior high schools today which is pointed out by A Study of Schooling data is to have purposes clarified. I firmly believe that each school staff, with its parents, should enter into serious discussion of what its purposes should be and why. The results of such discussion, combined with an assessment of what is currently occurring at the school should lead to the formulation of a thoughtful agenda for change at each school.

The aims of the junior high school listed in Chapter 2 were originally set forth in 1947.[30] Both our young people and our society have changed markedly since then. It is time for reconsideration. On the basis of my analysis of the data from A Study of Schooling presented in this book I would propose the following aims for our junior highs. I am hopeful that they can serve as discussion points as each school staff and parent group considers its own school.

AIM I. Integration

To provide active learning experiences in which students may use the skills, attitudes, interests, ideals and understandings previously and presently acquired in such a way that these will become integrated into effective and wholesome pupil behavior.

To engage students in critical thinking activity which will assist students in the development of integrative behavior.

359

AIM II. Exploration

To cause students to broaden and deepen the discovery and exploration of their interests, aptitudes and abilities as an activity of lifelong and intrinsic value.

To cause students to broaden and deepen their interest in, understanding of, and respect for the natural and physical world of which they are a part including the human beings with whom they share that world.

AIM III. Guidance

To assist students to make appropriate decisions about a variety of matters, including educational opportunities, peer relationships, and personal growth and development.

To motivate students to learn and adopt a lifelong attitude of inquiry.

AIM IV. Individualization

To provide, within a common curriculum for all and within heterogeneously grouped classes, the opportunity for each student to develop his/her interests, skills, aptitudes and abilities to their fullest.

AIM V. Socialization

To provide numerous interactive experiences for students which develop in them a healthy respect for themselves, their peers, and all humankind.

To develop in students a lifelong commitment to a sense of social responsibility which includes a willingness to become an active citizen and to take individual and collective action in the face of injustice.

Chapter X, Notes and References

1. William M. Alexander, et al., The Emergent Middle School, New York: Holt, Rinehart & Winston, Inc., 1968, p. 5.

2. William M. Alexander and Paul S. George, The Exemplary Middle School, New York: Holt, Rinehart & Winston, Inc., 1981, p. 3.

3. Alexander and George, The Exemplary Middle School, op. cit., p. 54.

4. Billy B. Reeves, Implementation Guide, I/D/E/A Change Program for Individually Guided Education, Ages 10-15, Dayton, Ohio: Institute for Development of Educational Activities, Inc., 1974.

5. The best book on vertical school reorganization is still: John I. Goodlad and Robert H. Anderson, The Nongraded Elementary School Revised Edition, New York: Harcourt, Brace & World, Inc., 1963. The one comprehensive presentation of horizontal organization I recommend is Robert H. Anderson, Teaching in a World of Change, New York: Harcourt, Brace & World, Inc., 1966. The best contemporary publication which places school organization into a realistic perspective vis-a-vis junior high education is Alexander and George, The Exemplary Middle School, op. cit.

6. John Naisbitt, Megatrends: Ten New Directions Transforming Our Lives, New York: Warner Books, 1982.

7. Chadwich F. Alger, A World of Cities: Or Good Foreign Policies Begin at Home, Columbus, Ohio: Mershon Center, Ohio State University, 1976.

8. Paul S. George and Christopher Rampachek, "Interscholastic Athletics and Early Adolescents: An Annotated Bibliography," Middle School Journal, Vol. 10 (May, 1979), pp. 20-21.

9. Seymour Papert, Mindstorms: Children, Computers and Powerful Ideas, New York: Basic Books, Inc., 1980.

10. Jere E. Brophy, "Teacher Behavior and Student Learning," Educational Leadership, Vol. 37 (October, 1979), p. 34.

11. Alexander and George, The Exemplary Middle School, op. cit., p. 229.

361

12. Kenneth A. Sirotnik, _What You See Is What You Get_..., op. cit., pp. 20-21.

13. David C. King, "Secondary School Programs," in James M. Becker (ed.) _Schooling for A Global Age_, New York: McGraw-Hill Book Company, 1979. p. 165.

14. See: John Dewey, _Democracy and Education_, New York: Macmillan Publishing Co., Inc., 1916, p. 192.

15. Baruk V. Rosenshine, "Recent Research on Teaching Behaviors and Student Achievement," op. cit.

16. David A. Squires, William G. Guitt, and John K. Segars, _Effective Schools and Classrooms: A Research-Based Perspective_, Alexandria, Va.: Association for Supervisors and Curriculum Development, 1983.

17. Lawrence Kohlberg, "Moral Education for A Society in Moral Transition," _Educational Leadership_, Vol. 33 (October, 1975), pp. 46-52.

18. Alexander and George, _The Exemplary Middle School_, op. cit., pp. 221-247.

19. Herbert Thelen, _Education and the Human Quest_, New York: Harper and Row, 1960.

20. Bruce Joyce and Marsha Weil, _Models of Teaching_, Englewood Cliffs, N.J.: Prentice-Hall, Inc., 1972. p. 47.

21. Ibid., p. 46.

22. Rosenshine, "Recent Research on Teaching Behaviors and Student Achievement," op. cit.

23. John Kinghorn and Barbara Benham, _The Advisor Role_, Dayton, Ohio: Institute for Development of Educational Activities (I/D/E/A), 1973.

24. Alexander and George, _The Exemplary Middle School_, op. cit., pp. 99-104.

25. A minimum reading list might include: J. Victor Baldridge and Terrence Deal (eds.), _Managing Change in Educational Organizations: Sociological Perspectives, Strategies, and Case Studies_, Berkeley: McCutchan Publishing Co., 1975; William G. Benis, et al., _The Planning of Change_ (3rd ed.), New York: Holt, Rinehart and Winston, 1976; Mary M. Bentzen, _Changing_

Schools: The Magic Feather Principle, New York: McGraw-Hill Book Company, 1974; John I. Goodlad, The Dynamics of Educational Change, op. cit.; Neal Gross, et al., Implementing Organizational Innovations: A Sociological Analysis of Planned Educational Change, New York: Basic Books, Inc., 1971; Ronald G. Havelock, Planning for Innovation through Dissemination and Utilization of Knowledge, Ann Arbor: Institute for Social Research, The University of Michigan, 1971; Everett M. Rogers, Diffusion of Innovations, op. cit.; Kenneth A. Tye and Jerrold M. Novotney, Schools in Transition: The Practitioner as Change Agent, New York: McGraw-Hill Book Company, 1975.

26. The DDAE Questionnaire can be found in Mary M. Bentzen, Changing Schools, op. cit., pp. 228-233.

27. Everett M. Rogers, Diffusion of Innovations, op. cit., pp. 81-86.

28. See, for example: Richard A. Schmuck, et al., The Second Handbook of Organization Development, op. cit. or Stephen M. Corey, Action Research to Improve School Practices. New York: Teachers College Press, Columbia University, 1953.

29. See for example: Kenneth A. Tye, "The Principal As A Change Agent: Given Certain Conditions," The National Elementary Principal, Vol. 49, No. 4 (February, 1970), pp. 41-51.

30. William T. Gruhn and Harl R. Douglas, The Modern Junior High School, op. cit., pp. 59-60.